DATE DUE			
MAY 1 9 '89 S			
6/9/89			
OCT 14 '91 S			
FEB 0 8 1993			
ILL 1588446			
JAN 02 1997 S			
AUG 2 1 2001			
ILL: 9560109			
FMB			

Cellular Automata Machines

Cellular Automata Machines

A new environment for modeling

Tommaso Toffoli
Norman Margolus

The MIT Press
Cambridge, Massachusetts
London, England

Third printing, 1988

This book was printed and bound in the United States of America.

Library of Congress Cataloging-in-Publication Data

Toffoli, Tommaso.
  Cellular automata machines.

  (MIT Press series in scientific computation)
  Bibliography: p.
  Includes index.
  1. Cellular automata.   I. Margolus, Norman.
II. Title.   III. Series.
QA267.5.C45T64   1987   511.3   86-33804
ISBN 0-262-20060-0

Contents

Acknowledgements

The writing of this book, like the worlds that it describes, could have gone on forever. We hope that the rest of the story will be written by our readers.

We are grateful for the help we received in our editorial task from Ed Barton, Charles Bennett, Tom Cloney, Ray Hirschfeld, Hrvoje Hrgovcic, Mark Smith, Pablo Tamayo, Thao Nguyen, Gérard Vichniac, and David Zaig.

We should like to thank Harold Abelson, Richard Brower, Arthur Burks, Nicola Cabibbo, Michael Creutz, Dominique d'Humière, Uriel Frisch, Peter Gacs, Bill Gosper, David Griffeath, Hyman Hartman, Brosl Hasslacher, Daniel Hillis, Giuseppe Iacopini, Leo Kadanoff, Rolf Landauer, Leonid Levin, Mike Levitt, Stewart Nelson, Giorgio Parisi, Yves Pomeau, Claudio Rebbi, Brian Silverman, Gerald Sussman, and Stephen Wolfram for useful discussions and suggestions. Charles Bennett made direct contributions to the book's contents.

The development of a family of cellular automata machines is an offshoot of more theoretical endeavors of the *Information Mechanics Group* at the MIT Laboratory for Computer Science. Encouragement and practical support were given by the director of the laboratory Michael Dertouzos, by Edward Fredkin—who led the group until recently and is behind many of the ideas presented in this book—and by the Provost, John Deutsch.

This research was supported in part by the following government agencies: Defense Advanced Research Projects Agency (Grant No. N00014-83-10-0125), National Science Foundation (Grant No. 8214312-IST), and U.S. Department of Energy (Grant No. DE-AC02-83-ER13082).

Tommaso Toffoli
Norman Margolus

November 5, 1986

Cellular Automata Machines

Introduction

In Greek mythology, the machinery of the universe was the gods themselves. They personally tugged the sun across the sky, delivered rain and thunder, and fed appropriate thoughts into human minds. In more recent conceptions, the universe is created complete with its operating mechanism: once set in motion, it runs by itself. God sits outside of it and can take delight in watching it.

Cellular automata are stylized, synthetic universes defined by simple rules much like those of a board game. They have their own kind of matter which whirls around in a space and a time of their own. One can think of an astounding variety of them. One can actually construct them, and watch them evolve. As inexperienced creators, we are not likely to get a very interesting universe on our first try; as individuals, we may have different ideas of what makes a universe interesting, or of what we might want to do with it. In any case, once we've been shown a cellular-automaton universe we'll want to make one ourselves; once we've made one, we will want to try another one. After having made a few, we'll be able to custom-tailor one for a particular purpose with a certain confidence.

A cellular automata machine is a universe synthesizer. Like an organ, it has keys and stops by which the resources of the instrument can be called into action, combined, and reconfigured. Its color screen is a window through which one can watch the universe that is being "played."

This book, then, is an introductory harmony and orchestration manual for "composers" of cellular-automaton universes.

Part I

Overview

Chapter 1

Cellular automata

> What has been done once can be done again.
>
> [Traditional clause to justify use of mathematical induction]

To *synthesize* a system means to "put it together" using a given repertoire of concepts, tools, and materials. The system may be an abstract mathematical structure, such as a differential equation, or a concrete piece of machinery, such as a telephone; we may be interested in the system for its own sake, or as a device for performing a certain function, or as a model of some other structure.

In this book, we shall explore the expressive power, for the purpose of system synthesis, of a particular repertoire of resources, namely the laws, structures, and phenomena supported by cellular automata—especially to the extent that these systems become effectively accessible to experimentation through the use of a cellular automata machine of adequate performance.

The present chapter is an introduction to cellular automata—it concludes with brief historical notes and references.

1.1 Basic concepts

Cellular automata are discrete dynamical systems whose behavior is completely specified in terms of a local relation, much as is the case for a large class of continuous dynamical systems defined by partial differential equations. In this sense, *cellular automata are the computer scientist's counterpart to the physicist's concept of "field."*

As noted in the Introduction, a cellular automaton can be thought of as a stylized universe. Space is represented by a uniform grid, with each site or *cell* containing a few bits of data; time advances in discrete steps; and the laws of the universe are expressed by a single recipe—say, a small look-up table—through which at each step each cell computes its new state from that of its close neighbors. Thus, the system's laws are *local* and *uniform*.[1]

Given a suitable recipe, such a simple operating mechanism is sufficient to support a whole hierarchy of structures and phenomena. Cellular automata supply useful models for many investigations in natural science, combinatorial mathematics, and computer science; in particular, they represent a natural way of studying the evolution of large physical systems. They also constitute a general paradigm for parallel computation, much as Turing machines do for serial computation.

1.2   Animate-by-numbers

Before asking a machine to run a cellular-automaton universe one should have a fair idea of how the same task could be performed by hand.

Take a pad of good-quality graph paper, in which the grid is printed exactly in the same position on each sheet. Starting with the last sheet and proceeding backwards through the pad you will draw a series of frames, one per sheet, which will make up a brief animation sequence.

Open the pad at the last sheet and draw a simple picture by filling in with black ink a few cells of the grid near the center of the sheet; this will be frame 1 of your "animation movie". Now turn a page, pulling the next-to-the-last sheet down on top of the last one: the figure of frame 1 will still be visible through one thickness of paper. Draw the next frame of the movie on the new sheet by the following INKSPOT recipe:

- Pick a cell, and look at the 3×3 area centered on it—its "neighborhood." If in this area you see (on the sheet just below) exactly three black cells, lightly mark your cell in pencil; also mark your cell if it is sitting directly on top of a black cell.

- Do the same for every cell of the grid. When you are finished, fill in with ink all the marked cells.

Construct frame 3 from frame 2 by turning to a new sheet and applying the same recipe; then construct frame 4 from frame 3, and so forth, until all the sheets have been used.

[1] "Local" means that to know what will happen here in a moment I only have to look at the state of things near me: no action-at-a-distance is permitted. "Uniform" means that the laws are the same everywhere: I can only tell one place from another by the shape of the surrounding landscape—not by any difference in the laws.

Now you can look at your flip-book. Close the pad, hold its edge between your thumb and forefinger, and let the sheets fall one by one in rapid sequence. What you will see is an inkspot that spreads in an irregular way—as through dirty fabric—producing capes and bays, leaving a few small areas untouched, and now and then shooting out a straight filament (Figure 1.1).

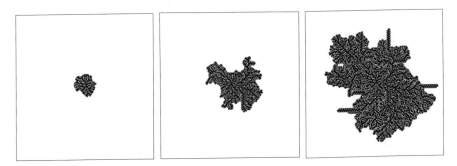

Figure 1.1: A few frames from a typical INKSPOT sequence. The scale is such that the individual cells are barely discernible.

This is, in essence, all there is to a cellular automaton. Change the initial conditions, and you'll get a somewhat different history. Change the recipe, and you get a new set of dynamical laws—a new universe. You can use a grid of different shape (say, hexagonal), or perhaps a three-dimensional one. The recipe may refer to a neighborhood of size and shape other than 3×3, and may involve more than one ink color; however, both the number of neighbors and the number of colors (i.e., the number of possible *cell states*) must be finite, because we want the updating of a cell to be a finite business.

Suppose our sheet contained 100,000 cells (this is somewhat coarser than the detail of a TV frame). If the recipe is not too involved, it will take a human animator a day to paint a new frame; the task is trivially simple, as in "paint-by-numbers," but long, tedious, and error-prone, A personal computer will do the job in a few seconds—generating new frames at the rate of a slide show. If we want to see real movement we need to go perhaps a thousand times faster: a super-mainframe computer might do, but at great cost and with a clear waste of resources. A more efficient approach is desirable.

1.3   Cellular automata machines

Let us frankly admit that the generality and flexibility of the cellular-automaton approach to system synthesis are achieved at a cost. Instead of few variables that may be made to interact in an arbitrarily assigned way, a cellular automaton uses many variables (one per cell) but demands that

these interact only locally and uniformly. In order to synthesize structures
of significant complexity it is necessary to use a large number of cells, and in
order for these structures to interact with one another and evolve to a significant extent it is necessary to let the automaton run for a large number of
steps. For elementary scientific applications, a satisfactory experimental run
may require the computation of billions of events (an *event* is the updating of
a single cell); for more substantial applications, a thousand or a million times
this value may be desirable (i.e., 10^{12}–10^{15} events): the limits are really set
by how much we *can* do rather than by how much we wish to do.

In this context, ordinary computers are of little use. The simulation of
a cellular-automaton event may require some thirty machine operations each
involving a few machine cycles—say, 10 μsec on a fast machine. To compute
10^{13} events with such an approach would take several years!

On the other hand, the structure of a cellular automaton is ideally suited
for realization on a machine having a high degree of parallelism and local and
uniform interconnections;[2] with an appropriate architecture one can achieve
in the simulation of cellular automata a performance at least several orders
of magnitude greater than with a conventional computer, for a comparable
cost.

Indeed, cellular automata machines having size, speed, and flexibility adequate for general experimentation, and moderate cost, have recently become
available to the scientific community at large (see Chapter 2). These machines provide a laboratory in which the ideas presented in this book can be
handled in a concrete form and applied to the synthesis of a great variety of
systems.

1.4   Historical notes and references

Cellular automata have been invented many times under different names, and
somewhat different concepts have been circulated under the same name. In
pure mathematics they can be recognized as a branch of topological dynamics,
in electrical engineering they are sometimes called iterative arrays, and high-
school kids may know them as a sort of home-computer game. They have been
used and abused by interdisciplinary scientists as well as interdisciplinary
bumblers. They have been the topic or the excuse for countless doctoral
theses. They have been much talked and written about, but until recently no
one had actually *seen* much of them.

---

[2]The term "non-von Neumann architecture" is often used to distinguish parallel computers of this kind from more conventional sequential computers. However, it should be noted
that the theory of cellular automata was introduced by von Neumann himself at about the
same time as he was working on the design of general-purpose electronic computers.

Since the present historical notes are for the benefit—not the confusion—of the reader, we shall touch only on those topics that we deem directly relevant to the purposes of this book.

Conventional models of computation, such as the Turing machine, make a distinction between the structural part of a computer—which is fixed, and the data on which the computer operates—which are variable. The computer cannot operate on its own "matter," so to speak; it cannot extend or modify itself, or build other computers.

Cellular automata were introduced in the late forties by John von Neumann, following a suggestion of Stan Ulam[64], to provide a more realistic model for the behavior of complex, extended systems[68]; in a cellular automaton, objects that may be interpreted as passive data and objects that may be interpreted as computing devices are both assembled out of the same kind of structural elements and subject to the same fine-grained laws; *computation* and *construction* are just two possible modes of activity. Though von Neumann was a leading physicist as well as a mathematician, explicit physical considerations are lacking in his work on cellular automata; his interest was directed more at a reductionistic explanation of certain aspects of biology. In fact the mechanisms he proposed for achieving self-reproducing structures within a cellular automaton bear a strong resemblance to those—discovered in the following decade—that are actually employed by biological life.

Near the end of the war, while von Neumann was building one of the first electronic computers, the german engineer Konrad Zuse was hiding from the Nazis in Austria; there, in the isolation of a mountain peak, he had the germs of many parallel ideas, including high-level programming languages and "computing spaces"[76]—i.e., cellular automata. Zuse was especially interested in digital models of mechanics, and physical motivation plays a primary role in his work. It is unfortunate that historical circumstances prevented his work from being more widely known at the time.

Von Neumann's work on self-reproducing automata was completed and described by Arthur Burks[68], who maintained an active interest in the field for several years afterwards. His *Essays on Cellular Automata*[10] are a good introduction to the questions that were asked about cellular automata in the formative years of computer science. In the same environment—i.e., the Logic of Computers Group of the University of Michigan—John Holland started applying cellular automata to problems of adaptation and optimization[27], and a general-purpose cellular automata simulator program was developed[7]. It was months of work with this simulator (cf. [55]) that convinced one of the authors (Toffoli) of the need for a more direct and efficient hardware realization—a cellular automata *machine*.

In the meantime, professional mathematicians had turned their attention to iterated transformations acting on spatially-extended, discrete-state structures[25]—cellular automata again! Lack of communication and of uniform terminology led to much duplication of work. An important characterization of cellular automata in terms of continuity in the Cantor-set topology, proved in twelve pages by Richardson[48], could actually have been written as a two-line corollary to previous work by Hedlund[25]. Similarly, a brute-force search for surjective cellular automata reported by Patt in 1971 (cf. [2]) had been conducted on a wider scale by Hedlund et al.[24] already in 1963!

Important theoretical questions on computability and reversibility, already touched on by Moore and by Myhill (cf. [10]), were studied by Alvy Smith[52], Serafino Amoroso[2], and Viktor Aladyev[1], among others, and this approach was continued by a still-flourishing Japanese school (cf. [40] and references therein).

John Conway's game of "life," introduced to the public by Martin Gardner's widely read Scientific American column[20], for a while enjoyed a popularity close to a cult—and turned 'cellular automata' into a household word for a generation of young scientists.

We are mostly interested in cellular automata as *autonomous* systems, i.e., as worlds in their own, rather than as *transducers* (systems that produce a steady output stream of information as a response to a steady input stream). For this reason, we shall not deal at all with the large literature concerned with iterative-circuit arrays in the context of arithmetic processing, image processing, and pattern recognition. Preston and Duff's book on *Modern Cellular Automata*[46] can be used as an introduction to these areas and as a reference to machines developed for these more specialized applications.

The question of whether cellular automata could model not only general phenomenological aspects of our world[3] but also directly the laws of *physics* itself was raised again by Edward Fredkin, who had also been active in more conventional areas of cellular automata research (cf. [3]), and by Tommaso Toffoli[55]. A primary theme of this research is the formulation of computer-like models of physics that are *information-preserving*, and thus retain one of the most fundamental features of microscopic physics—namely *reversibility*[17,58,35].

Models that explicitly reduce macroscopic phenomena to precisely defined microscopic processes are of prime methodological interest[13] because they can speak with great sincerity and authority (cf. Chapter 13). But, to let them speak at all, in general one has no choice but to implement in an explicit way the prescriptions of these models, actually bridging the scale gap between the microscopic level and the macroscopic one: cellular automata simulators capable of updating millions of cells in an extremely short time become indispensable tools. This is one of the issues that was addressed by our

---

[3]Such as communication, computation, and construction; growth, reproduction, competition, evolution, etc.

Information Mechanics Group, at the MIT Laboratory for Computer Science, with the design of high-performance cellular automata machines[59,60,36].

This approach has been used to provide extremely simple models of common differential equations of physics—such as the *heat* and *wave* equations[61] and the *Navier-Stokes* equation[23,18]—which can be thought of as limiting cases of a variety of extremely simple processes of combinatorial dynamics. In particular, cellular automata have been found to provide accurate models of fluid dynamics that are not only conceptually stimulating but also viable—at least in certain circumstances—from the viewpoint of computational efficiency[18,36,42].

A burgeoning branch of dynamical systems theory studies the emergence of well-characterized collective phenomena—ordering, turbulence, chaos, symmetry-breaking, fractality, etc.—in systems consisting of a large number of individuals connected by nonlinear couplings; here the motivations and the mathematical apparatus are more akin to those of macroscopic physics and materials science. Cellular automata provide a rich and continually growing collection of representative models where these phenomena can be isolated and studied with relative ease[66,15,5]. The systematic use of cellular automata in this context was vigorously pioneered by Stephen Wolfram[71,70,72,73,43]; his collection of papers on the *Theory and Applications of Cellular Automata*[74] is accompanied by an extensive bibliography.

In conclusion cellular automata seem to have found a permanent (and increasingly important) role as conceptual and practical models of spatially-distributed dynamical systems—of which physical systems are the first and foremost prototypes.

Chapter 2

The CAM environment

And so, rolling up his sleeves and summoning up all his mastery, Trurl built the king an entirely new kingdom....

"Have I understood you correctly?" said Klapaucius. "You gave that brutal despot ... a whole civilization to rule and have dominion over forever? Trurl, how could you have done such a thing?!"

"You must be joking!" Trurl exclaimed. "Really the whole kingdom fits into a box three feet by two and a half...it's only a model..."

"A model of what?"

[Stanislaw Lem]

A usual prerequisite for a harmony course is "familiarity with the piano." Of course, one can make harmony in a multitude of other ways—for instance with an organ, a guitar, or a choir. However, a standard environment makes it easier to keep the attention focused on issues of a more fundamental character: it will be up to the individual student to transfer to other contexts the expertise gained in mastering the resources of this environment.

In this book, the standard modeling environment, which will be gradually introduced starting with the present chapter, is represented by a specific, commercially-available cellular automata machine, namely CAM-6. The main reason for this choice is that the hardware and software of this machine are effectively accessible to a wide range of users.

2.1   The CAM-6 machine

CAM-6 is a cellular automata machine intended to serve as a laboratory for
experimentation, a vehicle for communication of results, and a medium for
real-time, interactive demonstration.

This machine was originally developed at the MIT Laboratory for Computer Science.[1] It is currently produced by SYSTEMS CONCEPTS (San Fran-
cisco, CA), from which it was commissioned with the explicit intention that,
after fulfilling MIT's internal needs, further output of the production line
would be made available to the scientific community at large, as inexpen-
sively as possible.

Physically, CAM-6 consists of a module that plugs into a single slot of the
IBM-PC, -XT, or -AT (or compatible models), and of driving software operating under PC-DOS 2. While this readily-available host computer provides
housing, shielding, power, disk storage, a monitor, and a standard operating
environment, the real work of simulating cellular automata at a very high
speed is all done by the module itself, with a performance comparable—for
this specific application—to that of a CRAY-1.

The control software for CAM-6 is written in Forth, and runs on the
IBM-PC with 256-K of memory. This software is complemented by a number of ready-made applications and demos, and includes complete annotated
sources.

The Forth system itself—derived from Laxen and Perry's F83 model[2]—is
in the public domain, and complete annotated sources accompany it.

In the rest of this book, we shall refer to CAM-6 simply as CAM.

2.2   Basic hardware resources

Here we briefly pass in review those basic hardware resources of CAM that are
visible to the user and constitute the "programmer's model" of the machine.
A fuller discussion of these and other resources is deferred to later chapters.

2.2.1   Storage: the bit-planes

In the animate-by-numbers example of Section 1.2, let us fix our attention on
a particular cell and follow its history from frame to frame. At any moment,
the given cell will be either white or black. Thus, each cell can be thought

---

[1]Machines of the CAM family have been in use for several years. An earlier version,
CAM-5, was described in *Physica D*[59], and popular articles related to it have appeared
in *Scientific American*[22], *High Technology*[63], and *Discover*[47]. CAM-6 is on permanent
exhibit at the Boston Computer Museum.

[2]Credit actually extends to a much longer list of people.

of as a two-state variable, or *bit*, and the whole grid as a two-dimensional array of bits, or *bit-plane*. It will be convenient to call ⓪ and ①—rather than "white" and "black"—the two possible values of a bit.

In many applications, cells with a wider range of states are required. Suppose we need four states. Instead of just ⓪ and ① we can use the symbols ⓪, ①, ②, and ③ as possible cell states. Alternatively, we can subdivide the cell into two sub-cells each containing a single bit, and write the four states as ⓪⓪, ⓪①, ①⓪, ①①; in this case, it is useful to visualize these two bits as piled on top of one another, rather than placed side by side. Then the whole array can be visualized as a set of two *bit-planes*, one overlaying the other.

In CAM, up to four bit-planes are available for encoding the state of a cell, and thus a cell can have up to 16 states. (However, there are certain restrictions on the collective use of the four bit-planes.)

2.2.2   Display: the color map

Treating the state of a cell as a pile of four bits is convenient for programming purposes. For display purposes, it is better to represent each cell by a colored dot, or *pixel*, on the monitor's screen. The color, of course, will correspond to the cell's state according to a definite assignment: the table that decides which color has been assigned to each of the 16 possible cell states is called the *color map*. In CAM the contents of the color map can be specified by the user to suit the requirements of each experiment.

2.2.3   Dynamics: the rule tables

During an update cycle of the cellular automata machine, the current frame—represented by the contents of all the bit-planes—is replaced by a new frame according to a specified recipe. The result is one *step* in the evolution of a particular cellular automaton, and that recipe is called the *rule* of this cellular automaton.

In CAM, the user is allowed to specify the rule in a rather discursive fashion, using constructs from a high-level programming language. Internally, however, this description is eventually converted into a rule *table*, which explicitly lists what the new state of a cell will be for any possible combination of states of its neighbors. Since each cell consists of four bits, it will be convenient to think of the rule table as consisting of four sub-tables or *components*, one for each of the bit-planes. In this context, we shall loosely speak of "the rule for plane 0" meaning "that component (of the overall rule) that specifies the new state of bit-plane 0."

2.2.4   Geometry in the small: the neighborhood

In writing a cellular automaton rule, we specify how each cell is going to be influenced by some nearby cells. More precisely, we specify how each of the four bits that make up a cell is going to be influenced by certain nearby bits; some of these may reside on the same bit-plane, and some may reside on the other three bit-planes. How far can this influence reach?

A bit is called a *neighbor* of another one if it has a chance to directly affect it, via the rule, in one step. In principle, a cellular-automaton rule could make use of an arbitrarily large number of neighbors. However, efficiency dictates a practical limit to the number and the span of direct neighbor connections; the hardware of CAM provides specific combinations of neighbor connections—or *neighborhoods*—that have been selected according to criteria of general utility and flexibility. Neighborhood selection is discussed in Chapter 7.

2.2.5   Geometry in the large: wrap-around

Returning to the animate-by-numbers example, how are we going to apply the INKSPOT rule when a cell lies at the edge of the sheet, and so some of its neighbors are missing from the frame? Of course we could make explicit provisions for this special case, but it would be better to avoid the need for "special cases" altogether.

In CAM, this problem is solved by the obvious *wrap-around* device; that is, the right edge of the sheet acts as if it were "glued" to the left edge (and likewise for the top and bottom edges). As in many video games, any object that tries to move off one edge of the screen will reenter the screen at the same position at the opposite edge.[3] One can visualize a frame as painted on the surface of a doughnut: no amount of walking will allow one to find the "edge of the world.[4]" Additional wrap-around options are mentioned in Section B.2.

2.3   Software: CAM Forth

The user of CAM is provided with access to its software at various levels, as explained in the documentation that accompanies the machine. For most ordinary applications, however, the software is transparent to the user, and one can view CAM much like an appliance—in which a few rows of buttons directly control, in an interactive manner, a number of functions and options.

However, if we wish to be able to add new items to our repertoire of universes, we will need a language—convenient for the user and understandable

---

[3]Several CAM modules can be combined so as to obtain a larger cellular automaton. In this case, edge "gluing" is appropriately modified so that the wrap-around applies correctly to the larger sheet.

[4]In more mathematical terms, the topology is that of a torus.

to the machine—for describing cellular automata rules. This rule-making process is formally introduced in Chapter 4, and is fully developed in the succeeding chapters.

The language we shall be using in this book is CAM *Forth*. Forth is an extensible programming language particularly suited for interactive tasks. This language has been extended so as to contain a variety of words and constructs useful for conversing with CAM; in particular, for defining cellular automata rules and for constructing, documenting, and running experiments.

Forth was adopted as a standard by the International Astronomical Union to facilitate the exchange of procedures for aiming telescopes and controlling their ancillary equipment. Here, we shall be using it to adjust the settings of a new kind of "scope," one that gives a view into a variety of synthetic worlds.

For the purpose of defining cellular automata rules, very little Forth is actually needed. On the other hand, the texture of Forth is unusual, and even people who are already familiar with more conventional programming languages (such as PASCAL or BASIC) may appreciate a minimum of introduction. Appendix A provides a brief tutorial covering the most basic concepts; one should glance at it before proceeding. Sections A.12 and A.14 in particular contain information which is specific to this version of Forth. Some of the tutorial material will be recalled and expanded in the course of the book; constructs that are more intimately tied to the operation of CAM will be introduced as the occasion arises.

To achieve a more comprehensive command of the language, the reader may turn to Leo Brodie's "Starting Forth" [8], which is an excellent introduction to the subject.

Chapter 3

A live demo

I now saw very plainly that these were very
little eels, or worms, lying all huddled up together and wriggling; just as if you saw, with
the naked eye, a whole tubful of very little eels
and water, with the eels a-squirming among
one another: and the whole water seemed to
be alive with these multifarious animalcules.

[Leeuwenhoek]

Read this brief chapter once through without worrying too much about details. Imagine that a friend is sitting at the console of a CAM machine, showing
you a brief cycle of experiments and explaining along the way what he is doing and why. You may put off a question to avoid interrupting him, and in
many cases the question will be answered by what you see on the screen.
Eventually you may want to go over a few points in more detail.

At the end of the session you don't expect to "know everything." However, you want to feel that there was a definite connection between stated
goals, actions performed, and results seen; and that, with a better knowledge of available commands and resources, you might be able to run some
experiments yourself.

As the subject for this demo we have chosen the game of "life." This is by
no means the only, or even the most interesting, rule for cellular automata—
just the most widely known—and appears here more for historical reasons
than for any direct relevance to the themes of this book.

3.1   The game of "life"

In 1970, the mathematician John Conway introduced a delightful cellular
automaton which caught the attention of science amateurs and professionals
all over the world[20]. LIFE may be thought of as describing a population
of stylized organisms, developing in time under the effect of counteracting
propagation and extinction tendencies.

An individual of this population is represented by a cell in the $\boxed{1}$ state,
while a $\boxed{0}$ represents empty space; for brevity, one can speak respectively of
"live" and "dead" cells. At every step, each cell responds to the state of its
immediate environment—consisting of its eight nearest neighbors—according
to the following directions:

Death: A live cell will remain alive only when surrounded by 2 or 3 live
   neighbors; otherwise, it will feel either "overcrowded" or "too lonely"
   and it will die.

Birth: A dead cell will come to life when surrounded by exactly 3 live neighbors. Thus, birth is induced by the meeting of three "parents."

In CAM, the machinery "knows" that the same rule must be applied to all
cells (there are 256×256=65,536 of them), and therefore it will be sufficient
to express the rule for a "generic" cell, called CENTER (the *center* of attention). The eight neighbors of this cell are called, with self-explanatory names,
NORTH, SOUTH, WEST, EAST, N.WEST, N.EAST, S.WEST, and S.EAST.

To write the rule for LIFE in CAM Forth, we'll first define a word 8SUM
which counts the number of live neighbors, and then use this count as an
address to locate in a table the entry that corresponds to that particular
count; the entry itself specifies the cell's new state. There are two tables in
our program, one for the case of a "dead" center cell and the other for a "live"
one.

```
                          : 8SUM ( -- count)
        NORTH SOUTH WEST EAST        \ count ranges
    N.WEST N.EAST S.WEST S.EAST      \  from 0 thru 8
              + + + + + + + ;
                          : LIFE
            CENTER 0= IF
8SUM { 0 0 0 1 0 0 0 0 0 } ELSE      \ dead-cell table
8SUM { 0 0 1 1 0 0 0 0 0 } THEN      \ live-cell table
                  >PLN0 ;            \ rule for bit-plane 0
```

At this point, you don't have to understand the exact meaning of the above
piece of Forth program (though it might be helpful to take a look now at
the tutorial of Appendix A). At any rate, an inspection of the definition of
8SUM should make it plausible that this Forth word adds up eight quantities

(there are eight terms and seven + 's). The expression in parentheses, (--
count) , is just a comment, and reminds us that the result of 8SUM is the
desired neighbor count. Similarly, it should appear plausible to you that the
Forth word LIFE may somehow use the value of 8SUM to select a particular
entry in a list of nine objects, and that the value of CENTER may determine
which of the two given lists is actually used. Finally, the word >PLN0 tells
the software that the object specified by this recipe is the new state of the
bit in bit-plane 0 of CAM.

Let's start the screen with a "primeval soup" in which $\boxed{0}$'s and $\boxed{1}$'s are
distributed at random in equal proportions (Figure 3.1a). After a few dozen
steps of wild activity the population will have thinned down (Figure 3.1b);
a little later, most of the screen will be quiet except for a few places where
things keep smoldering and occasionally flare up in sudden bursts of activity,
in a way reminiscent of brush fire (Figure 3.2a). Eventually, all activity may
subside except for a few isolated "blinkers" or other cyclic patterns of short
period (Figure 3.2b).

To allow a static picture to give some feeling of dynamic behavior, the
frames of Figure 3.2 are actually time exposures.

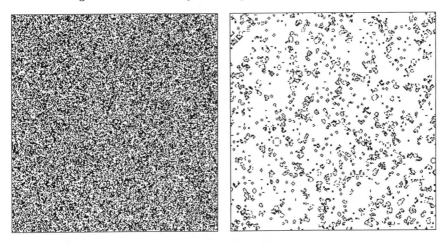

Figure 3.1: A LIFE gallery: (a) Initial random configuration. (b) A few dozen steps
later the "primeval soup" has grown thinner.

The above transcript is typical of LIFE "in the wild," in the sense that behavior having similar chaotic features will occur starting from almost any initial configuration; on the other hand, closer observation will reveal a number
of well-defined effects which can be brought under our control by a suitable
choice of initial conditions (cf. Section 3.4). This phenomenology is abun-
dantly documented elsewhere[6]; here, we use LIFE only to provide a definite
context in illustrating a number of methodological points.

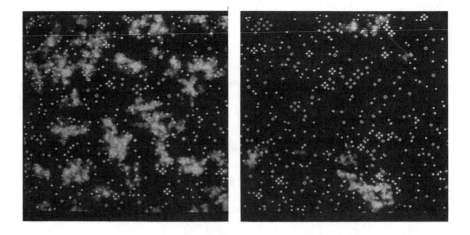

Figure 3.2: (a) Hundreds of steps later activity is concentrated in a few smoldering areas, with occasional flares. (b) A few thousand steps later, most action has died out.

3.2   Echoing

When we watch LIFE on CAM's screen, a lot of things happen at the same time all over the place, and we may want to slow down the simulation or even stop it for a while in order to observe some details. However, just when the pace is slow enough to allow us to view at leisure an individual frame, all feeling of movement is lost; things that at full speed looked quite different from one another because of their state of motion now look disappointingly the same, and it's hard to remember which cells carried the action and which belonged to a static background. To paraphrase Zeno, by the light of an electronic flash it's hard to tell a flying bullet from a piece of chewed gum. What we need is a way of coloring with the hues of "velocity" the black-and-white postcard representing current "position."

The cells of LIFE consist of one bit each. Thus, LIFE uses a single bit-plane of CAM and could be displayed as black-on-white. But CAM has several bit-planes available, and can drive a color monitor. When we construct in plane 0 the new state of a cell, instead of discarding the old state we can temporarily save it on a second bit-plane, say, plane 1 (here, one may think of plane 1 as an *echo* of the past). In this way, we can put together a two-bit value from a new state and an old state, and we can instruct CAM's color map to display a different color for each of the four combinations $\boxed{0}\boxed{0}$, $\boxed{0}\boxed{1}$, $\boxed{1}\boxed{0}$, and $\boxed{1}\boxed{1}$.

The rule that makes plane 1 echo plane 0 with a delay of one step is simply

: ECHO

```
CENTER >PLN1;
```

Note that, even though this is a rule for the new state of plane 1, CENTER still denotes the center neighbor from plane 0; the center neighbor from plane 1—called CENTER' —is not "sensed" at all by this rule, since the echo is discarded after one step.

If we rerun the experiment of Section 3.1 with ECHO on, using the color assignment of table (3.1), LIFE becomes much more colorful. Static objects will look red, moving objects will look whitish with a green leading edge and a blue trailing edge—*and the colors will stay even when the simulation is stopped.*

The colors used for representing on the color monitor the four possible states of a four-bit cell are red, green, blue, and black, as in the table below; this color scheme also applies to the color plates, which were taken directly from the monitor's screen. A different scheme is necessary, of course, for the black-and white figures; this scheme is indicated in the same table.[1] To avoid confusion, actual colors will be mentioned in the rest of this book only when referring to the color plates; for the other illustrations, we shall imagine having a custom "paper monitor" capable of displaying black, white, and two intermediate shades of gray. Figures involving a single bit-plane, such as Figure 3.1, will of course use black for ⬛1⬛ and white for ⬜0⬜.

CELL STATUS (LIFE with ECHO)	PLANE 0 1	PRINTED PAGE	COLOR MONITOR	
cell stayed alive	1 1	Black	Red	(3.1)
cell was just born	1 0	Dark gray	Green	
cell just died	0 1	Light gray	Blue	
cell stayed dead	0 0	White	Black	

3.3 Tracing

The ECHO feature enriches the display with a small amount of short-term memory. In principle, one could prolong the echo by using more auxiliary bit-planes to hold, in a pipelined fashion, an after-image of the last few steps. However, bit-planes are expensive, and at any rate there are limits to the amount of historical information that can be effectively displayed on the screen by color- or intensity-coding.

A simpler *tracing* technique will be effective in many situations, in particular when there are a limited number of objects evolving on a uniform background—as in LIFE. We shall let each live cell in plane 0 leave a trace of its presence on plane 1, as with ECHO, but this time the trace will be a

---

[1] On the paper, large background areas are better left white (no ink), rather than shown in black as on the monitor.

permanent one (in a way, we are adding to the monitor's cathode-ray tube
an "infinite-permanence" phosphor layer). The TRACE mode is turned on by
specifying for plane 1 the rule

```
                 : TRACE
        CENTER CENTER' OR >PLN1 ;
```

Using the same color coding as with ECHO (the interpretation is, of course,
slightly different), moving objects will leave a light-gray trace behind, and a
retreating tide will leave the shore painted light-gray up to the high-water
mark. When the tracing sheet is too messed up, we start a fresh one by doing
at least one step in the ECHO mode (this wipes out the long-term history)
and resuming the TRACE whenever desired.

Let's proceed with our monitoring of LIFE in the wild. We will notice
that active areas occasionally eject a a small fluttering object, called a *glider*,
which steadily scuttles away on a diagonal path until it crashes into something
else. The spontaneous production of a glider is not a rare event; however,
under ordinary conditions the mean free path of a glider (from production to
disintegration) is quite short, and most of them will escape our notice. Now
we turn on the TRACE; in a few moments the screen will have recorded a
number of rectilinear gray traces left by gliders, as in Figure 3.3a.

ECHO and TRACE are perhaps the simplest examples of *image-enhancing*
aids useful in cellular-automaton experiments. Some experience, a good familiarity with the available resources, and most of all a good knowledge of
the phenomenology of a particular cellular-automaton universe will suggest
a whole array of observation aids of suitable sensitivity and selectivity, analogous to the staining techniques used in microscopy to differentiate specific
tissues, or to the the cloud chambers used in particle physics to "materialize"
the tracks of specific events.

3.4   How to breed gliders

TRACE'ing will stain a glider's path, but a short path will remain short and
hard to see. Can we prepare a "culture" in which gliders will be longer-
lived? Can we "isolate" a glider? Using CAM's plane editor, let's construct
on the screen a mask consisting of all $\boxed{0}$'s except for a circular island of $\boxed{1}$'s
in the middle, and store this mask in a buffer in the host computer. Now,
we run LIFE from the usual primeval soup for, say, a hundred steps—when
conditions for the birth of gliders are quite favorable. At this point we AND
the saved mask with the configuration on the screen,[2] to retain only the

---

[2]The logical operator AND acts on two binary inputs and returns one binary output; to
AND two configurations, one applies the operator to each cell site, AND'ing the corresponding
two bits. CAM has provisions for such logical operations between host buffers and CAM
configurations.

central portion of the picture. Gliders produced on the shore of this island
and moving into the surrounding ocean will be able to swim a long distance
unhindered (Figure 3.3b).

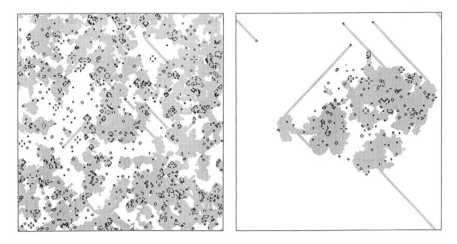

Figure 3.3: Glider breeding: (a) Wild gliders have a short life. (b) Gliders swimming
away from shore into open ocean; by blotting out the island, we will be left with a
pure glider culture.

On a lucky run we may find many gliders in the ocean at the same time!
When this happens, we'll be ready with a new mask (all ⊡'s except for a
large round hole of ⓪'s) to blot out what is left of the island; now the gliders
will be able to pursue their paths without risk of crashing into other objects.
They may still collide with *one another*, of course—but what else would one
collect gliders for?

This breeding experiment illustrates how, by setting up initial conditions
that are far from equilibrium, one can increase the chances of observing situations that otherwise would be quite improbable. (Note that the exact shape
and size of the island do not matter much.)

A further stage in the understanding of a world is reached when we can
identify, at some level of aggregation, a number of primitive materials and
mechanisms that we can use in the construction of structures having a well-
identified, repeatable behavior. At this stage, science turns into technology.
To build arbitrarily complex machinery we may have to control in great detail
the initial conditions of an extended portion of the world.

Figure 3.4a shows the complete plans for a "glider gun," a machine which
at regular intervals shoots a new glider along a well-defined path; the discovery
of this device—as well as of many other interesting phenomena of LIFE, is
attributed to Bill Gosper. Finally, in Figure 3.4b we use this "technology" to

set up a colliding-beam experiment, where two streams of gliders are made
to cross and interact.

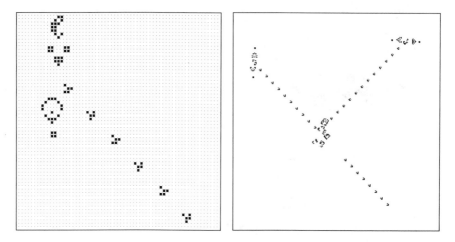

Figure 3.4: (a) Glider gun (shown enlarged). (b) Colliding-beam experiment using
two glider guns.

Chapter 4

The rules of the game

> I shall omit the discussion of republics.... I shall turn only to the principate, and go on weaving according to the order written above, disputing how one is able to govern and maintain these principates.
>
> [Niccolò Machiavelli]

In this chapter we shall look at cellular-automaton rules from the viewpoint of their format, or "grammar," rather than of their specific contents.

A cellular-automaton rule happens to be a function on a finite set, and thus can be explicitly given by a look-up table, i.e, by writing next to each possible input value the corresponding output value. Indeed, this is the internal format used by CAM's hardware, mainly for reasons of speed.

On the other hand, people usually prefer to develop more structured (though not necessarily more compact) descriptions of the functions they are required to handle. The choice of a suitable description language makes it easier to specify, identify, or remember functions of a particular class, and to a certain extent "comprehend" their behavior.

4.1 The choices of creation

A cellular automata machine is sitting on our desk, waiting for us to give a *rule*—the law that will govern a world. Where do we start?

Well, how much choice do we have? In other words, what does a rule look like?

Take an arbitrary configuration on the screen, pick a cell, and look at the bit pattern formed by its neighbors. (In this chapter, for simplicity we shall consider cellular automata utilizing only two states per cell and five neighbors.) We may find, for instance,

$$\begin{array}{c} \boxed{0} \\ \boxed{1}\boxed{0}\boxed{1} \\ \boxed{0} \end{array} \quad .$$

Does our rule specify a $\boxed{0}$ or a $\boxed{1}$ for the new state of the cell, as a "consequence" of this particular pattern? If we are making up the rule now, we are free to choose. Let's choose $\boxed{1}$, and make a record of it:

It is clear that the rule must specify the new state of the center cell for *any* neighborhood pattern. To proceed in an organized way, let's print a form listing all possible neighbor patterns (for graphic convenience, we have written the five neighbors in a row and labeled them with abbreviations of CENTER, NORTH, SOUTH, WEST, EAST):

Rule: ...

EWSNC	c_{new}	EWSNC	c_{new}	EWSNC	c_{new}	EWSNC	c_{new}
00000		01000		10000		11000	
00001		01001		10001		11001	
00010		01010		10010		11010	
00011		01011		10011		11011	
00100		01100		10100		11100	
00101		01101		10101		11101	
00110		01110		10110		11110	
00111		01111		10111		11111	

(4.1)

To make up a rule, one just fills out the form by writing a 0 or a 1 in each of the 32 boxes.

At first, you might just want to toss a coin for each choice.[1] For every rule that you get in this way run a few experiments[2] starting from different kinds of initial conditions (randomness, a little blob on a uniform background, a face, etc.). Much of the time the results will be quite disappointing; the initial pattern will grow in a chaotic way until the whole screen is filled with "static," or will shrivel and settle into a frozen arrangement. However, even at this casual level of experimentation some rules will show interesting traits,

---

[1]This process can be automated, of course.

[2]Section 5.6 explains how an arbitrary table can be coded in CAM Forth.

and once in a while you'll get a real nugget. The authors once obtained the following table

Rule Name: **HGLASS**

EWSNC	c_{new}	EWSNC	c_{new}	EWSNC	c_{new}	EWSNC	c_{new}
00000	0	01000	0	10000	0	11000	0
00001	1	01001	0	10001	0	11001	1
00010	1	01010	0	10010	0	11010	0
00011	1	01011	1	10011	0	11011	0
00100	0	01100	0	10100	0	11100	0
00101	0	01101	0	10101	1	11101	1
00110	0	01110	0	10110	0	11110	1
00111	0	01111	0	10111	0	11111	1

$$(4.2)$$

Run this rule for different initial conditions (in particular, starting from a blob of 0's in a sea of 1's), and see how much variety of behavior is packed in a mere 32-bit table. Figure 4.1 and Plates 1, 2 provide a few examples.

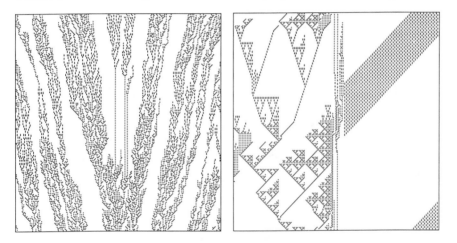

Figure 4.1: Behavior of **HGLASS** (a) from random conditions and (b) from a simple seed.

After generating a few hundred rules at random (it's hard to avoid falling into the gambler's syndrome, "Just one more!"), you may conclude that this is not a particularly effective way of constructing interesting worlds (or at least obviously interesting worlds).

A fundamental aspect of good computer programming is a well-matched interplay between algorithms and data structures. In a similar way, with cellular automata the synthesis of useful systems usually arises from a good match between choices made in the "rule" space (the set of look-up tables) and choices made in the "state" space (the set of configurations).

What is the size of the rule space? In other words, in how many different ways can one fill out the above form? Since there are $2^5 = 32$ boxes and 2 choices per box, the total number of rules is 2^{32}, or approximately 4 billion! For cellular automata with 2 states and 9 neighbors (the "format" of LIFE), this number climbs to $2^{2^9} = 2^{512}$—the square of the estimated number of elementary particles in the universe![3]

4.2   Rules in words

Having acquainted ourselves with what a cellular-automaton rule looks like from a *cell*'s viewpoint, we shall now discuss how to express it in a way that is convenient for *us*. Specifying the individual entries of a large table is a tedious and error-prone job; what's more, we don't want to stagger through the enormous space of rules without a sense of direction, a structured approach to rule-writing, and meaningful constraints arising from the nature of the problem at hand.

What we need is a language for expressing a rule in whatever terms we find most suitable, and a mechanism for interpreting our requests and translating them into a look-up table. In practice, any extensible programming language that is reasonably easy to use will serve these needs. The lowest-level tasks of this translation process may be supplied by the machine designer as additional, specialized primitives of the language; higher-level tasks may take the form of general-purpose utilities; finally, problem-specific needs may be addressed by the user by suitably combining these utilities or adding to the language new terms or constructs.

Note that, with the CAM approach, a table entry that may be used billions of times in the course of an experiment need only be constructed once, before the experiment starts; the efficiency of the process that translates the specifications for a rule into a look-up table in no way affects the speed at which the cellular automaton will run on the machine. Therefore, in expressing a rule in the chosen language one can take a relaxed attitude, and concentrate on convenience and clarity of description rather than worry about programming tricks that would improve execution efficiency.

A simple example will illustrate the route that leads from describing a cellular automaton in words to running it on CAM. A rule suggested by Edward Fredkin of MIT in the early years of cellular automata[3] specifies that a cell will "follow the *parity* of its neighborhood," i.e., that it will become live or dead depending on whether its neighborhood currently contains an odd

---

[3]CAM can handle a number of different cellular-automaton neighborhoods, and for each neighborhood the internal look-up tables provide up to 8192 entries; thus the number of rules one can explore with CAM is on the order of $2^{8192} \approx 10^{2467}$! Moreover, by rule composition one can greatly extend this range.

or even number of live cells. More formally,

$$\text{CENTER}_{\text{new}} = \text{CENTER} \oplus \text{NORTH} \oplus \text{SOUTH} \oplus \text{WEST} \oplus \text{EAST} \qquad (4.3)$$

(where $\oplus$ denotes "sum mod 2"). Evaluating this expression for all possible values of the arguments would yield the following look-up table

Rule: PARITY

EWSNC	c_{new}	EWSNC	c_{new}	EWSNC	c_{new}	EWSNC	c_{new}
00000	0	01000	1	10000	1	11000	0
00001	1	01001	0	10001	0	11001	1
00010	1	01010	0	10010	0	11010	1
00011	0	01011	1	10011	1	11011	0
00100	1	01100	0	10100	0	11100	1
00101	0	01101	1	10101	1	11101	0
00110	0	01110	1	10110	1	11110	0
00111	1	01111	0	10111	0	11111	1

$$(4.4)$$

but this is exactly what we wish done automatically, without even wanting to bother to see the result. In CAM Forth, we might code expression (4.3) as follows

```
N/MOORE
                              : PARITY
        CENTER NORTH SOUTH WEST EAST
              XOR XOR XOR XOR
                  >PLN0 ;
```

The declaration N/MOORE states that for this experiment we plan to use the *Moore* neighborhood, in which the neighbor words CENTER, ..., EAST are available.[4] The colon ':' tells Forth that we are going to add a new word to its dictionary, namely PARITY. The body of the definition, terminated by ';', is a simple expression in reverse Polish notation; XOR is the Forth word for the $\oplus$ operation. The word PARITY will never be called by us directly; rather, it will be passed as an argument to another word, MAKE-TABLE, which will know what to do with it. The following activity will then ensue

- MAKE-TABLE will run through the list of all possible neighbor configurations; for each configuration, it will assign to the predefined words CENTER, ..., EAST the values that the corresponding neighbors have in the configuration, and will call PARITY.

- Every time it is called with a fresh set of neighbor values, PARITY will calculate the corresponding new value for the center cell and store it in the appropriate entry of a table associated with plane 0 (>PLN0 knows where this table is located, and acts as a middleman).

---

[4]Each CAM neighborhood is accompanied by its own set of appropriate neighbor words, as explained in Chapter 7. The corresponding "wiring" of the machine allows a cell to receive information from those neighbors.

- Finally, MAKE-TABLE will ship the complete table to the CAM machine proper, where it is stored in a fast-access memory, ready to be used as many times as necessary in the course of an experiment.

At this point, all we have to do is "run" CAM. Let's initialize the screen with, say, a little square in the middle and hit the RUN key. With the PARITY rule, the square will rapidly evolve in a pulsating fashion, producing "Persian rug" patterns as in Figure 4.2.

Figure 4.2: Patterns produced by the PARITY rule, starting from a 32×32 square pattern, after approximately (a) fifty and (b) a hundred steps.

One feature of PARITY which is not at all obvious from the look-up table (4.4), and instead is brought out quite clearly by the structured description (4.3), is its *linearity*.[5] From this property one can formally draw important conclusions; for instance, waves emerge unaffected after going through one another. Another property that can be proved from (4.3) by means of formal arguments is that, for *any* initial figure on a uniform background, this figure will be found exactly reproduced in five copies after a suitable lapse of time (and later on in twenty-five copies, etc.).

Though one should not be tempted to ascribe miraculous powers to it, the choice of an appropriate notation in expressing the laws of a system often provides insights into significant aspects of its behavior.

Algorithms are often used as compressed representations of large data tables having a certain amount of regularity. In our situation—where the

---

[5]Take any two initial configurations and follow them in two separate experiments for, say, a hundred steps, and then add the two final configurations together (add corresponding sites mod 2). The result will be the same as if the two configurations had been added at the beginning and then followed for a hundred steps in a single experiment.

tables are of at most a few thousand bits—the advantage of using algorithms rather than tables in describing rules is not so much one of conciseness as of structural clarity. For example, the string of 32 bits that make up the C_{new} column in form (4.4) can be written, in hexadecimal digits, as 6DD6D66D, and this string could even be used as a *canonical* name of the rule; however, who would recognize in

```
088E8EE38EE3E3308EE3E330E3303000
8EE3E330E3303000E330300030000000
8EE3E330E3303000E330300030000000
E33030003000000030000000000000000
```

the rule **LIFE** of Chapter 3?

Systematic naming schemes—where a rule of a certain class can be reconstructed from its name—have some use, but only in specialized contexts (cf. [55,66,71,38]).

Part II

Resources

Chapter 5

Our first rules

> See Spot.
> See Spot run.
> Run, Spot, run!
> Run, run, run ...
> Spot can run fast.
>
> > [My Little Red Reader]

In this chapter we shall discuss cellular-automaton rules that use CAM's most basic resources in a straightforward way.

Even this simple class of rules is already capable of yielding a rich phenomenology, applicable to a variety of models. Moreover, a good familiarity with the basic building blocks will make it easier to deal with the more complex constructs that will be introduced in the following chapters. (As in ordinary programming, CAM's primitive resources can be organized and structured by means of a number of conceptual techniques, and turned into a hierarchy of tools suited to specific tasks.)

All of the rules discussed in this chapter will use a single bit-plane and the Moore neighborhood (cf. 7.3.1), consisting of the center cell and its eight nearest neighbors.

5.1 Unconstrained growth

Let us clear the CAM screen (all $\boxed{0}$'s) and run the following rule

```
                         : SQUARES

     N.WEST   NORTH    N.EAST
     WEST     CENTER   EAST
```

```
      S.WEST   SOUTH    S.EAST
OR OR OR OR OR OR OR OR  >PLNO ;
```

The screen will remain white. But as soon as we place a single ⊡ on it, there
will arise out of this "seed" a a black square growing at a uniform rate; in
a few seconds the black area will have filled the screen. If we sprinkle more
seeds, an equal number of squares will arise, and in their growth they will
overlap one another (Figure 5.1a).

This is a simple example of monotonic,[1] unconstrained growth.

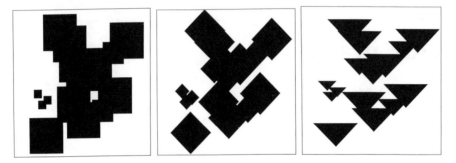

Figure 5.1: Monotonic growth from a few seeds: (a) SQUARES, (b) DIAMONDS, and
(c) TRIANGLES.

In the SQUARES rule above, the OR expression utilizes nine neighbors
arranged in a 3×3 square pattern having the center cell in the middle; the
result is "square" growth. In a similar way, the DIAMONDS rule

```
                    : DIAMONDS
           NORTH
    WEST CENTER EAST
           SOUTH
          OR OR OR OR  >PLNO ;
```

utilizes a diamond-shaped pattern of five neighbors,[2] and the result is "diamond" growth (Figure 5.1b). Before attempting to make generalizations on
this trend, let's try a pattern where the four-fold symmetry is broken; for
instance, a triangle pointing north, as in

```
                    : TRIANGLES
           NORTH
    WEST CENTER EAST
              OR OR OR  >PLNO ;
```

---

[1]I.e., once turned on a cell will remain on.

[2]The typographical arrangement of this piece of Forth code is, of course, irrelevant, and
has been chosen only for clarity.

The resulting growth (Figure 5.1c) is one of triangles pointing *south*! In general, any term in the OR expression whose position in the neighborhood is away from the center in a certain direction will produce growth in the *opposite* direction. This is not surprising, since neighbors act as *sources* of information for the center cell.

To further clarify this point, observe that the rule that is used by CAM when you press the DOWN-ARROW key in order to shift the whole screen southwards is

```
       : SHIFT-SOUTH
NORTH  >PLN0 ;
```

That is, information that moves to the south must come from the *north*, and that's where we should be looking for it.

The *light-cone* of an event (an updating of a cell) consists of all events in the past which can affect the outcome, and all events in the future which will be influenced by the outcome. In a cellular automaton, the *speed of light* (the maximum speed of propagation of information) may be different in different directions, and thus the shape of the light-cone of the cellular automaton spacetime may in reality be a skewed pyramid. In any case, the cells which can be influenced in one step (a cross section of the future light-cone) are arranged in a point-reflected image (rather than an identical copy) of the neighborhood (a cross section of the past light-cone).

5.2 Constrained growth

In the SQUARES rule of the previous section, a black area grows "as fast as it can" (i.e., at the speed of light) because a cell comes to life soon as it sees a live cell in its neighborhood. One can make the growth process more selective by limiting the number of cases in which a cell is allowed to turn on. For example, in the following rule a cell turns on only if it sees *exactly one* live cell among its eight neighbors, and will remain unchanged otherwise. (The word 8SUM was used in the LIFE example of Section 3.1.)

```
          : 1-OUT-OF-8
8SUM 1 = IF
        1 ELSE
CENTER THEN
       >PLN0 ;
```

The resulting growth, shown in Figure 5.2a, is much sparser that with SQUARES. Note the regular fractal pattern.

A whole set of constrained-growth rules can be obtained by playing variations on the "counting" theme, using the following scheme (for brevity, we define the word U—for "unchanged"—as an abbreviation of CENTER):

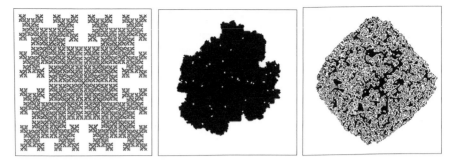

Figure 5.2:   Constrained   growth: (a) `1-OUT-OF-8`, (b) `LICHENS`, (c) `LICHENS-WITH-DEATH`.

```
                          : U
                CENTER ;
                          : LICHENS
    8SUM { U U U 1 U U U 1 1 }
                >PLNO ;
```

The construct within braces is a *case statement*, containing one entry for each possible value of its argument (`8SUM` $= 0, \ldots, 8$). Here, this construct is used as a straightforward decision table: a `1` in position n means that the cell will turn on if n neighbors are on, and a `U` means that it will remain unchanged. In the above example, growth is allowed only when the number of live neighbors is 3, 7, or 8; a seed of at least three cells is necessary to initiate growth, and, depending on the shape of the seed, growth may continue or stop after a while (Figure 5.2b). The `INKSPOT` rule of Section 1.2 works in a similar way.

5.3   Competitive growth

If in the above decision table one replaces some of the entries by `0`'s there will be situations where white grows back at the expense of black. In this case, the long-term results are in general very hard to predict; in fact, it is well known in computation theory that extremely simple competitive-growth mechanisms are capable of supporting processes that are computation-universal.

The following rule is obtained from `LICHENS` above by changing a single entry into a `0`:

```
                      : LICHENS-WITH-DEATH
    8SUM { U U U 1 0 U U 1 1 }
                >PLNO ;
```

The resulting growth pattern (Figure 5.2c) is radically different.

The game of `LIFE`, discussed in Chapter 3, belongs to this class of rules, and actually could have been defined more concisely as follows

```
                          : LIFE
    8SUM { 0 0 U 1 0 0 0 0 0 }
                    >PLNO ;
```

5.4 Voting rules

The rules discussed in the previous two sections are *counting* rules, in which the behavior of a cell depends on just *how many* neighbors are in a given state—irrespective of their detailed spatial arrangement. A further specialization arises when each neighbor's contribution is interpreted as a "vote" in favor of a certain outcome; any number of votes above a certain threshold will yield that outcome.

In the following rule, a cell will follow the state of the majority of its neighbors. The cell's own vote is counted by 9SUM, analogous to 8SUM; this leads to a range of 10 distinct possibilities, $0, 1, \ldots, 9$, which can be evenly split by setting the threshold between 4 and 5 ("simple majority").

```
                        : MAJORITY
    9SUM { 0 0 0 0 0 1 1 1 1 1 }
                    >PLNO ;
```

It's quite obvious that areas in which black initially has even a slight majority will tend to consolidate this majority, and similarly for white. What is not obvious is what will happen where the two colors meet: will the boundary be sharp or fuzzy? will it be stable? will it tend to become straighter or more wiggly? We'll see that the behavior of the boundary can be profoundly affected by small variations in the rule.

With MAJORITY, if one starts the screen with a random distribution of ⓪'s and ①'s in a few steps the whole screen will have rearranged itself into interpenetrating black and white domains, maintained by stable "alliances." If one starts with a low percentage of ①'s, the white area will end up being mostly connected, leaving black islands surrounded by a white ocean; the situation gradually reverses as the initial fraction of ①'s is increased (cf. Figure 5.3a). Models of this kind are useful in the study of *nucleation* and *percolation* phenomena.

An interesting variation of this rule was constructed by Gérard Vichniac[67]. By swapping the two table entries that are adjacent to the threshold, as follows

```
                        : ANNEAL
    9SUM { 0 0 0 0 1 0 1 1 1 1 }
                    >PLNO ;
```

one encourages reshuffling at the boundary between black and white domains, where the majority is marginal. The net effect is one of gradual *annealing* of

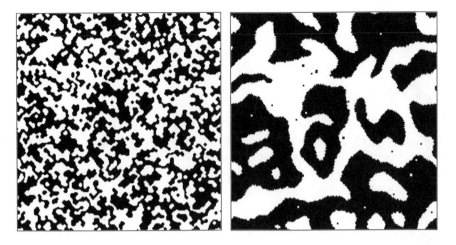

Figure 5.3: Voting rules, starting with 50% of 1's at random: (a) With simple majority one gets stable, quite fragmented domains. (b) Annealed majority (ANNEAL) leads to continual consolidation of domains; here ECHO is on.

domains: in the long term, each cell behaves as if the vote reflected not only the state of the immediate neighbors, but also, with decreasing weights, that of cells that are further and further away from it. Domains form as before, but now the boundaries are in continual ferment; each cell can "feel," so to speak, the curvature in its general vicinity, and will dynamically adjust its state so as to make the boundary straighter (Figure 5.3b): "bays" are filled and "capes" are eroded—as shown in Figure 5.4a. On a macroscopic scale, the detailed mechanics of the rule is blurred away, and what is left is a good model of *surface tension*, where boundaries behave as stretched membranes that exert a pull proportional to their curvature (Figure 5.4b) and Plate 3. In Part III we shall discuss other cases in which discrete microscopic mechanisms provide good models for familiar continuum phenomena.

5.5   Bank's computer

At the end of Section 3.4 we remarked that in the world defined by a given cellular-automaton rule one may find "materials" and "mechanisms" capable of being assembled into complex machinery with a definite plan and purpose. Can one build a computer inside a cellular automaton? This is actually one of the first questions that was asked by von Neumann in his search for a mathematical "universe" capable of supporting the most essential features of life. Von Neumann eventually managed to design a universal computing/constructing "robot" living inside a cellular automaton; his design

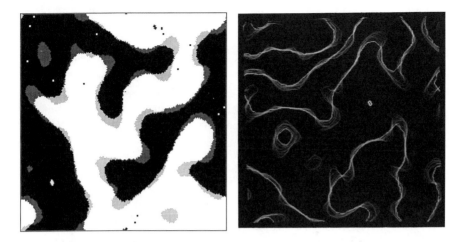

Figure 5.4: Surface tension in the ANNEAL rule: (a) Two superposed snapshots taken at an interval of 400 steps; bays are filled and capes eroded. (b) Time-exposure recording the wandering of the boundaries.

uses 29-state cells and five neighbors, and occupies several hundred thousand cells[68]. Later on, Codd[11] achieved similar results with an 8-state cellular automaton.

Banks[3] discusses even simpler solutions, using different trade-offs between number of states, number of neighbors, compactness of construction, and texture of the environment in which the robot performs its tasks. Here we shall present the simplest of Bank's approaches, which is suitable for building computing circuitry of arbitrary complexity.

Bank's rule is completely specified by the following three entries

$$\begin{array}{c}\boxed{1}\\\boxed{0}\boxed{1}\boxed{1}\\\boxed{0}\end{array}\mapsto\boxed{0}\qquad\begin{array}{c}\boxed{0}\\\boxed{1}\boxed{0}\boxed{1}\\\boxed{1}\end{array}\mapsto\boxed{1}\qquad\begin{array}{c}\boxed{1}\\\boxed{1}\boxed{0}\boxed{1}\\\boxed{1}\end{array}\mapsto\boxed{1}$$

(with the understanding that the four rotated versions of each entry lead to the same result); for all other entries of the table the rule specifies "no change" for the center cell. With reference to a pattern of $\boxed{1}$'s on a field of $\boxed{0}$'s, the rule essentially says "fill pockets, erase corners." In CAM Forth, using U for "unchanged" as before,

```
                         : CORNER?
NORTH SOUTH = IF U ELSE 0 THEN ;
                         : BANKS
   NORTH SOUTH WEST EAST + + +
   { U U CORNER? 1 1 } >PLN0 ;
```

If the number of ⊞neighbors (without counting the center cell) is 2, we have to decide whether they are on a straight line or at 90°; in the latter case we force the corner to be ⓪. This is the only case where "death" can arise.

If we run this rule starting from random initial conditions, after a few steps we obtain the pleasant but undistinguished texture of Figure5.5a; in a few places we can make out little pockets of activity, with signals shuttling back and forth. Can we "tame" this activity, and turn it to more purposeful tasks?

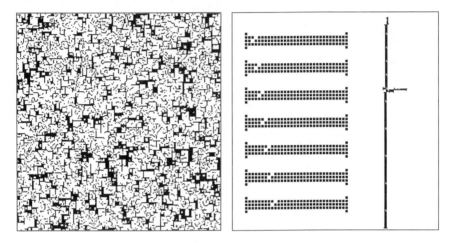

Figure 5.5: BANKS rule. (a) Pattern evolved out of random initial conditions. (b) Deliberate artifacts: signal propagating on a wire (left, enlarged), and interference between two streams of signals generated by clocks of different periods.

It turns out that signals can easily be made to run on "wires." In fact, if you cut a slanted notch on the edge of a solid black area, the notch will move one position at every step; with the opposite slant, the notch will move in the opposite direction. To support a signal, the black area need only be three cells deep—this will be our *wire*. The left half of Figure 5.5b shows the propagation of a signal; a signal reaching the end of the wire will die out.[3]

With a lot of patience (the details are in [3]) one can show that signals can be made to turn corners, to cross, and to fan out. Finally, it is possible to build a "clock" that generates a stream of pulses at regular intervals, much like the "glider gun" of Section 3.4, and a two-input, one-output gate that performs the logical function *a* AND NOT *b*. This is all that is needed to build a general-purpose computer. The right half of Figure 5.5b shows a clock

---

[3]The corners at the free end of a wire must be protected by a little "serif" as shown in the figure, or they will be eroded.

of period 16 shooting signals down a line, and another clock of period 32 intercepting and killing every second pulse.

5.6 "Random" rules

Occasionally one may want to use rules for which there is no simple logical or arithmetical recipe, or have the freedom to arbitrarily redefine the response of a given rule to specific neighborhood patterns. In such cases, the only practical solution may be to deal with a full-blown table. For example, the rule for HGLASS given in table (4.2) can be coded as follows

```
                               : VONN-INDEX ( -- 0,..,31)
   EAST 2* WEST + 2* SOUTH + 2*
           NORTH + 2* CENTER + ;
                               : HGLASS
VONN-INDEX { 0 1 1 1  0 0 0 0
             0 0 0 1  0 0 0 0
             0 0 0 0  0 1 0 0
             0 1 0 0  0 1 1 1 }
                        >PLNO ;
```

where VONN-INDEX numbers from 0 to 31 the thirty-two neighborhood patterns of the von Neumann neighborhood, in the same order as they appear in form (4.1).

Chapter 6

Second-order dynamics

> "I am the Ghost of Christmas Past!"...
> "I am the Ghost of Christmas Present!"...
> "I am in the Presence of Christmas Yet to Come?" said Scrooge.
>
> [Dickens]

In this chapter, we allow the rule to look at a second bit-plane—set up as an ECHO of the first, as in Section 3.2—in order to put a little short-term memory into the dynamics. Unlike the earlier situation, where ECHO was used only to enhance the display of LIFE, here the ECHO component is an essential part of the rule. This approach leads to the construction of a variety of *second-order* dynamical systems, including ones that display remarkable analogies with Newtonian mechanics.

6.1 Firing of neurons: a three-state rule

In introducing LIFE, we touched upon the analogy with population dynamics; this provided some suggestive terminology—but there was no pretense of modeling a real system. In a similar vein, the following rule can be interpreted as describing the dynamics of information patterns in a "brain" consisting of all neurons and no axons: neurons are tightly packed and communicate by immediate contact with their neighbors.[1]

The rule involves cells having *three* states, $\boxed{0}$ ("ready") $\boxed{1}$ ("firing") and $\boxed{2}$ ("refractory"). A ready cell will fire when exactly two of its eight neighbors

---

[1]This rule was suggested by Brian Silverman; the "neuron" interpretation is ours.

are firing; after firing it will go into a refractory state, where it is insensitive to stimuli, and finally it will go back to the ready state. In tabular form,

$$
\boxed{0} \mapsto \boxed{1} \quad \text{(only when two neighbors are in state } \boxed{1}\text{)}
$$
$$
\boxed{1} \mapsto \boxed{2}
$$
$$
\boxed{2} \mapsto \boxed{0}
$$
. \hfill (6.1)

Using two bit-planes as in Section 3.2 (Echoing), we shall encode the neuron states as follows

CELL STATUS (BRAIN)	STATE	PLANE 0 1
ready	$\boxed{0}$	$\boxed{0}\ \boxed{0}$
firing	$\boxed{1}$	$\boxed{1}\ \boxed{0}$
refractory	$\boxed{2}$	$\boxed{0}\ \boxed{1}$
not used	$\boxed{3}$	$\boxed{1}\ \boxed{1}$

(6.2)

Since with this coding scheme plane 0 records which cells are firing and plane 1 which ones are refractory, it's easy to express the overall rule (6.1) by means of two separate rule components, one for plane 0 and one for plane 1.

Observe that a cell will be refractory right after firing; therefore, the rule for plane 1 is simply ECHO (discussed in Section 3.2 and repeated below for convenience), which puts in plane 1 a copy of plane 0 with a one-step delay.

```
              : ECHO
      CENTER >PLN1 ;
```

As for plane 0, we define first a word that returns a 1 only if the appropriate STIMULUS is present, and one that tells us if cell is READY. The cell's new state is then determined by AND'ing these two conditions:

```
                      : READY    ( -- 0|1 )
        CENTERS { 1 0 0 0 } ;
                      : STIMULUS ( -- 0|1 )
    8SUM { 0 0 1 0 0 0 0 0 } ;
                      : BRIAN'S-BRAIN
      STIMULUS READY AND >PLN0 ;
```

In the code for READY, we have used a new "neighbor word," namely CENTERS. This word expresses the joint status of CENTER and CENTER' as a single variable having values 0, 1, 2, and 3 —as in table (6.2).[2]

Even if by carelessness of the experimenter the initial configuration should contain any cells in state $\boxed{3}$ ("not used"), with the rule as given the anomaly will vanish after one step.[3]

---

[2] All the neighbor words available in CAM Forth are discussed in Chapter 7. To all purposes, CENTERS = CENTER + 2 × CENTER'. Of course, we could have defined READY in terms of the OR of CENTER and CENTER'; however, here we wanted to spare the reader the subtleties of arithmetic/logic conversion (cf. Section A.14).

[3] During that step, these cells will behave as firing cells.

An interesting aspect of BRIAN'S-BRAIN is that there are no static structures. All activity is fast-paced, and is continually refreshed by the mutual stimulation of firing patterns. Figure 6.1a—a brief time-exposure—can hardly do justice to what one sees on the screen.

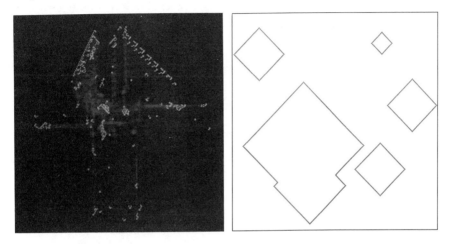

Figure 6.1: (a) Short time-exposure of BRIAN'S-BRAIN. (b) GREENBERG rule: isolated dots grow into rings, which merge into larger rings.

Once a trick has been learned it takes little effort to apply it to a variety of different situations. In conjunction with ECHO, the word READY can be used as an "inhibiting" component for *any* rule running on plane 0. For example, we can take DIAMONDS (Section 5.1), which by itself leads to trivial, unconstrained growth, and write

```
                           : GREENBERG
CENTER NORTH SOUTH WEST EAST        \ this part is
      OR OR OR OR                   \   DIAMONDS
           READY AND >PLN0 ;
```

This rule, some aspects of which have been studied by Greenberg and Hastings[21], has several "modes" of activity depending on the initial conditions. A single dot will grow into a diamond-shaped wave front (with a hollow interior) traveling at the speed of light; when two of these "rings" meet their common boundary is annihilated, resulting in a larger hollow structure with a continuous boundary (Figure 6.1b). If plane 1 is initially empty, the inhibition wave in this plane closely trails the firing wave in plane 0, creating a "guard ring" that prevents any activity from penetrating inside: when the excitement is all over, nothing is left on the screen. However, sustained activity is possible if the ring is broken at one point: this gap becomes a stable,

localized source of periodic waves of a certain frequency. There also exists a
pattern that produces waves of twice that frequency.

A good way to experiment with this rule is to use as an initial configuration
one containing of a small fraction of ⬚1's placed at random in planes 0 and 1.
By slowly varying this fraction from run to run, different modes of behavior
are encouraged. Figure 6.2 is a sequence obtained from 3% of ⬚1's.

Figure 6.2: GREENBERG: Initial, intermediate, and steady-state behavior, starting
with 3% of 1's at random in one plane and a different 3% random pattern in the
other.

6.2 Going into reverse gear

An essential feature of the rules of the previous section is that the new configuration of plane 0 (the "future") is constructed by looking at both the
current configuration of this plane (the "present") and its *previous* configuration (the "past"); the latter was saved in plane 1 by ECHO . In other words,
if we consider the sequence of configurations

$$\ldots c^{t-2}, c^{t-1}, c^t, c^{t+1}, c^{t+2} \ldots \qquad (6.3)$$

traversed by the system in the course of time, each configuration is completely
determined by the previous two. This characterizes a *second-order* system.

As mentioned above, a simple way to construct a second-order rule is to
start with an ordinary (or *first-order*) rule and add to it a term containing
a reference to the past. Here we shall consider the case in which the past
enters in the rule in a very simple way, namely, it is XOR'ed with the value
produced by the original first-order rule. For example, starting from PARITY
of Section 4.2, we can construct the new rule

```
                    : PARITY-FLIP
  CENTER NORTH SOUTH WEST EAST
         XOR XOR XOR XOR
```

```
          CENTER' XOR
          >PLN0  ;
```

in which the value formerly returned by PARITY is further XOR'ed with CENTER' (the current value in plane 1 is the previous value of plane 0, since ECHO is on) before being used as the next value for plane 0.

With the new rule, the past is simply copied into the future, either "as is" (when the value returned by the original rule is 0) or after *complementing* it (when that value is 1). The first-order piece of the rule may be visualized as a "force field" which the state of the system must traverse in going from the past to the future; depending on the value of this force, this state may re-emerge unchanged or "flipped."

As a first experiment with this rule, start for simplicity with a small square of ⊡'s in plane 0 and an all-blank configuration in plane 1, and run a thousand steps (Figure 6.3a). The dynamic behavior has a quite different character from that of the original PARITY: on all scales, growth alternates with steady retreat rather than sudden collapse. Now *swap* the contents of the two bit-planes[4] and run a thousand more steps: *the movie will run in reverse*, and you will come back to the original starting point. Continue for a few more steps—you are now traveling into the (as yet unexplored) system's past! Swap past and present again, and the system will resume traveling forward in time. PARITY-FLIP is a *time-reversible* system—and we have access to its "reverse gear."

Though the visual appearances are similar, this experiment in reversibility is quite different from conventional "trick cinematography." In ordinary life, one can make a movie showing scattered debris "unexplode" and come together to form, say, a house; but this only at the cost of storing on film *all the individual frames* of the direct process, and then showing them in reverse order. When the movie is projected, there is no causal connection between the individual frames (they were put in that particular order by the trickster, who could have chosen a different order with even more miraculous results). In our experiment, instead, we store just the last pair of frames, and then let the rule re-generate in real time the system's past history according to principles of strict causality.

A fuller treatment of reversibility in cellular automata will be given in Chapter 14; in particular, theoretical background for the above example is given in Section 14.2.

---

[4]Commands for swapping planes are, of course, directly available in CAM.

Figure 6.3: (a) Eight stages in the evolution of `PARITY-FLIP`, followed by the same evolution backwards in time. (b) `TIME-TUNNEL` from a square, after thousands of steps.

6.3   An impenetrable shield

We shall run an experiment with another reversible rule of the second-order kind, namely

```
                          : TIME-TUNNEL
CENTER NORTH SOUTH WEST EAST
    + + + + { 0 1 1 1 1 0 }        \ return 1 if not all the same
          CENTER' XOR >PLNO ;      \ XOR with the past
```

(`ECHO` is again the rule for plane 1). A small square of $\boxed{3}$'s[5] in the middle will act as a steady source of waves. Since our cellular-automaton space is wrapped around (cf. Section 2.2.5), these waves will travel full circle—or, better, full *torus*—and come back to interfere with themselves in a nonlinear way, giving rise to a whole sequence of increasingly more complex shuffles. Eventually the whole screen will be filled with a "turbulent" pattern, as in Figure 6.3b (the four-fold symmetry of the initial configuration is, of course, indefinitely preserved by this rule, which is rotation-invariant).

Observe that throughout all this the outline of the square is not destroyed (in fact, it keeps originating waves going inwards as well as outwards). The same experiment starting with a big circle—(a) in Figure 6.4—yields pattern (b) after 4000 steps. Since the dynamics is reversible, if we go back in time for the same number of steps we come back to (a): the turbulence has been "undone." Let's do all this again, but this time, when we are at (b), before

---

[5]I.e., 1's in *both* planes, as in table (6.2).

reversing gears let's change just one bit of plane 0, outside of the circle. When we run backwards, this "error" will rapidly grow, destroying all the subtle correlations hidden in (b), and the resulting "$t = 0$" pattern will be (c) instead of (a): total chaos—outside the circle. However, inside the circle we have come back to the initial orderly pattern: the disturbance has not propagated to the circle's interior.

It is clear that the boundary of the circle acts as an impenetrable shield, completely isolating what's inside from what's outside and vice versa. With these initial conditions, the system is effectively partitioned into two *decoupled* subsystems.

The fact that the edges of the circle are conserved is an expression of a simple *conservation law*. Conservation laws in cellular automata are discussed in [35] and [45].

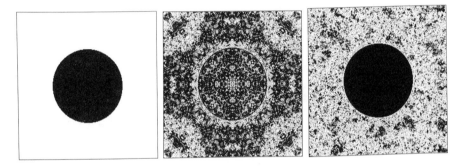

Figure 6.4: TIME-TUNNEL: From (a) to (b) forward in time, and from (b) to (c) backwards after having changed a single bit in (b).

6.4   Other examples

There are many reversible rules closely related to the TIME-TUNNEL example of the previous section. For instance, take the case statement which appears as part of TIME-TUNNEL's definition, and replace it with any other table in which all cases return the same value except for the maximum or minimum neighborhood counts (or both). All of these rules exhibit two causally disconnected regions when started from the configuration of Figure 6.4a. Generalizations to any other symmetric neighborhood in which neighborhood counts which aren't the maximum or minimum are all treated alike also have this property. This property arises because cells adjacent to the black/white boundary in Figure 6.4a don't see maximum or minimum counts—complementary pairs along the boundary will always remain complementary.

The PARITY-FLIP rule of Section 6.2 can also give rise to a family of related reversible rules. This family includes any rule that depends on the

XOR of any set of neighbors in the present, XOR'ed with the center cell in the past. All of these rules share the property with `PARITY-FLIP` of being linear (see footnote 5 of Section 4.2).

You can take any first-order rule and find a closely related second-order reversible rule by XOR'ing the result of this rule with the center cell in the present, and also with the center cell in the past. The latter operation makes the rule reversible (see Section 14.2) while the former insures that patterns which don't change in the first-order rule are also unchanging in the second-order version.

Space does not permit us to give an extensive phenomenological discussion of reversible second-order rules. Further examples appear in Chapter 9 and in Part III of this book.

Chapter 7

Neighbors and neighborhoods

In this chapter we present in a systematic fashion the sources of information to which a cell of CAM has access for the purpose of computing its new state.

Recall that CAM does computation by table look-up. Functionally, CAM behaves as if each cell owned its own copy of the rule table and all cells were updated at the same time. In reality the table exists in a single copy which is time-shared by the cells in a sequential fashion; however, all the multiplexing, buffering, and pipelining machinery necessary to turn this sequential process into an effectively parallel one is hidden from view, and the user will never have to be concerned with it.[1] In particular, one knows that while the cellular automaton is constructing the values for time $t+1$ (this is cellular-automaton time, and increments by 1 at every step) only values from time t appear at the inputs of the table: the new value constructed by a cell during the sequential updating of the array is hidden from view, while its current value remains visible until the whole array has been updated.

The rule table produces a new value for each of the bits that make up a cell. The potentially useable sources of information are too numerous to all be presented simultaneously to a look-up table of practical size.[2] An

---

[1]The only parameter worth remembering when attaching external hardware to CAM is the period of the internal clock—about 180 nsec. At every pulse of the clock a set of neighbor values appears at the inputs of the table; at the next clock pulse the new value for the cell to be updated is read from the table output and a fresh set of input data is supplied to the table. The table could (and in fact can) be replaced by any combinational-logic circuit which, given a set of arguments, settles down to a definite result within a clock period.

[2]The number of inputs to a look-up table can never be large, since the table's size grows exponentially with the number of inputs (it doubles for each additional input); on the other hand, the number of signals that exist on the CAM board and for which one might conceivably find a use at one time or another as arguments to a table approaches one-hundred.

important aspect in the design of CAM was the selection of functional groups of variables that, used jointly or alternatively within the constraints set by table size, would yield the richest range of possibilities in the exploration of cellular automata dynamics.

In many contexts the rule will be able to use, besides the ordinary spatial neighbors, additional *pseudo-neighbors*. These variables may carry space- or time-dependent information, parameters communicated by the host computer, and signals supplied by external hardware (such as a random-number source or even a video camera).

7.1   A weakly coupled pair

The CAM machine is functionally organized as two identical "halves," called CAM-A and CAM-B. Each half consists of two bit-planes (planes 0 and 1 for CAM-A, 2 and 3 for CAM-B) and a look-up table, and is capable of running a cellular-automaton rule quite independently of the other. However, each of the two halves can see some of what is going on in the other; thus, the two halves can also be run as a single cellular automaton consisting of two coupled subsystems. This coupling is normally relatively weak: only the CENTER and CENTER' neighbors of each half can be sensed by the other half.

For special applications the coupling between the two subsystems can be strengthened by custom-configuring the machine. In CAM, all relevant input and output lines are brought out to a *user connector*, so that various portions of the internal cell-updating circuitry can be complemented or replaced by external circuitry, which in many cases of practical interest may consist of just a few jumpers.

Another way to couple the two halves is to join them edge-to-edge, so as to have a single cellular automaton of larger size. This mode of operation is briefly discussed in Section B.2.

Some of the resources on the CAM board are shared by CAM-A and CAM-B; namely the color map, which encodes the overall contents of the two halves into a single color picture, and the cell-event counter, which is fed by a distinguished output of the color map. The symmetry between the two halves extends to the way they use the common resources.

For the above reasons, in programming CAM it is convenient to direct one's attention to just one of the two halves of the machine at a time. Because of the symmetry between the two halves, one and the same set of terms will serve for either context; for example, in CAM-A the word NORTH refers to a cell's north-neighbor bit of plane 0; in CAM-B, to that of plane 2.

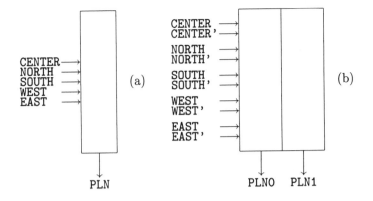

Figure 7.1: The rule of a cellular automaton as a black box. Each bit of neighborhood state contributes one input, each bit of the cell's new state requires one output.

7.2   The magic number twelve

In Chapter 4 we considered, for sake of illustration, a simple class of cellular automata, namely those consisting of one bit-plane (i.e., one bit per cell) and utilizing five neighbors. For any automaton of that class the rule could be encoded in a table of 2^5 (=32) entries. Such a table can be visualized as a "black box" (Figure 7.1a) having five input lines and one output line. The inputs represent the five neighborhood bits seen by a cell, and the output represents the bit that is to make up the cell's new state. On the other hand, if the cellular automaton consisted of two bit-planes, 0 and 1, and thus had two bits per cell, each of the five neighboring cells would contribute two bits—one for plane 0 and one for plane 1—and the new state of a cell would also consist of two bits; the corresponding black box would have 10 inputs and 2 outputs, as in Figure 7.1b. The table itself would consist of 2^{10} (=1024) entries, with each entry consisting of two bits; it will be convenient to visualize such a table as consisting of two *columns*, each one-bit wide and 1024-bits long, producing outputs labeled PLN0 and PLN1 .

The look-up table actually used in each half of CAM is four columns wide, as shown in Figure 7.2. (The other two columns are used for auxiliary functions to be discussed later.) The length of the table is 4096 entries—corresponding to 12 input (or *address*) lines; this number 12 will be the key constraint in the following considerations, since it sets an upper bound to the amount of information that can directly be used by the table in computing the new state of a cell.

Let us visualize the meaning of this constraint. Inside each of CAM-A's cells we have an identical copy of a black box similar to that of Figure 7.2,

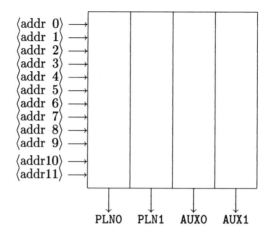

⟨addr 0⟩ —→
⟨addr 1⟩ —→
⟨addr 2⟩ —→
⟨addr 3⟩ —→
⟨addr 4⟩ —→
⟨addr 5⟩ —→
⟨addr 6⟩ —→
⟨addr 7⟩ —→
⟨addr 8⟩ —→
⟨addr 9⟩ —→
⟨addr10⟩ —→
⟨addr11⟩ —→

PLN0   PLN1   AUX0   AUX1

Figure 7.2: The look-up table of CAM-A. (For that of CAM-B, replace 0 and 1 in the output labels by 2 and 3. The twelve input "probes" can be connected to a variety of signals.

with four output ports and twelve cables dangling from its input connectors. Imagine the input cables to be terminated by a test clip or "probe" which can be hooked to any variable we want to sense. Say, we want to run a demo of LIFE as in Chapter 3. We connect the first nine probes to the nine neighbors of that cell, sensing only the bits of plane 0, namely CENTER, NORTH, ..., S.EAST. (Since either in CAM-A or in CAM-B there is only one black box—which is time-shared between all the cells—in our scenario we have to imagine that whatever we do with the probes of one cell is imitated by all the cells of the array.) Assuming that the PLN0 column of the table inside the box has been appropriately filled, this is enough to run LIFE with no frills; whatever comes out of the first output port is going to be the cell's new state—again, only as far as plane 0 is concerned.

If we want to run the ECHO feature, we suitably fill also the PLN1 column of the table, and whatever comes out of the second output port is going to be the new state of the bit in plane 1; we don't have to use more probes, because all we need for ECHO is knowledge of the CENTER bit, which we have already tapped with the very first probe. Three probes are still unused.

Now we want to run the TRACE feature. Since we want to sense not only the center cell's bit in plane 0 but also that in plane 1 (namely CENTER'), we have to connect one more probe. Only two probes left!—and think that of plane 1 we are seeing just one of the nine bits contained in the 3×3 window centered on the given cell. With only 12 probes, we'll never be able to see at the same time the nine bits of plane 0 *and* the nine of plane 1.

And there are more things we may want to look at: a few bits from the other two planes (those of the other half of the machine), some spatial information (can we make a "checkerboard" cellular automaton in which white and black squares follow somewhat different rules?), some time-dependent information supplied by the host computer, external inputs, random sources, etc. In certain cases it will be possible to combine in a meaningful way information coming from different sources and route it to a single probe.

Computation by table look-up is fast, but demands careful allocation of the most vital resource, namely the table's address lines. In early prototypes of CAM the "probes" were literally implemented as wires that one could move at will, by hand. Extra pieces of circuitry could be inserted here and there. Coming back to the machine after other people had been using it was always a surprise! In the official version of CAM this do-it-yourself approach is still possible, though in a slightly more disciplined form, through access to the user connector. However, it is important to be able to configure the machine in a number of standard "modes" suitable for a wide range of applications. They must be software-selectable, well-documented, and always available—we want our experiments to be communicable and repeatable.

These are the issues addressed by CAM's "neighborhoods."

7.3 Neighborhood declarations

The following considerations apply independently to each half of CAM, i.e., either CAM-A or CAM-B.

In CAM, a *neighbor* is defined as any one-bit source of information to which one of the 12 "probes"—or address lines of the look-up table—is connected. A *neighborhood* is an assignment of some or all of these lines to definite neighbors. In general, we will make a *major* assignment, which explicitly attaches *ten* of the lines to a specific set of signal sources, by means of a declaration of the form

$$N/\langle \text{major assignment} \rangle \quad ,$$

(where N/ is a mnemonic for "neighborhood"); the sources for the remaining two lines are specified by an optional *minor* assignment, of the form

$$\&/\langle \text{minor assignment} \rangle \quad .$$

A new major assignment overrides the previous one, and nullifies the previous minor assignment.

We can make distinct neighborhood choices for the two halves of CAM. The words **CAM-A** and **CAM-B** are used to indicate that subsequent neighborhood assignments should be transmitted only to the corresponding half of the machine. **CAM-AB** directs assignments to both halves—this is the choice that is in effect at the beginning of a new experiment.

The user will have no need to keep track of the identity of the 12 address lines, since each neighborhood declaration assigns to them convenient symbolic names.[3]

7.3.1 Major assignments

The *Moore neighborhood* declaration, `N/MOORE`, makes the following ten neighbor words available for use in defining a rule in CAM Forth

```
CENTER    NORTH    SOUTH    WEST    EAST
          N.WEST   N.EAST   S.WEST  S.EAST
CENTER'
```

At the same time, it connects the corresponding physical signals to the first ten inputs of the look-up table.[4] This is the neighborhood we have been using in the previous chapters.

Unless explicitly noted, all "neighbor words" in CAM Forth represent binary variables, with values 0 and 1.

Also the *von Neumann* neighborhood, `N/VONN`, provides ten signal sources, but the selection in this case is the following

```
CENTER    NORTH    SOUTH    WEST    EAST
CENTER'   NORTH'   SOUTH'   WEST'   EAST'
```

Thus, the entire contents of five cells becomes accessible, and within the scope of that reach one can program with full generality a cellular automaton having four states per cell.

Especially in this context, it may be more convenient to deal with five 4-state variables, called

```
CENTERS   NORTHS   SOUTHS   WESTS   EASTS ,
```

rather than with ten 2-state variables. In CAM Forth, whenever both the primed and the unprimed version of a neighbor word are available in a given neighborhood, the "plural" version (ending in 'S') is also available. For example, `CENTERS` is defined as $CENTER + 2 \times CENTER'$, and takes on the values 0, 1, 2, and 3.

The specific pair `CENTER`, `CENTER'` (and consequently `CENTERS`) is included in every major assignment.

The third major assignment, called the *Margolus* neighborhood, will be presented in Chapter 12. It comes in three flavors, called `N/MARG`, `N/MARG-PH`, and `N/MARG-HV`.

---

[3]For reference, these assignments are listed in tables (7.2) and (7.3).

[4]Signals and table are those of CAM-A or CAM-B, depending on the context.

As we have already remarked, the above declarations are mutually exclusive: any one of them will supersede the previous one. But where are these ten probes parked *before* we assign a neighborhood? Actually, there is a fourth, default option, called *user* neighborhood, which is automatically selected at the beginning of a new experiment and to which one can revert by explicitly saying `N/USER`. Its sources are

```
CENTER
CENTER'
⟨user 2⟩    ⟨user 3⟩    ⟨user 4⟩    ⟨user 5⟩
⟨user 6⟩    ⟨user 7⟩    ⟨user 8⟩    ⟨user 9⟩    .
```

The last eight neighbors correspond to pins on the user connector and may be fed with arbitrary signals from the external world. Note that we haven't assigned a name to these sources, since it will be more convenient for the user to provide the desired mnemonics according to what is actually connected to them. To associate, say, the neighbor name 'CAMERA' to address line ⟨addr 7⟩ (cf. Figure 7.2)—which in the present neighbor assignment is directly connected to the external input signal ⟨user 7⟩—one simply writes

$$7 \ == \ \text{CAMERA} \ . \tag{7.1}$$

Of course, existing neighbor words can be renamed at any time to suit one's taste. For example, it is always legitimate to write

```
        : UNDERLAY
CENTER' ;
```

and then refer to `UNDERLAY` rather than `CENTER'` in the body of a rule.

7.3.2   Minor assignments

Having made our major purchases, we have some change left—namely two address lines—which we may want to invest in some little extras. Eventually, it will become clear that these extras carry a lot of power.

The minor assignment `&/CENTERS` connects our last two probes to the other half of the machine, giving us a 1×1 window on the other two planes; these extra neighbors are called

```
&CENTER
&CENTER'
```

or, collectively, `&CENTERS`.

A general and quite powerful method of extending the range of behavior that can be explored with a cellular automata machine is by *rule composition*.

That is, by doing one step with a given rule *a*, one with rule *b*, and so on through an assigned sequence, we can effectively construct a "super-rule" with properties that are beyond the reach of the individual components.

Downloading a new rule from the host computer to CAM before every step takes some time.[5] In many cases we will be able to preload the look-up table with several rules at once (they will occupy different portions of the table) and then run them in a cyclic sequence without interruptions. We can visualize the whole table as a single super-rule which switches from *a* to *b* etc. on successive steps. The time-dependent information necessary to do this switching is provided by *pseudo-neighbors* which can be manipulated between steps by the host computer (pseudo-neighbors are sensed by the rule just as if they were ordinary spatial neighbors).

The declaration **&/PHASES** connects the two extra probes to two of these pseudo-neighbors, namely

&PHASE
&PHASE'   ,

also known to CAM Forth by the collective name **&PHASES**. (Note that **&PHASE** and **&PHASE'** follow the usual primed/unprimed naming scheme for a pair of related variables; however, they are not intrinsically associated with specific planes. Also note that CAM's built-in pseudo-neighbors, such as **&PHASE** and **&PHASE'** as well as **&HORZ** and **&VERT** introduced below, exist in a single copy shared by CAM-A and CAM-B.)

Finally, the minor assignment **&/HV** selects two pseudo-neighbors called

&HORZ
&VERT

(*horizontal phase* and *vertical phase*), which provide some space-dependent information; in particular, they allow one to make up rules that follow a "striped" or a "checkerboard" pattern, and they support the partitioning technique discussed in Chapter 12. They will be explained in more detail in Section 11.1 below. The collective name for this pair of pseudo-neighbors is **&HV** ($=$**&HORZ**$+2\times$**&VERT**).

Minor assignments too are mutually exclusive. The default assignment is **&/USER**, by which we may complement the major selection with a couple of external lines; that is, this selection introduces two (unnamed) neighbors

⟨user 10⟩
⟨user 11⟩

associated with two more pins on the user connector.

---

[5]Typically, one step-time for a precompiled rule that has been stored as a table in the host's memory; much longer if the rule must first be compiled.

7.4 Summary of neighborhoods

We stress again that the number of neighbors available at any moment equals the number of address lines of a look-up table, as shown in Figure 7.2.

The construct '⟨address line⟩ == ⟨neighbor name⟩' used in (7.1) above is in fact used by the CAM software for generating the neighbor names associated with the various neighborhoods. With this notation, the overall picture for the major neighborhoods can be summarized as follows

addr	N/MOORE	N/VONN	N/MARG	N/MARG-PH	N/MARG-HV	N/USER
0 ==	CENTER	CENTER	CENTER	CENTER	CENTER	CENTER
1 ==	CENTER'	CENTER'	CENTER'	CENTER'	CENTER'	CENTER'
2 ==	S.EAST	EAST'	CW	CW	CW	⟨user 2⟩
3 ==	S.WEST	WEST'	CCW	CCW	CCW	⟨user 3⟩
4 ==	N.EAST	SOUTH'	OPP	OPP	OPP	⟨user 4⟩
5 ==	N.WEST	NORTH'	CW'	CW'	CW'	⟨user 5⟩
6 ==	EAST	EAST	CCW'	CCW'	CCW'	⟨user 6⟩
7 ==	WEST	WEST	OPP'	OPP'	OPP'	⟨user 7⟩
8 ==	SOUTH	SOUTH	⟨user 8⟩	PHASE	HORZ	⟨user 8⟩
9 ==	NORTH	NORTH	⟨user 9⟩	PHASE'	VERT	⟨user 9⟩

$$(7.2)$$

(the Margolus neighbors will be explained in detail in Chapter 12). In addition, each neighborhood makes available as an added convenience the appropriate joint version of every unprimed/primed pair (such as CENTERS for 'CENTER *and* CENTER' ')—as well as HV for the pair HORZ – VERT.

In a similar way, the minor neighborhoods provide the following options

addr	&/CENTERS	&/PHASES	&/HV	&/USER
10 ==	&CENTER	&PHASE	&HORZ	⟨user 10⟩
11 ==	&CENTER'	&PHASE'	&VERT	⟨user 11⟩

$$(7.3)$$

with analogous provisions for joint neighbor pairs.

7.5 Custom neighborhoods

You may have a need for a neighborhood that uses a different mix of signals than those provided by any of the standard neighborhoods listed above, or you may want to use some signals that are available on the user connector but are not routed at all to one of the standard neighborhoods. In such cases it is easy to turn a user neighborhood (major, minor, or both) into a *custom* neighborhood, by connecting a few jumpers across the user connector. This procedure is explained in Section 9.7.

7.6 Making tables

As we have seen, CAM contains several tables—namely the color map and the two look-up tables associated with CAM-A and CAM-B. All of these tables may be in use in a complex experiment, and their contents may change in the course of the experiment. It is important to have a general procedure for specifying the desired make-up of the relevant columns of these tables.

The command MAKE-TABLE ⟨table descriptor⟩ fills one or more look-up table columns as specified by ⟨table descriptor⟩, a user-defined Forth word containing the desired specifications.

The "rules" that we have used in the previous chapters, such as

```
              : ECHO
      CENTER >PLN1 ;
```

are typical examples of such descriptors; in fact, the command

```
              MAKE-TABLE ECHO
```

overwrites column PLN1 with the ECHO table, leaving all other columns unchanged (cf. Section 4.2).

More than one column can be filled at once. For example, the sequence

```
CAM-A  N/VONN
                          : PARITY-WITH-ECHO
   CENTER NORTH SOUTH WEST EAST
        XOR XOR XOR XOR >PLN0
              CENTER >PLN1 ;
MAKE-TABLE PARITY-WITH-ECHO
```

would write in in columns PLN0 and PLN1 the information required to run the rule PARITY (cf. Section 4.2) with the ECHO feature on.

This two-stage procedure—where one defines a descriptor and then passes it as an argument to a command—provides the flexibility required in complex situations.

To have more control one could have defined PARITY as in Section 4.2, and then prepared the following descriptors

```
                      : ECHO
          CENTER >PLN1 ;
                      : TRACE
   CENTER CENTER' OR >PLN1 ;
                      : BARE
          0 >PLN1 ;      \ keep plane 1 clear
```

so that, after starting an experiment with

```
MAKE-TABLE PARITY
MAKE-TABLE BARE
```

the ECHO or TRACE modes could be turned on and off at will by issuing the
appropriate MAKE-TABLE commands.

Note that in ordinary circumstances one won't have to *type* these commands during the course of a simulation; CAM Forth provides the means for
"attaching" an arbitrary command or sequence of commands to an individual
key, thus turning the keyboard into a dedicated control-panel for running an
experiment in real time.

In the above examples it was natural to separately specify the contents of
columns PLN0 and PLN1 of the table, since there the two bit-planes play quite
independent roles. In other situations it is more convenient to return the new
state of a cell as a single four-state variable. The word >PLNA accepts a four-
state argument and writes it as a two-bit table entry, i.e., across columns
PLN0 and PLN1. For example, to make a cell cycle through the states $\boxed{0}$
through $\boxed{3}$ one would write

```
                 : 4CYCLE
      CENTERS 1+ 4 MOD  >PLNA ;
MAKE-TABLE 4CYCLE
```

The sequence 4 MOD divides the argument on the stack by 4 and returns the remainder, thus insuring that after reaching state $\boxed{3}$ a cell will go back to $\boxed{0}$.[6]

The corresponding "column dispatcher" words for CAM-B are, of course,
>PLN2, >PLN3, and >PLNB. Analogous words, such as >AUX0, >AUXA, etc.
are used for filling the auxiliary columns of a look-up table (cf. Section 7.2).

7.7 The color map and the event counter

The color map, briefly introduced in Section 2.2.2, has a structure analogous
to that of the look-up tables, namely

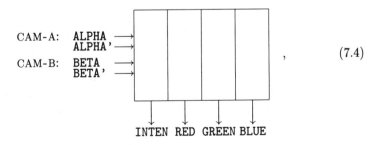

$$(7.4)$$

---

[6]Since Forth encodes integers as 16-bit binary numbers and >PLNA only ships to the
table the least significant two bits of its argument (cf. Section A.14), the construct 4 MOD
is redundant in this case.

and its contents is specified in a similar way, i.e., by giving a table descriptor as an argument to the command `MAKE-CMAP`. The columns labeled `INTEN`, `RED`, `GREEN`, and `BLUE` are filled by the "dispatcher" words `>INTEN`, `>RED`, etc.

The two pairs of inputs, `ALPHA`, `ALPHA'` and `BETA`, `BETA'`, come respectively from CAM-A and CAM-B. Normally they are connected to planes 0 through 3, and thus directly see the four bits that make up the current *state* of a cell. A second option is to connect them to the auxiliary outputs `AUXO` through `AUX3` of the look-up tables (cf. Figure 7.2); in this way, it is possible to send to the color map an arbitrary *function* of a cell's *entire neighborhood*. We shall assume that these two options are selected by the commands `SHOW-STATE` (default selection) and `SHOW-FUNCTION`.

For example, the color map of table (3.1) is defined as follows

```
                           : ECHO-MAP
                       0 >INTEN
ALPHA       ALPHA'        AND >RED          \ 1 in both planes
ALPHA       ALPHA' NOT    AND >GREEN        \ 1 in plane 0 only
ALPHA NOT   ALPHA'        AND >BLUE  ;      \ 1 in plane 1 only
```

`MAKE-CMAP ECHO-MAP`

Other examples are found in Sections 9.2 and 12.8.2.

By itself or in conjunction with the auxiliary tables the color map may be made to perform—in parallel with the simulation proper—a substantial amount of preprocessing of the array's contents before sending it to the monitor for real-time *visual* analysis. But often one needs "hard" data, to be subjected to concurrent or subsequent *computer* analysis. For this purpose, the "intensity" output is also fed to an *event counter*, which at each step records the number of intensified pixels; the value of this counter is directly accessible to the host computer.

By suitably programming the input to the counter one can detect and count specific events of a local nature, compare the contents of the planes, compute correlations "on the fly," accumulate statistics, and have the simulation automatically pause when certain conditions occur. By performing multiple passes with the counter,[7] different kinds of events can be classified. Even though the counter's discriminating power is limited by the usual constraints of *locality* and *uniformity*, it can be used to substantially cut down the number of situations in which the host is required to suspend the simulation, read all or part of the bit-planes' contents, and extract the relevant information.

---

[7]This entails, of course, "marking time" for one or more steps.

Chapter 8

Randomness and probabilistic rules

The rules described in the previous chapters are all *deterministic*, i.e, the new state of a cell is uniquely determined by the current state of its neighbors: from the same initial conditions one invariably obtains the same evolution.

In a *probabilistic* rule, the same current situation may lead to several different outcomes, each with a given probability. Say, we look at a certain entry of the look-up table in order to determine the new state of a cell, and instead of finding a single value we find two values, a and b, and a message, "Toss a coin to make your final choice!" If the coin is fair, a will be chosen with probability one-half. A loaded coin will give a different probability, and thus a different rule: by turning a knob, as it were, on the source of randomness, one can obtain from the same look-up table a whole set of probabilistic rules— spanning in a continuous way the range bounded by the two deterministic entries 'always a' and 'always b'.

Probabilistic rules are useful in many modeling contexts.

In CAM, each entry of the look-up table contains a single, well-defined value. However, one can easily synthesize nondeterministic outcomes. For example, one may connect one of the table inputs (cf. Chapter 7) to a binary random variable: for a given assignment of values to all other inputs, the output will come from one or the other of two distinct table entries, depending on the current value of the random variable. Thus, the look-up table will return probabilistic results with a probability distribution directly related to that of the random variable.

This approach can be generalized. We shall use the term *noisy neighbor* for any quantity that can play the role of a random variable in the definition of a rule. Noisy neighbors may be supplied by external hardware, or may be generated within CAM using a variety of techniques.

8.1   Exponential decay

Consider a large number of lighted candles put out in the rain. Whenever a candle is hit by a raindrop it fizzles out. The fewer candles there are left, the fewer extinctions will be observed in the next second: the total illumination will decay exponentially.

We shall use plane 0 to represent the array of candles ($\boxed{1}$ = "lit," $\boxed{0}$ = "blown out"). At each step we want certain candles to be hit by raindrops: how many, and which ones? In other words

- How do we create a random raindrop pattern?

- How do we make it influence the array of candles?

- How do we produce a fresh random pattern step after step?

We shall describe first an impractical but conceptually very simple solution. Plane 1 will be used to represent the raindrops, ($\boxed{1}$ = "drop," $\boxed{0}$ = "no drop"). Before each step we fill plane 1 *by hand* with a fresh random pattern, and then we run a step: each raindrop blows out the corresponding candle (if still lit). Candles are affected by raindrops according to the following DECAY rule (we have renamed CENTER' for convenience):

```
              : RAND
     CENTER' ;
              : DECAY
RAND { CENTER 0 } >PLN0 ;
```

That is, if there is no raindrop (RAND = $\boxed{0}$) a candle will remain in its current state; however, a raindrop (RAND = $\boxed{1}$) will put the candle out.

We'll run the experiment with a color map that makes the contents of plane 1 (the random source) invisible, and displays only the contents of plane 0 (the candles). The experiment will start with all candles lit. Let's fill plane 1 with a random pattern having a certain density. For instance, we may toss a coin five times, and if we get heads all five times we put a raindrop in the first cell of the array; this will happen with probability $p = 1/2^5$. We repeat this for the second cell, and so on, until every one of the N (=256×256) cells has had a chance to be filled: about pN (=2048) cells will contain a raindrop. When the pattern is complete, we take one step of the DECAY rule. A good number of candles will be blown out. We repeat the whole procedure, and some more candles will go out. In this way the whole array of candles will be gradually extinguished, with the desired exponential-decay law, as shown in Figure 8.1

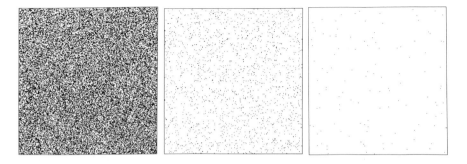

Figure 8.1: Exponential decay driven by a random source.

8.2 A simple noise generator

Producing a random pattern by hand is extremely slow. To speed things up, we may ask the host computer to generate random bits with probability p and insert them in the array, but even this is slow—it takes several seconds to generate a screenful of random bits. What we really need is something capable of producing random bits as fast as CAM can use them, i.e., about six million per second.

It is easy to build an external circuit that will produce a new random bit for every CAM clock pulse.[1] We may inject the output of this source into, say, pin ⟨user 11⟩ of CAM. As explained in Chapter 7, the definition

11 == RAND

will create the name RAND for this pseudo-neighbor, and the assignment

&/USER

will connect the physical signal ⟨user 11⟩ to address line 11 of the look-up table.

By making recourse to external hardware, one can obviously avail oneself of a random source approximating any desired statistical properties. But, if CAM is good at modeling a great variety of systems, why not try to use CAM itself also for this purpose, thus making experiments easy to set up and to reproduce on a standard installation? Indeed, although for certain critical applications an external random number generator may be mandatory, the internal-generation approach is more than adequate for most of the probabilistic models described in this book.

---

[1]A linear-feedback shift register of moderate length (say, 31 bits) will provide a "synthetic coin" that for most practical purposes is indistinguishable from a theoretical fair coin[44]. A more substantial amount of circuitry is needed if we want 1's to be produced with a probability that is adjustable in small increments all the way from zero to one— rather than with a fixed probability of 1/2.

The exponential-decay experiment of Section 8.1 used plane 1 as a passive receptacle for a hand-generated random pattern. Here we shall turn this plane into a continually stirred "bit soup" containing a new random pattern at each step. A suitable rule is (using `N/VONN`)

```
                              : STIR
CENTER' NORTH' WEST' SOUTH' EAST'
        AND XOR XOR XOR >PLN1 ;
```

With the neighbors in the order given, the `XOR`'s guarantee that in the long run the soup will yield an even mix of $\boxed{0}$'s and $\boxed{1}$'s (cf. footnote 3 on page 72); by putting some nonlinearity in the rule, the `AND` insures that the system won't get stuck in a short cycle.

This soup will be immediately usable if we start it with a random pattern containing 50% of $\boxed{1}$'s; however, one obtains a usable soup from virtually any initial pattern by pre-stirring for a few hundred steps.[2] The statistical properties of this noise generator are good enough for our purpose. We could use the raw bits of plane 1 directly as raindrops, but that would give a very strong rain ($p = 1/2$). To get a lower value for p we shall introduce a noise "sampler" that returns a 1 (a raindrop) only when several adjacent bits of the soup are in the $\boxed{1}$ state:

```
                         : RAND ( -- 0|1 )
CENTER' NORTH' SOUTH' WEST' EAST'
        AND AND AND AND ;
```

With this version of `RAND`, which will replace that of the previous section, the probability of a raindrop at any place is $p = 1/2^5$—just as if we were tossing a coin five times.

As far as plane 0 is concerned, the word `RAND` acts as a pseudo-neighbor whose value varies at random from cell to cell and from step to step with a well-defined probability distribution. The possible values of this noisy neighbor are 1 and 0; p can be coarsely adjusted (in powers of two) by varying the number of terms that are `AND`'ed by `RAND`. We shall discuss later how to obtain a wider range of values, a wider range of probabilities, and a finer resolution in the probability settings, and how to avoid correlations.

8.3   Voting rules, revisited

A random number generator may be used to inject some "thermal noise" in an otherwise deterministic rule.

In Section 5.4 we had considered a voting rule, `9MAJ`, that in a few steps turns a random initial configuration into domains of all $\boxed{0}$'s and domains of

---

[2]This is the time that it takes for a signal to go "all the way around the world" a few times (CAM's screen is 256×256).

all ⬚1⬚'s separated by extremely irregular boundaries—a frozen pattern of local alliances. To encourage the growth of more compact domains we had slightly altered the rule: the new rule, ANNEAL, shakes up those areas where the majority is marginal—namely the boundaries between domains—and forces the system to explore the viability of longer-range alliances.

Here we proceed in an analogous way, this time using noise rather than frustration as a means of maintaining fluidity on the boundaries. The random number generator will be that of the previous section; i.e., noise is generated in plane 1 by STIR and is sampled by RAND.

We shall start with a majority rule that uses only five neighbors, that is,

```
                        : 5SUM ( -- n )
CENTER NORTH SOUTH WEST EAST
                    + + + + ;
                        : 5MAJ
      5SUM { 0 0 0 1 1 1 } >PLNO ;
```

this produces domain boundaries similar to those given by 9MAJ, though a little more jagged (Figure 8.2a).

In 5MAJ, the two middle entries (... 0 1 ...)—located just below and just above the 50% threshold—correspond to "marginal" situations, where neither party has an overwhelming advantage; we are going to replace them with probabilistic outcomes: the 0 below the threshold will be replaced by RAND of the previous section, which returns a 0 most of the time but occasionally returns a 1 (with probability $p = 1/32$); similarly, the 1 above the threshold will be replaced by RAND's complement, -RAND, which returns a 1 most of the time but occasionally returns a 0:

```
                    : -RAND ( -- 0|1 )
              RAND 1 XOR ;
```

The resulting rule, illustrated in Figure 8.2b, is

```
                    : RAND-ANNEAL
    5SUM { 0 0 RAND -RAND 1 1 }
                    >PLNO ;
```

The fact that the two random variables RAND and -RAND are strongly correlated (one is the complement of the other!) need not worry us, since for any particular cell we are going to use either one or the other—never *both*.

If we increase the value of p, the annealing is driven faster until finally, when p reaches 1, the rule becomes a 5-neighbor version of ANNEAL.

In Figure 5.3b, note that the ANNEAL rule had missed smoothing out a few rare spots: it's hard for a deterministic rule to guarantee "smoothness" on the scale of only a few cells; on the other hand, with a nondeterministic rule such as RAND-ANNEAL (with p not 0 or 1) such stuck patterns are eventually melted away.

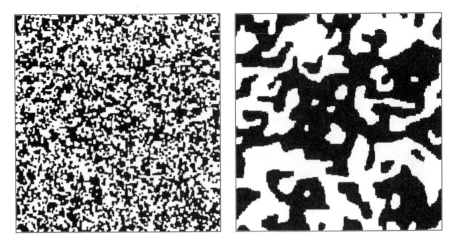

Figure 8.2: The frozen boundaries (a) produced by **5MAJ** are thawed in (b) by the thermal noise provided by a probabilistic variant of this rule, namely **RAND-ANNEAL**.

8.4   Remarks on noise

We shall approach noise generation in a more systematic way in later chapters. For the moment, let us make a few observations based on the previous example; these observations are immediately extendible to rules that use more neighbors and more states per cell.

More outcomes. The five neighbors **CENTER'** , ..., **EAST'** that appear in **RAND** can be used to produce more than just two distinct values. For example, the quantity

$$\text{CENTER'} + 2 \times \text{NORTH'}$$

takes on the values **0**, **1**, **2**, and **3**, and thus can be used to simulate the outcome of throwing a 4-sided die. It is clear that by looking at all five neighbors one can resolve up to 32 distinct outcomes. (By using nine neighbors, 512 outcomes become available).

A probability dial. Those thirty-two outcomes all have equal probabilities.[3] The version of **RAND** given in Section 8.2 utilizes just one of them, and thus produces a probability $p = 1/32$. One can construct a more sophisticated outcome sampler: by making up a Forth word that returns **1** for n of the outcomes (chosen once and for all) and **0** for the remaining $32 - n$,

---

[3]The proof of this is rather technical. Briefly, if one considers an indefinitely extended cellular automaton, the presence of the two XOR's as the last two operations of **STIR** insures that the cellular automaton's global map is *surjective*, and therefore that all its iterates are *balanced* (cf. [24,39]). As a consequence, almost all initial configurations (i.e., all configurations except perhaps a subset of measure zero) yield a steady-state distribution where all patterns of finite size are present with the same weight.

one obtains a probability $p = n/32$. Thus, by varying n, the probability p can be adjusted from zero to one in thirty-two equal steps (512 steps, when using nine neighbors).

Interchangeability. In the previous sections we considered three different random sources, namely (a) data directly written in plane 1, (b) external random source, and (c) internal shuffling and AND'ing of bits in plane P'. We have used the same word RAND in all three cases to stress that from a programming viewpoint it doesn't matter which method is used: the different versions of RAND are functionally interchangeable. Typically, one would write a probabilistic rule in terms of a "generic" noisy neighbor RAND, explore the rule's behavior using any quick-and-dirty version of RAND, and turn to a more refined version only when the accuracy of the experiment demanded it.

Modularity. So far, we have run both the desired probabilistic cellular automaton—such as DECAY or RAND-ANNEAL—and the associated random source on only half of the machine, say CAM-A. STIR and RAND use up about half of the resources of CAM-A;[4] that doesn't leave much to run the main rule on. To retain all of CAM-A's resources for the main rule the recommended practice is to implement the random source in CAM-B; this also encourages a more structured approach to experiment design. If even more sophisticated sources of randomness are needed a second CAM machine can be used as a dedicated noise generator.

Avoiding correlations. Since a cellular automaton's rule is local, information can only slowly propagate away from a site. The correlations entailed by the "finite speed of light" constraint can be virtually eliminated by a technique that uses two CAM modules and randomly offsets their updating origins, as explained in Section 15.6.

Fine resolution. So far we have considered scrambling rules that eventually yield an even proportion of $\boxed{0}$'s and $\boxed{1}$'s in the bit-plane used as a random-number generator even when the initial seed contains a different proportion. In Chapter 12 we'll introduce rules that *conserve* the number of $\boxed{1}$'s in a bit-plane (they are treated as indestructible particles) while still producing efficient randomization. In this way one can finely adjust the p—in increments of $1/65{,}536$—by just changing the number of "particles" in the bit-plane.

8.5 Caveat emptor!

A neighbor word such as CENTER is really a shorthand for a whole collection of *state variables*—one for each cell of the array and for each time-step; similarly, RAND represents a whole collection of *random variables*, one for each cell and

---

[4]Namely, one of the two planes and five of the ten N/VONN neighbors.

for each step. However, most practical implementations of RAND use and reuse a single mechanism (a coin, a program within the host computer, a cellular-automaton system within CAM, or an external circuit) to produce values for all of these variables.

Won't this *sharing* of one mechanism result in some *correlations* between the random variables? This is indeed the case for *any* pseudo-random number generator.[5] Well, then—if we are willing to pay enough can't we have a random number generator having an "amount of correlation" guaranteed to be less than a given bound?

Unfortunately, correlation is too complex a concept to be satisfactorily quantified by a single numerical parameter: correlations that are negligible in one context may in another context alter the very nature of an experiment. Fortunately, we can often make an educated guess as to whether the correlations characteristic of a certain noise-generating mechanism may adversely affect an experiment.

Intuitively, a mechanism R disturbs a system S in a *random* way if its dynamics is so *alien* from that of S that the latter has no effective way of predicting what R will do next. Thus, to be usable as a noise source for S, R need not be more cunning than everyone else in the world (that would be an *ideal* random source); it only has to surprise S—and S may be quite slow-witted, or just too busy with other things to have resources to spare for a guessing game. By using our knowledge of S's limitations in this respect, we can often synthesize an adequate noise source R by amazingly simple means.

8.6   A noise-box

For the experiments of the next chapter we shall use CAM-B as a simple noise generator producing the four values [0], [1], [2], and [3] with equal probabilities. Planes 2 and 3 will be driven by a stirrer similar to that of Section 8.2, and will be initialized with a random seed. From CAM-A, this noise will be visible through the 1×1 window on CAM-B provided by the minor neighborhood assignment &/CENTERS (see Section 7.3.2).

For reference, this noise generator is defined as follows

```
CAM-B N/VONN
                                      : NOISE-BOX
    CENTER NORTH WEST SOUTH EAST
    AND XOR XOR XOR   CENTER' XOR
                    >PLN2
CENTER' NORTH' EAST' SOUTH' WEST'
```

---

[5]The qualifier "pseudo" shouldn't make one think of somewhat fraudulent practices. No one in the world knows how to make an "ideal" random number generator, and it isn't even clear whether this mathematical abstraction is a well-defined one.

```
AND XOR XOR XOR   CENTER XOR
                >PLN3 ;
```

Note the cross-coupling terms (e.g., the center of plane 2 is XOR'ed onto plane 3), and the different positioning of the neighbors with respect to AND and XOR.[6]

---

[6]Refer to Knuth[31] for comments on such superstitious practices.

Chapter 9

A sampler of techniques

When you first start out, you'll undoubtedly try a lot of rules, perhaps even using randomly-generated tables, just to see what they do. You'll want to get familiar with the idea that a cellular automata machine can indeed translate a rule on the paper into a world full of activity.

We shall now start to proceed in a more deliberate way, setting ourselves goals—modest at first—and trying to see if and how they can be achieved with the available resources. The objective is to gain some expertise—to arrive at a point where, confronted with a new problem, we can try to "divide and conquer" it by reducing it to previously solved ones.

In this chapter we shall explore some of the possibilities offered by the CAM neighborhoods, using only ordinary "compass" neighbors (NORTH, SOUTH, etc.). The use of pseudo-neighbors will be treated later on.

9.1   Particle conservation

Suppose we want a rule that will make a *histogram* of the contents of a bit-plane; the height of each column of the histogram will represent the number of 1's contained in the corresponding column of the plane. The idea is to draw a horizontal line—the base of the histogram—at the bottom of the screen, and let the "tokens" (i.e., the ①'s) fall down gently and pile up above this line, column by column.

The tokens to be counted will be in plane 0, and the baseline for the histogram will be drawn in plane 1. The rule for plane 1 will be "no change:" we want the baseline to remain where it is. The rule for plane 0 will be an elaboration of SHIFT-SOUTH (cf. end of Section 5.1). Let us start with plane

1 all clear except for a row of ⬚1's at the bottom—our base line. Plane 0 can
be filled at random, or with whatever pattern you prefer.

The most important point of this exercise is that we don't want to lose or
gain any tokens as we move them around. As long as everything is supposed
to be shifting down at a constant speed, each cell can just copy the contents of
the cell above it, confident that its own contents will be picked up by the cell
below. However, the moment we interpose obstacles this blind trust won't
work any longer; the cell below us may already be full, and *we* won't know
if the cell below *that* one will be capable of accepting its contents. To avoid
dropping bits, a cell will have to make a move only when (a) it knows that
the move is possible *and* (b) it knows that its neighbors know it too. That
is, we'll have to establish a handshake protocol.

Before worrying about obstacles—e.g., the growing histogram to which tokens will stick—let us solve on a *local* basis the problem of particle-conserving
motion in this context. The relevant question is, "What area of the array is
visible at the same time by me and, say, my north neighbor?" That area,
and only that, can be the object of negotiation between the two of us. Since
we are dealing with a one-dimensional system (each column of the array is
treated independently of the others), the overlapping area is just two cells, i.e.,
CENTER and NORTH for me, and CENTER and SOUTH for my north neighbor.
A safe token-passing rule will be:

- If I'm empty and my *north* neighbor is full, I'll make a copy of its
  contents (I know he will erase his).

- Conversely, if I'm full and my *south* neighbor is empty, I'll erase my
  own contents (I know he will make a copy of it).

Note that these two conditions can't be true at the same time, and thus can
be examined and processed independently.

- Otherwise I'll do nothing.

Translated into CAM Forth:

```
                          : TAKE? ( -- F|T)
    CENTER 0=   NORTH 0> AND ;
                          : GIVE? ( -- F|T)
     SOUTH 0= CENTER 0> AND ;
                          : SAFE-PASS
                   CENTER
    TAKE? IF DROP NORTH THEN
    GIVE? IF DROP SOUTH THEN
                   >PLN0
        CENTER' >PLN1 ;   \ no change on plane 1

MAKE-TABLE SAFE-PASS
```

The current state of the cell is put on the stack by `CENTER`, and is passed on "as is" to `>PLN0`, unless one of the two conditions is true, in which case it is modified first. For example, if `TAKE?` is true the phrase `DROP NORTH` will drop the item on the stack and replace it with `NORTH`.

Run this rule now (plane 1 isn't used yet). Isolated particles will fall downwards at the speed of light; in crowded areas different parts will move at different speeds, shrinking and stretching like an earthworm; any solid area will get its bottom eroded and its top piled up with new stuff; "bubbles" will move upwards at the speed of light. But everything will eventually shift downwards—and tokens will be *conserved*. Note that the same kind of rule would work even if there were tokens of different "colors;" each color would be conserved.

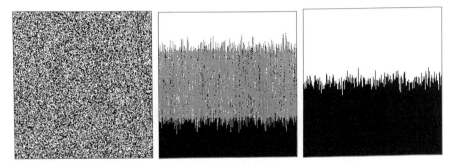

Figure 9.1: The tokens in (a) gradually condense on the baseline (b), eventually giving rise to histogram (c).

At this point, we only have to add a new constraint; that is, inhibit the execution of **SAFE-PASS** across the histogram baseline drawn in plane 1. For sake of generality, we'll make the inhibition work with any kind of obstacle, treating the north edge of an obstacle (i.e., any place in plane 1 where there is a 0 immediately to the north of a 1) as an impassable boundary. Again, what really matters is that both cells involved in a transaction use equivalent criteria to recognize the existence of the constraint. For the lower cell, the boundary is indicated by the condition

```
CENTER' 0> NORTH' 0= AND
```

and for the upper one by

```
SOUTH' 0> CENTER' 0= AND
```

If we inhibit with these extra constraints the "green lights" given respectively by `TAKE?` and `GIVE?`, that is, if we replace `TAKE?` in the above rule by

```
                                 : TAKE? ( -- F|T)
CENTER' O> NORTH' O= AND NOT
CENTER  O= NORTH  O> AND  AND ;
```

(and similarly for GIVE?), the rule will have the desired behavior. Figure 9.1 shows three stages in the production of the histogram.

The issue of particle conservation—and reversible dynamics in general—will be taken up again after the introduction of *partitioning* neighborhoods (such as the Margolus neighborhood), which provide the means to automatically guarantee inter-cell coordination for this purpose.

9.2   Differential effects

In the experiment of Section 6.3 we compared two runs of the same rule, starting from initial conditions that differed by just one bit. If the perturbation is introduced where there is already active and complex behavior, it becomes hard to tell to what extent the new history differs from the original one. Of course, one can record in full the two histories and subsequently compare them, but this requires a large amount of storage and, eventually, a lot of data movement for the "collating" work.

The ideal situation would be to concurrently run two *copies* of the system—identically prepared except for a small, deliberate perturbation.[1] On a cellular automata machine this kind of experiment is performed quite easily; not only can one use the two halves of CAM (or two machines, for more ambitious undertakings) for the two copies of the system, but one can compare the two histories, cell by cell, even as they unfold themselves, and display any differences on the screen; the event counter can be used for a more quantitative analysis.

We shall repeat the experiment of Section 6.3 with a duplicate system set up as follows in CAM-A and CAM-B:

```
CAM-A N/VONN
                                 : TIME-TUNNEL/A
   CENTER NORTH SOUTH WEST EAST
       + + + + { 0 1 1 1 1 0 }
            CENTER' XOR >PLN0
               CENTER >PLN1 ;
MAKE-TABLE TIME-TUNNEL/A

CAM-B N/VONN
                                 : TIME-TUNNEL/B
```

---

[1] In physical experiments this is usually hard to do, since extraneous perturbations differently affect the two copies and may in the long run swamp the effects one desires to observe.

```
CENTER NORTH SOUTH WEST EAST
    + + + + { 0 1 1 1 1 0 }
         CENTER' XOR >PLN2
             CENTER >PLN3 ;
MAKE-TABLE TIME-TUNNEL/B
```

Note that the neighbor names are the same in the two halves of the machine: whether a rule is sent to CAM-A or CAM-B is decided by the "dispatcher" words (>PLN0 and >PLN1 refer to table columns in CAM-A, >PLN2 and >PLN3, in CAM-B). The physical neighbors are wired in place by the assignments CAM-A N/VONN and CAM-B N/VONN.

The second half of this program could have been replaced simply by the word B=A, which duplicates both the tables and the neighborhood selections.

In order to show on the screen the *differences* between corresponding planes rather than the planes themselves, we shall replace the color map we've been using so far (ECHO-MAP, Section 7.7) with a suitably modified one. In DIFF-MAP, instead of telling us that a bit in plane 0 is *on*, green will tell us that this bit *differs* from that in plane 2 (i.e., the homologous bit in CAM-B); similarly, blue will flag differences between plane 1 and plane 3, and red will flag those cells where a difference appears in *both* planes. With this color coding nothing will appear on the screen as long as the two histories are identical; to see at least a ghost of what is happening, we'll route the contents of plane 0 to the intensity signal.

```
                      : DIFF
         ALPHA  BETA  XOR ;      \ plane 0 vs plane 2
                      : DIFF'
         ALPHA' BETA' XOR ;      \ plane 1 vs plane 3
                      : DIFF-MAP
              ALPHA >INTEN       \ ghost of plane 0
DIFF      DIFF'      AND >RED    \ diff. on both planes
DIFF      DIFF' NOT  AND >GREEN  \ diff. on 0 only
DIFF NOT  DIFF'      AND >BLUE ; \ diff. on 1 only
```

MAKE-CMAP DIFF-MAP

If we had wanted to *count* the differences, we would have routed DIFF to >INTEN and read off the counter's value after each step, as explained in Section 7.7.[2]

At this point we are ready to run. As we did in Figure 6.4, we start with a big circle (this time in *both* pairs of planes), we run for 4000 steps, and we stop. So far the two copies have kept in lockstep, as we can tell by the absence of any colors from the screen (the faint gray image on the screen produced

---

[2]Since with this rule plane 1 lags behind plane 0 by one step, and similarly for planes 3 and 2, there is no point in counting *both* differences.

by the intensity bit allows us to monitor what is going on). Now we change a single bit in plane 0 (the spot will turn bright green, as only one of the two copies is perturbed) and run backwards in time. The cancer will spread its tendrils and start enveloping the circle (Plate 4); as remarked in Section 6.3, the interior of the circle is protected by an impenetrable shield and will not be affected by the perturbation.

9.3   Coupling the two halves

Having used CAM-A and CAM-B as two independent systems, we are now ready for an experiment in which the two halves of CAM are coupled into a single dynamical system.

We shall model a reef of *tube-worms*; these animals have plumes that look like delicate flowers, but at the slightest disturbance the "flower" retracts into a tube and waits a good fraction of a minute before coming out again. Our tube-worms will be so sensitive that the disturbance created by n active neighbors will be enough to make them go into hiding (we reserve the right to play with the parameter n).

The "clock" by which a worm times its retreat will be represented by the state of the CAM-B half of a cell. In CAM-A, plane 0 will encode the status of the worm ($\boxed{1}$ = "active," $\boxed{0}$ = "hiding"); plane 1 will sense the stimuli, and ring the alarm when a sufficient number of active neighbors is present. The sequence is the following:

1. A worm is out; its timer is stopped at $\boxed{0}$; the stimulus detector continually tracks the number of active neighbors.

2. If this number exceeds the threshold, an alarm is posted on plane 1.

3. On seeing the alarm, the timer sets itself to $\boxed{3}$.

4. The worm gets pulled into the tube, while the timer ticks down to $\boxed{2}$.

5. The count-down continues: ...$\boxed{1}$, $\boxed{0}$.

6. When it sees $\boxed{0}$, the worm emerges. The timer remains at $\boxed{0}$, and we are back at point 1.

Of course, this recipe admits of various shades of interpretation; here is ours:

```
CAM-A N/MOORE &/CENTERS
                                : 8SUM
          NORTH SOUTH WEST EAST        \ add up stimuli
     N.WEST N.EAST S.WEST S.EAST
                    + + + + + + ;
                                : ALARM
```

```
8SUM { 0 0 1 1 1 1 1 1 1 } ;        \ ring if two or more
                          : TUBE-WORMS
   &CENTERS { 1 0 0 0 } >PLN0        \ emerge if time over
              ALARM > PLN1 ;         \ post alarm where
                                     \   CAM-B can see it
CAM-B N/MOORE &/CENTERS
                          : TIMER
    &CENTER &CENTER' AND IF          \ if "worm out" and "alarm"
                  3 ELSE             \   set timer to 3,
    CENTERS { 0 0 1 2 } THEN         \   otherwise count down
                  >PLNB ;
MAKE-TABLE TUBE-WORMS
MAKE-TABLE TIMER
```

&CENTER means "the CENTER bit of the other half CAM;" to CAM-A, that means the bit of plane 2, but to CAM-B it means the bit of plane 0.

The stimuli in CAM-A cannot be seen directly by the timer in CAM-B, since the minor neighborhood assignment &/CENTERS only allows the latter to access the *center* bits of CAM-A. We have to go through a two-stage process: (a) in CAM-A, where we have access to all nine of the neighbors, we count the stimuli, compare the count with a threshold, and store the result in the center cell of plane 1; (b) at the next step, CAM-B picks up the result from there.

Start this experiment with random configurations in all four planes, so that the relative phasing of the worms' cycles is random. In a short time coherent phase ripples will be visible; these will grow and coalesce, yielding a pattern reminiscent of shifting sand-dunes (Figure 9.2a).

Rules of this kind are very sensitive to the details of the feedback loop. With $n = 2$, as above, the pattern develops very rapidly and the ripples are rather minute. With $n = 3$, waves are broad and progress is slow (Figure 9.2b); soon self-sustained centers of activity develop, usually taking the form of paired spirals ("ram's-horns"). With $n = 4$, large areas eventually lock their phases, and little interesting activity is left. Perhaps the most interesting behavior is obtained with the following "alarm" condition

$$8SUM \ \{ \ 0 \ 0 \ 1 \ 0 \ 1 \ 1 \ 1 \ 1 \ \} \ ,$$

which is a sort of "annealing" version of $n = 3$ (cf. **ANNEAL** in Section 5.4); this is shown in Figure 9.2c. The same three rules are illustrated in Plates 5, 6, 7.

Systems of this kind provide good models for certain kinds of competitive/cooperative phenomena such as the well-known Zhabotinsky reaction[75].

There is a strong analogy between this model and that of "firing neurons" described in Section 6.1. In both cases the stimulus is provided by the presence of a certain number of neighbors, and the individuals are characterized

Figure 9.2: Spatial reactions: (a) and (b) use different values of a feedback parameter, while (c) is a non-monotonic threshold version of (b).

by a certain recovery time. However, there is a substantial difference in the nature of the feedback loop. In the neuron model feedback is *positive*: only the firing of neurons may trigger new firings. Such a system has, broadly speaking, two stable modes: (a) "activity that breeds activity," and (b) "inaction that breeds inaction." In the worm model feedback is *negative* at a short distance: the presence of worms tends to *inhibit* rather than *favor* the presence of more worms in the immediate neighborhood. However, the "delay line" represented by the timer makes it such that for certain frequencies and wavelengths the feedback is positive ("If there are worms *present* here now, there will be few in the neighborhood in a moment, and that means that on the ring just outside that neighborhood there will be better chances for worms to be *present* again."). In this model, the characteristic periods and wavelengths that are observed correspond to spacetime patterns for which the feedback factor is approximately one.

9.4   Genetic drift

Using a random-number generator, we can take a first shot at modeling a kind of behavior that is quite interesting on its own account—and is also an important ingredient in more complex recipes. What we have in mind is *diffusion*. We wish to think of a $\boxed{1}$ as a "particle" in an "empty space" of $\boxed{0}$'s; at every step, we want this particle to take a step at random in one of the four possible directions.

The idea is quite simple. We can put the particles in plane 0, and noise in planes 2 and 3 (with the noise-box of Section 8.6). A particle will look at the two random bits on which it is sitting, and use them as coin tosses to decide whether to go up or down, left or right. Naively, we might write down the following rule

: **NAIVE-DIFFUSION**

```
&CENTERS { NORTH SOUTH WEST EAST }
                >PLNO ;
```

The random value of &CENTERS (this is the two-pack version of &CENTER and &CENTER') ranges from 0 through 3, and we use it to select one of the four directions.

Let's try this rule starting from a solid disk. Indeed, black and white diffuse into each other: the disk breaks up into tongues of fire (the split-screen of Figure 9.3a shows "before" and "after"). However, even after a long wait we still get flakes on the screen rather than a uniform mixture. If we compare this pattern with that of Figure 9.3b (which was produced by a less naive diffusion algorithm, discussed in Section 15.1) we see that something is wrong. Moreover, if we *count* the particles step after step, we see that their number fluctuates: particles are not conserved.

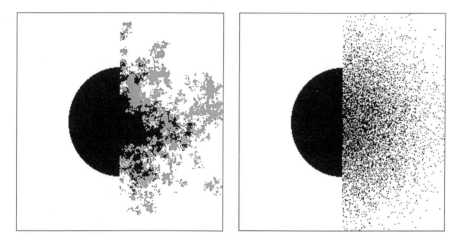

Figure 9.3: (a) Pseudo-diffusion, obtained with a "copy from a random neighbor" rule, vs genuine diffusion (b). Both figures are split-screen, starting from a disk, showing half "before" and half "after."

All this shouldn't come as a surprise. In a cellular automaton, a cell has no jurisdiction over, say, its south neighbor's cell: it cannot just "deposit" a particle there. As explained in Section 5.1, all a cell can do to make something move to the south is throw away its own contents and "copy" that of its north neighbor. Without a handshake (cf. Section 9.1), losses and duplications are bound to occur. All we can hope for is that particles will be conserved *on average*.

Even though we may have failed in our original goal, the rule we are left with actually constitutes a plausible model of *genetic drift*[29,12]. Genes do diffuse by having copies of them made, and in a situation of selective equilibrium each occurrence of a gene leaves on average one copy of itself at each generation. The above experiment can be repeated using four gene "species" rather than two, using both bits of CAM-A to encode which of the four species is represented by a given cell (CAM-B is still used as a noise generator). The rule is, of course,

```
                              : GENETIC-DRIFT
&CENTERS { NORTHS SOUTHS WESTS EASTS }
                    >PLNA ;
```

If we start with a uniform (random) spatial distribution for the four species, the steady state achieved after a while will show a mottled distribution (Figure 9.4a and Plate 8): the same species may be over- or under-represented in different areas.

Finally, we shall study genetic drift in small, isolated populations. To this end, we shall divide the screen into a large number of squares; this is achieved by drawing a grid in plane 1 and making the rule of plane 0 interpret this grid as a barrier to gene transfer (since only plane 0 remains available for the genes, we shall have only two species). The above NAIVE-DIFFUSION rule is modified as follows to take the grid into account:

```
                          : GENE-CIDE
                    &CENTERS
      { NORTHS SOUTHS WESTS EASTS }
      DUP 1 > IF DROP CENTER THEN    \ use CENTER if neighbor is grid
                    >PLN0
            CENTER' >PLN1 ; \ keep grid in place
```

Together with the randomly-chosen neighbor, say, NORTH, we also pick up the corresponding bit in the grid plane, i.e., NORTH' (the two bits come together in NORTHS). The phrase DUP 1 > makes a copy of what we have picked up and checks whether it's actually a piece of the grid (states 2 or 3 mean "grid"), in which case we drop it and replace it with the current value of the cell. In other words, the grid acts as a mirror in which each gene sees an image of itself in that particular direction.

Even if we start with an even distribution of $\boxed{0}$ and $\boxed{1}$ genes, fluctuations will be violent in such small populations, and after a while some of the populations will be left with only one species, as shown in Figure 9.4b; this loss is irreversible.

9.5 Poisson updating

An ordinary cellular automaton is by definition a time-discrete system: cells are updated at integral values of time. It is often useful to consider models in which the updating of a cell (which is still a discrete business in the *state* domain) can take place at an arbitrary moment along a *continuous time* axis.

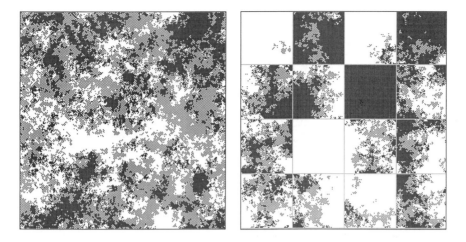

Figure 9.4: Genetic drift: (a) A large population shows mild fluctuations in its genetic make-up. (b) Permanent impoverishment of the gene pool may occur in isolated populations.

A chief example is given by Poisson processes, where events occur at random with a uniform distribution in time, and thus the probability that the *next* event will occur between times t and $t + dt$ equals $\lambda e^{-\lambda t} dt$. In a *Poisson cellular automaton* the updating of each cell is governed by an independent Poisson process. With this continuous-time updating the probability that two cells will be updated at *exactly* the same moment is zero; therefore, in writing the updating rule for a cell one may safely assume that that cell is the *only* one that may change state; with this assumption, the handshake protocols that may be necessary to insure respect of certain constraints (cf. Section 9.1) can be greatly simplified.

In this section we'll first give a simple example of a system for which the two updating methods yield radically different behaviors; then we'll show how Poisson updating can be emulated to an arbitrary degree of approximation by an ordinary cellular automaton.

Consider the following "soil erosion" problem. A piece of soil, represented by a ⎡1⎤, will stay in place if there is some soil somewhere on the north side of it (i.e., in one of the three north neighbors N.WEST, NORTH, N.EAST), as well as somewhere on the south, somewhere on the west, and somewhere on the east. In the first three cases shown below the soil in the center of the 3×3 neighborhood is "stable," while in the fourth it is "loose" (since none of its three east neighbor sites is occupied):

```
101     010     010     010
010     110     111     110
010     001     010     110
```

Loose soil will be blown away by the following rule

```
                            : STABLE ( -- 0|1)
    N.WEST NORTH N.EAST OR OR
    S.WEST SOUTH S.EAST OR OR
    N.WEST  WEST S.WEST OR OR
    N.EAST  EAST S.EAST OR OR
              AND AND AND ;
                            : SOIL
        CENTER STABLE AND >PLN0 ;
```

STABLE is a bit-mask that is AND'ed with the current state of the cell. If the value of this mask is 1 the soil remains in place; if 0, it is wiped out.

If you run this rule starting with solid soil, nothing will happen. If you remove an isolated piece of soil here and there no further erosion will occur. If you keep removing pieces at random eventually you'll get places where two or three adjacent pieces have been removed; depending on the shape of such a "hole," the walls may "cave in" enlarging the hole itself. As long as the amount of soil that is removed remains below a certain critical level (about 17%), such cave-ins are generally self-healing and the soil remains stable over-all (Figure 9.5a). However, when the fraction of soil removed goes above that level some of the holes exhibit unbounded growth—they become *nucleation centers*[66]—and eventually all the soil is blown away (Figure 9.5b).[3]

Stop the random poking just before reaching the critical threshold—when the soil is still stable—and survey the situation. Now, if instead of proceeding at random you are careful not to take away pieces that are essential to their neighbors' stability, you can manage to remove up to *half* of the soil without triggering a chain reaction (for instance, a checkerboard pattern is stable). A safe rule of thumb for a lone "land developer" just parachuted in the area would be to remove a piece of soil only if it has soil *directly* to the NORTH, SOUTH, WEST, and EAST; you can verify that this will not create any instabilities. The rule can be encoded as follows

```
                            : SAFE ( -- 0|1)
        NORTH SOUTH WEST EAST
              AND AND AND ;
                            : NAIVE-DEVELOP
      CENTER STABLE AND
        SAFE NOT AND >PLN0 ;
```

Again, SAFE NOT is used as a mask. A piece of soil will remain if it is "stable," as before, *and* if it is not deemed "safe" to remove it.

---

[3]The transition is very sharp; i.e., the probability of a chain reaction remains close to zero even when one comes very close to the threshold, and then rapidly swings to values close to one as soon as one passes the threshold.

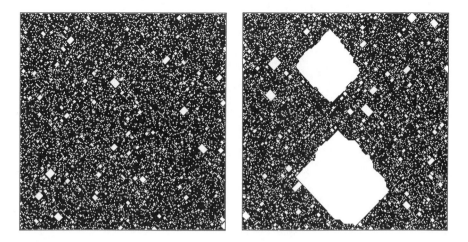

Figure 9.5: Nucleation: (a) As long as soil removal does not exceed a critical level the pattern generally remains stable. (b) Above this level nucleation centers appear and grow without bounds.

However, if you run this rule on an ordinary cellular automaton, starting from the stable configuration of Figure 9.5a, you may have a surprise. The rule is applied to all cells at the same time. If, unaware of one another's intentions, two developers concentrate at the same moment on adjacent plots, they may "undercut" one another and eventually find themselves surrounded by desert (Figure 9.6a): this NAIVE-DEVELOP game is safe only when played by one person at a time. To prevent mishaps, more sophisticated forms of inhibition would have to be introduced if more than one developer is operating in the area.

With Poisson updating, instead, the chances of a mishap like the above are zero, and the long-term result is a prairie covered with an irregular tiling of cottages (Figure 9.6b).

That was, of course, an extreme example. In general, though, updating at random times is useful for systems in which a synchronously updated model would introduce spurious, undesired symmetries.

To emulate a Poisson process having a characteristic rate λ, one can provide each cell with a random-number generator as explained in Chapter 8, and update the cell only on steps when the generator returns a 1. For this to work satisfactorily, the probability p that a cell will be updated at any time step must be kept low, and one must imagine the time axis magnified by a correspondingly large factor $k = \lambda/p$ (so that k steps of the cellular automaton correspond to one unit of time in the simulated system). In the limit as $p \to 0$, the probability that during one unit of *system time* two adjacent cells will be updated at the same instant goes to zero.

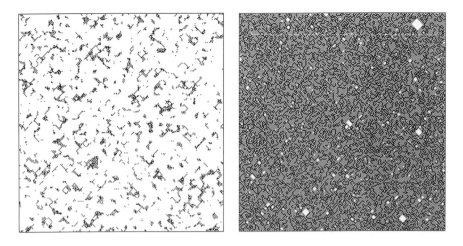

Figure 9.6: Prairie development: (a) With ordinary updating, destructive chain reactions are likely to be started; the large white areas are spreading dust-bowls. (b) Completed development, achieved with Poisson updating.

For the present example, the Poisson-updated rule is, of course,

```
               : SOUND-DEVELOP
    CENTER STABLE AND
            RAND IF
    SAFE NOT AND THEN
           >PLNO  ;
```

where **RAND** is the output from the random-number generator, which could be installed in CAM-B.

The noise-box of Section 8.6 is not suitable for this purpose, since each of the two planes provides a probability of $1/2$, and even AND'ing them would give $1/4$. With the approach of Section 8.2, and using nine rather than five neighbors in the sampler, one can obtain probabilities as low as $1/512$, which is adequate in many cases. In Section 15.6 we shall discuss a method for achieving a wider dynamic range for the random-number generator.

An alternative way to rule out "misunderstandings" between developers is to permit the updating of only every other cell—in a checkerboard pattern—at one step, and of the remaining cells at the next step. This approach is discussed in Section 11.6 and used in Chapter 17.

9.6   Asynchronous deterministic computation

In the genetic drift experiments of Section 9.4, each cell was forced to unconditionally "hatch a copy" of one of its neighbors selected at random. One may imagine a more selective outcome for this encounter; for instance, the cell may be allowed to retain its identity unless it faces an opponent that is in some sense "stronger." Rules of this kind were brought to our attention by David Griffeath.

In this context, a monotonic ranking of cell states obviously leads to saturation: in the long term all activity dies out (much as in the experiment of "candles in the rain" of Section 8.1). Let us consider instead a *cyclic* rank order, where 0̄ can be displaced only by 1̄, 1̄ by 2̄, 2̄ by 3̄, and 3̄ by 0̄—no one state is absolutely strongest.[4]

Then the state of a cell can be interpreted as a *phase variable* which is irregularly but inexorably driven through a four-state cycle. Our rule will use both planes of CAM-A for encoding a cell's phase, and will rely on CAM-B as the source of noise—as in the previous examples.

```
                    : BEATS-ME ( rank -- flag)
        CENTERS { 1 2 3 0 } = ;
                    : CYCLIC-RANK

              &CENTERS
{ NORTHS SOUTHS WESTS EASTS }
       DUP BEATS-ME NOT IF
       DROP CENTERS THEN
               >PLNA ;
```

The word BEATS-ME compares the rank of the selected neighbor with that of the cell itself.

Started from random initial conditions, this system shows self-organizing behavior similar to that discussed in Section 9.3, as shown in Figure 9.7 and Plate 9. Bands of a given phase lose ground on one edge and gain on the other; instabilities lead straight bands to fold over, and self-sustaining spirals develop.

Similar mechanisms can be used for enforcing *causal coherence* in asynchronously-updated parallel computers.

Consider, for example, a cellular automaton whose cells are updated by a number of independent-minded "workers." There may be available fewer workers than cells, workers may take their breaks at random times, they may get tired of working always in one place or at one task, they may be delayed or interrupted by external factors; etc. There is no hope that the cells will all be updated at the same time—say, at the signal of a foreman's whistle.

In spite of all that, we want the asynchronous system to evolve *isomorphically* to one that is updated in a strictly synchronous manner. If a cell is temporarily ahead of the others, it must have the state that it would have

---

[4]This is similar to the well-known two-person game of "paper, scissors, stone," where the paper wraps the stone, the stone dulls the scissors, and the scissors cut the paper.

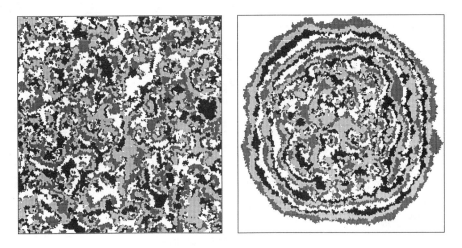

Figure 9.7: Phase waves in cyclic-rank systems: (a) from uniform randomness, and (b) from a small patch of randomness.

had if all other cells had kept step with it. Though timing will not be deterministic, at each place we want the right events to happen in the right sequence; this entails also that the correct causal relationship between events occurring at different places must be preserved.

Not only can this be achieved, but it can be achieved by relatively straightforward means. The solution (which is applicable to computers having arbitrary structure—not just cellular automata), hinges on the following three provisions:[5]

a. The cell state is *buffered*; i.e., the new state for a cell is computed and stored in a separate register, while the current state remains visible to the neighbors. Only when all the neighbors have computed their own new states will the current state of the cell itself be replaced by the new one. Note that, with this approach, a single updating step of the original system will be replaced in the asynchronous model by an *updating cycle* consisting of several steps.

b. In addition to the *current state* register, which is publicly shown, and the *next state* register, which is a private affair of the cell, the cell is provided with a *phase variable* (in this case, an integer from 0 through 3) that indicates its progress through the updating cycle. This variable is also visible to the neighbors, to permit inter-cell coordination.

c. At no time shall a cell advance by one step of its updating cycle if it is already one step ahead of at least one of its neighbors. This prescription

---

[5]This canonical solution to the synchronization problem is discussed in [56].

is motivated below.

Here we shall be directly concerned only with points *b* and *c*; that is, we shall implement only the phase variable and its evolution rule (in Section 12.8.3 we'll give an example where a definite computation is made to run with such an asynchronous discipline). If we start with a flat "phase sheet" spread over the array—that is, if all cells initially have the same phase—we'll allow this sheet to develop peaks and valleys as it advances through time in an asynchronous fashion, but never "rips" corresponding to loss of causal coherence.

From the viewpoint of each cell, the four values of the phase variable correspond to the following stages of dialogue with its neighbors:

0 I'm still looking at some of you (don't change your state yet); some of you may be looking at me (I cannot change my state yet).

1 I'm no longer looking at any of you (go ahead and post a new state if you wish—I have already used the old one for computing my next state, which I have stored in a private place); some of you may still be looking at me (I'll keep my new state to myself and still display the old one).

2 I'm not looking at any of you. None of you should be looking at me (I can now post my computed new state on the publicly visible register, superseding the previous one).

3 I'm again looking at you (if you have already posted your new state, hold it there; if not, proceed at your leisure—I'll wait for it as long as necessary); none of you should be looking at me yet.

At the prompt of an asynchronous clock the cell will look at the phases of its neighbors, and perform a transition to the next phase of the above cycle only if the situation permits it; otherwise it will mark time. Unlike the example of Section 9.5, we are not concerned here with whether adjacent cells may be activated at the same time. There we wanted to simulate an asynchronous system by a synchronous one; here we want to do just the opposite, and an occasional relapse into synchronism will not hurt.

We shall use CAM-A for the phase variable and a noise-box in CAM-B for the Poisson clock. In CAM Forth the rule is as follows

```
                    : STIMULUS? ( -- F|T)
          &CENTERS 0= ;    \ Time to do something!
                    : CENTERS+1 ( -- next-phase)
      CENTERS { 1 2 3 0 } ;
                    : TRANSIT? ( -- F|T)
   NORTHS CENTERS   =       \ Am I even with north neigh.
   NORTHS CENTERS+1 = OR    \  or just behind ?
```

```
        SOUTHS CENTERS   =         \ Same for south
        SOUTHS CENTERS+1 = OR
         WESTS CENTERS   =         \ Etc.
         WESTS CENTERS+1 = OR
         EASTS CENTERS   =
         EASTS CENTERS+1 = OR
               AND AND AND ;
                         : ASYNC
    STIMULUS? TRANSIT? AND IF      \ If I can (and have to)
            CENTERS+1 ELSE         \   I'll advance,
            CENTERS THEN           \   otherwise, manana!
                  >PLNA ;
```

CENTERS+1 simply defines the next phase in the cycle. TRANSIT? checks whether
there is some slack for the phase to advance. With the noise-box we've been using
all along, at every step a "worker" has a probability $p = 1/4$ to be prodded (by
STIMULUS) to mind the shop; different rates can be achieved by tuning the random-
number generator.

We shall start all cells at phase $\boxed{0}$, corresponding to the situation where
all cells are displaying their current state and none of them has computed
its next state (recall that the *state* component of the system is not explicitly
represented in the present example; only the *phase* component is). As the
random clock ticks, some cells will advance to phase $\boxed{1}$. Eventually, some cells
will be surrounded by all $\boxed{1}$'s, and will be able to move to phase $\boxed{2}$ (in the
state-component of the system, at this point part of the array will already be
displaying a new state, ahead of the rest of the array). And so on.

Different parts of the phase "sheet" will float at different time levels. The
phase difference between distant cells may attain several full cycles (one phase
cycle corresponds to one step of the synchronous automaton that is being
simulated in an asynchronous way). The maximum possible time separation
is one cycle over four units of distance: beyond that, the "pull" of lagging
phases in the neighborhood becomes irresistible and no further progress is
possible until a cell's neighbors pick up the slack.

Figure 9.8a shows a typical phase distribution at a time when memory
of the initial "flat" phase assignment is completely lost; in Figure 9.8b, the
asynchronous clock has been stopped for one cell,[6] and eventually the whole
system grinds to a halt, earlier for the nearest cells and later for the ones
farther away.

9.7   One-dimensional cellular automata

When dealing with a one-dimensional system, the resources of a two-
dimensional cellular automata machine of size $m \times n$ can be redirected in

---

[6]This was actually done by setting its phase two steps behind that of its neighbors.

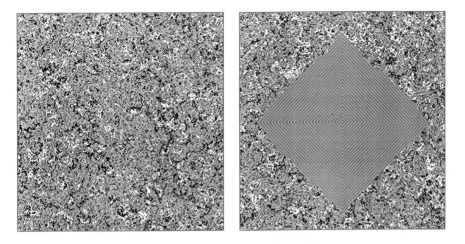

Figure 9.8: (a) Typical contour levels for the phase "sheet." In (b), the sheet has been "nailed down" at one spot by permanently deactivating one cell's clock.

several ways. For instance:

1. One can run multiple copies of the system—one in each row of the array—starting each copy from different initial conditions, as in Figure 10.2. This may be useful for statistical studies.

2. One can simulate the system in a single row of the array. In this case, the remaining $m - 1$ rows can be used to record the history of the system, from the most recent state all the way back to the $(m - 1)$-th step in the past, as in Figure 10.1. In this way, a view of the system's spacetime history is "scrolled" through the array.

3. One can connect the rows end-to-end in a spiral fashion, thus synthesizing a one-dimensional machine of size mn.

Approach 1 is trivial to implement. If the rule uses only the west, east, and center neighbors one automatically has a one-dimensional system. For wider neighborhoods, see Section 9.8.

With Approach 2 it is necessary to mark a row (say, the bottom one) as the one on which the evolution takes place; this mark, which we shall call the NOW line, can be stored in another plane—or can be obtained from the hardware as a pseudo-neighbor, as we'll explain below. The rule will sense this line and operate regularly on the cells that are on it; on the other rows of the array the rule will simply "shift north." In this way the most recent state will be at the bottom of the array and the oldest one that is still visible will be at the top; the time axis will be oriented downwards (physicists may prefer to change the rule so that it shifts the other way).

For a very simple example, let's make a one-dimensional random-number generator using the approach discussed in Section 8.2. The NOW line will be placed at the bottom of plane 1, and the generator will be in plane 0. The rule is

```
N/VONN
                               : NOW ( -- 0|1)
                  CENTER' ;
                               : ONED-RAND
               NOW IF          \ If on NOW line
WEST CENTER EAST OR XOR ELSE    \    run the rule
              SOUTH THEN        \    else shift north
                  >PLN0
          CENTER' >PLN1 ;       \ The NOW line stays put
```

The evolution of this random-number generator, which has been studied by Stephen Wolfram[73], is shown in Figure 9.9a.

If we want to avoid wasting one plane for the NOW line we can use a signal called -VFF, which is provided by the internal circuitry and is available on the user connector.[7] To make a custom neighborhood in which this signal is available we would use, for instance, the minor neighborhood assignment &/USER, which feeds address lines 10 and 11 of the look-up table from the user connector. On this connector, we would connect a jumper from the -VFF pin to the USER10 pin of CAM-A. Finally, we would assign the neighbor name -NOW to address line 10, and define NOW as the complement of -NOW:

```
10 == -NOW
                               : NOW ( -- 0|1)
                  -NOW 1 XOR ;
```

The jumper can stay in place even when it is not needed, since it will be used only when &/USER is in force.

For Approach 3, intuitively we have to "slice" the torus (cf. Section 2.2.4), say, along the left edge of the array, and reconnect the two ends after having offset them by one row with respect to one another, thus obtaining spiral wrap-around. The mechanism for achieving this is to have cells on the right edge of the cut treat as **EAST** what is actually N.**EAST**, and cells on the left edge treat as **WEST** what is S.**WEST**. The position of the cut may be marked by a vertical line stored in a plane or taken from the pseudo-neighbors -H00 and -HFF available on the user connector (cf. footnote 7).

---

[7]-VFF returns a 0 for the cells on the *bottom row* (FF is 255 in hexadecimal), and a 1 elsewhere. Also available are -V00 (the top line), -H00 (the leftmost column) and -HFF (the rightmost column).

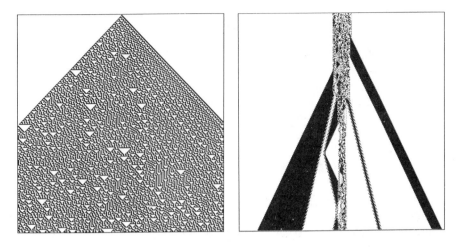

Figure 9.9: (a) One-dimensional random-number generator. (b) Sample spacetime history from SCARVES—a one-dimensional mechanical microcosm.

A simple but very interesting rule, which is a one-dimensional analog of the SPINS-ONLY rule of Section 17.3, has been studied by Charles Bennett. SCARVES is a second-order reversible rule (cf. Section 6.2) which looks not only at the first neighbors, WEST and EAST, but also at the *second* neighbors, WEST-OF-WEST and EAST-OF-EAST (see the next section for ways to get hold of these extra neighbors). In going from the past to the future, a cell will flip if there are presently two ⓪'s and two ①'s among its four neighbors. When working in one dimension with Approach 2, there is no need to store the past state of a cell (needed by the second-order rule) in an extra plane, since this state is already available in an adjacent row of the same plane, where it can be seen as the NORTH neighbor.

The cellular-automaton world defined by this rule is a veritable microcosm of mechanical and statistical mechanical effects (Figure 9.9b). It supports a great variety of elementary and complex "particles" (analogous to the gliders of Section 3.4)—some small and fast, some large and sluggish. Particles may be dismembered by a collision and emerge as new combinations of particles; however, an *Ising-like energy*[8] is conserved in the collisions[45]. If you start with a cloud of "hot gas"—a random patch on a clear background—the cloud will slowly lose heat by expansion and evaporation and various levels of ordered structures will appear.

---

[8]A quantity that counts how many of the present neighbors "disagree" with the past value of the cell under consideration; cf. Sections 6.2, 17.2.

9.8   Neighborhood expansion tricks

Several techniques are available for sensing the second neighbors needed by
this rule, and, in general, for bringing within the neighborhood scope cells
that do not fall within the 3×3 window provided by CAM; we shall barely
touch on two of them, namely *gathering* and *pleating*.

Suppose you want to "gather" your second neighbors, which we shall call
WEST-WEST and EAST-EAST, into the neighborhood fold. You can copy the
current contents of plane 0 onto, say, plane 1, then shift plane 1 one position to
the right, and WEST-WEST will now be visible as WEST'. The extra step taken
by the shift slows down the simulation, but you have gained one neighbor.
As usual, a custom neighborhood and some ingenuity may be needed to make
the most of the available resources.

A more efficient way to get the extra neighbors is to "pleat" the array so
that it will become narrower in the west-east direction and correspondingly
gain in thickness; the extra thickness is provided by a second bit-plane. This is
illustrated by the following diagrams, in which letters represent cells; one five-
cell neighborhood is given in upper-case letters. We start with a configuration
in which cells are arranged in one bit-plane

$$a \quad b \quad c \quad D \quad E \quad F \quad G \quad H \quad i \quad j \quad k \quad l \,,$$

and we rewrite this configuration as one in which the same cells are arranged
into two bit-planes

$$\begin{array}{cccccc} a & c & E & G & i & k \\ b & D & F & H & j & l \end{array} \cdot$$

In this configuration, all five neighbors of cell F are no more than one cell
away from F, even though some are in the other bit-plane.

With this pleating technique, the SCARVES rule becomes

```
NEW-EXPERIMENT N/VONN &/CENTERS
                                    : NOW
                         &CENTER  ;
                                    : 4SUM0
   EAST CENTER' WEST' WEST + + +  ;
                                    : 4SUM1
   EAST EAST' CENTER WEST' + + +  ;
                                    : PLEATED-SCARVES
                         NOW IF
4SUM0 2 = NORTH   XOR >PLN0              \ the past just
4SUM1 2 = NORTH'  XOR >PLN1 ELSE         \   scrolled north
              SOUTHS >PLNA THEN
              CENTER >PLN2       ;
MAKE-TABLE PLEATED-SCARVES
```

Since the array has been compressed in the east-west direction, one unit of space is now half the size of one unit of time, and the light-cone spans a narrower angle, as is apparent from Figure 9.9b.

Chapter 10

Identity and motion

> A farmer was complaining that his feet got cold: the comforter was too short. "That's easy," said his wife, "I'll cut a good strip off the top and sew it on at the bottom!"

Competitive growth of the kind discussed in previous chapters can give rise to some sort of motion. Say, a blob of matter is eroded on one side and grows by accretion on the other side: it will appear to have moved—amoeba-like. In this context, identity and motion are statistical features which vanish when we examine the phenomenon on the scale of a single cell.

Several rules we've introduced give rise not only to such statistical motion, but also to a more microscopic kind of motion. For example, the gliders of **LIFE** (Section 3.1) are patterns which, on a background of 0's, are reproduced by the rule after a number of steps in a displaced position. There is a recognizable object which has moved. The **SCARVES** rule of Section 9.7 also supports a rich spectrum of such particles.

The simplest particle would be a $\boxed{1}$ or a $\boxed{0}$ moving on a uniform background of $\boxed{0}$'s or $\boxed{1}$'s. Therefore in this chapter our techniques for dealing with identity and motion on a microscopic scale will be based on rules that yield exact, deterministic, microscopic conservation of $\boxed{1}$'s and $\boxed{0}$'s. Once we have mastered the conservation of such "material" objects, it will be easy to extend our methods to the conservation of more abstract quantities such as energy or momentum, and of that most abstract quantity of all, namely *information*.

For simpler experiments with conservation of material objects we will use only the resources already introduced. Eventually, it will be desirable to use the additional resources which CAM provides for this explicit purpose, which embody directly in hardware some of the techniques employed in these simple experiments.

10.1   A random walk

In a cellular automaton, to "transport" a particle from here to there one has to *make a copy* of it there and *erase* it from here. Though performed at *different* places, these two actions must take place as the two halves of an *indivisible* operation—lest particles multiply or vanish—and thus must be carefully coordinated, as we have seen in Section 9.1. Here we shall consider the worst possible situation: the decision to move or not to move, or to go in one direction or the other, is taken by the particle on the spur of the moment, so that explicit travel arrangements cannot be made in advance.

Small particles of ink suspended in water are seen through the microscope to be in a state of continual, irregular motion—the result of innumerable collisions with the water molecules in thermal agitation. In this *Brownian motion*, the behavior of an individual ink particle can be approximated by a *random walk*: at each step the particle moves one unit right or left[1] depending on the outcome of a coin toss.

As long as we have *only one particle*, this model is not hard to realize on a cellular automaton. In CAM, for instance, we can use plane 0 for the particle and plane 1 as a random-number generator, interpreting a $\boxed{0}$ in the latter plane as "left" and $\boxed{1}$ as "right." In words, the directives for a cell are:

- If you have the particle, erase it: it will be picked up by one of your neighbors.

- If the particle is on your right and the underlying random bit says "left," make a copy of the particle.

- Similarly, if the particle is on your left and the random bit says "right," make a copy of the particle.

The result is shown in Figure 10.1a (where the second dimension shows the progress of the particle in time, as explained in Section 9.7).

The machinery of a cellular automaton is wasted on a single particle. However, difficulties arise when we want to model more than one particle: what shall we do when two particles, one coming from the right and one from the left, try to step onto the same square? Shall we provide a separate bit-plane for each particle?[2] Shall we modify the rule so that particles somehow

---

[1]For simplicity, we restrict our attention for a moment to one-dimensional models.

[2]In this case, no economy of machinery can be achieved, and the model is more efficiently handled by a conventional computer.

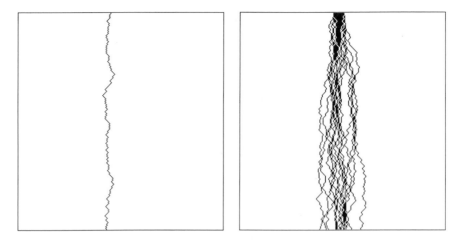

Figure 10.1: Random walk: (a) Spacetime history of a one-particle system, using the "left/right" approach. (b) A many-particle system, using the "swap" approach.

"repel" one another? But then the path of a single particle won't be an ideal random walk, since it will depend on factors external to the particle.

It should be clear that the difficulty is a *conceptual* one, not one of implementation:

- With one bit-plane per particle, the paths are true random walks. However, an arbitrarily large number of particles may end up in the same site; this is not observed in nature, where molecules are essentially impenetrable to one another.

- With a single bit-plane, it would seem that we have no choice but to steer a particle away from its randomly chosen course when a contention arises. However, this would spoil the statistics of the *ideal random walk*; yet, on the scale we are considering, it is *that* statistics that is observed in nature.

Well, how does *nature* do it?

10.2 A random shuffle

In Brownian motion, particles do not travel in a *vacuum*. At each place we have either ink *or water*—which is also impenetrable. When a particle moves, it *swaps* places with some water; if there is a particle next to it, it can swap places with the other particle.

Let us then build a new mental picture. Our model will consist of particles filling all of space and having *identical* dynamical properties. We'll take the liberty of painting some of these particles black ("ink") and leave the others white ("water"). Using Poisson updating (Section 9.5), we shall choose a pair of adjacent sites—which we shall call a *block*—and *swap* their contents. As a result of this swap, at every tick of the "Poisson clock" a particle will take a step left or right depending on its place within the cell pair. If *two* particles are present, they will exchange places;[3] they will never attempt to occupy the *same* place. Note that with this approach the random decision to swap or not to swap is associated with a whole two-cell block, not with a single cell.

The swap rule is "data blind:" that is, the exchange takes place in the same way no matter what the contents of the block is. We could update the array *without even looking at it!* This is our guarantee that the path of an individual particle will have the same statistics whether the particle is alone or in company!

Poisson updating guarantees that at any moment we'll try to update only one block. In fact, the above "swap" recipe is meaningless if applied to two overlapping blocks:

$$\cdots \overline{a\;\underline{b}\;c} \cdots \quad ; \tag{10.1}$$

that is, the contents of cell b cannot be swapped *at the same time* with that of a and that of c. On the other hand, ideal Poisson updating can be simulated in a synchronous cellular automaton only in the limit of an infinitely slow simulation, as explained in Section 9.5. A much faster simulation can be achieved by introducing a suitable updating discipline. That is, we shall divide the blocks into two groups—*even* and *odd*—as shown below

$$\cdots \overset{\text{even}}{\overline{0\;\underline{1}}}\;\overset{\text{even}}{\overline{2\;\underline{3}}}\;\overset{\text{even}}{\overline{4\;\underline{5}}}\;6 \cdots \quad ,$$
$$\text{odd}\quad\text{odd}\quad\text{odd}$$

and permit the updating of a block of one type only on even-numbered steps; of the other type, on odd-numbered steps.

We'll run the new model of a random walk on CAM, using plane 0 for the particles, plane 1 for the random-number generator that will supply the Poisson clock, and plane 2 to store an alternating 0/1 pattern which will be used for telling how the cells are paired in blocks. Since this is a one-dimensional model, we'll be able to run a different copy of the system on each row of the array.

The main emphasis in the following construction is to make a *cell rule*—which is the only kind provided by CAM—act as if it were a *block rule*;[4] that is, the two cells of a block must act at the same time—whenever they act at all—and separately perform the two halves of an indivisible operation

---

[3]If the ink particles only come in one color, this case is indistinguishable from the case of no movement at all.

[4]In Section 16.5 we shall briefly examine a second approach to this problem.

("swap" in this case). This construction will be the starting point for our discussion of the Margolus neighborhood in Chapter 12.

We shall separately define different "pieces" of our machinery and put them all together in the end.

. *Alternating block pattern.* Before beginning the experiment, let us store on each row of plane 2 the pattern

$$010101010101\cdots,$$

where 0 will be used to identify the left element of a block and 1 the right element. At the next step, we would like to have the pattern

$$101010101010\cdots,$$

and so on in alternation; this is taken care of by the simple rule component

```
( CAM-B )                        : CHANGE-GRID
              CENTER NOT >PLN2 ;
```

which complements the pattern. (The comment CAM-B is a reminder that we are operating in the CAM-B context, since we are giving a rule for plane 2.)

To allow us to run multiple copies of the system, the row of alternating 0's and 1's was repeated on each line of the screen, so that plane 2 contains alternating vertical stripes of 0's and 1's (cf. Section 14.3).

The "left/right" markers will be used by CAM-A, where they will be visible under the neighbor name &CENTER; for clarity, we shall define

```
( CAM-A )                        : LEFT/RITE ( -- 0|1)
                   &CENTER ;
```

Neighbor multiplexing. No matter which kind of block we are in, the relevant neighbor for the CENTER cell of plane 0 is the one *opposite* to it in the block, i.e., EAST for the left cell and WEST for the right cell. For this reason, it will be convenient to define

```
( CAM-A )                        : OPPOSITE
        LEFT/RITE { EAST   WEST  } ;
                                 : OPPOSITE'
        LEFT/RITE { EAST' WEST' } ;
```

so that from now on, given a cell as the current 'CENTER' of attention, one can refer to its block companion as the 'OPPOSITE'.

Block clock. Plane 1 will contain the usual rudimentary random-number generator (Section 8.2), defined by

```
( CAM-A )                        : STIR
        CENTER'
        NORTH' WEST' SOUTH' EAST'
           AND XOR XOR XOR >PLN1 ;
```

At each step, this generator will provide a different random outcome for each cell. To make both cells of a block see the same activation signal, we process these two bits so that the result is the same for the two cells:

```
( CAM-A )                              : POISSON-CLOCK ( -- 0|1)
                CENTER' OPPOSITE' XOR ;
```

Since **STIR** provides an even mixture of 0's and 1's, the XOR of two random bits will also give an even mixture, and thus this Poisson clock will tick on average once every two steps.

Swapping, at last!   A this point we are ready to write the main component of the rule, namely that for the particles in plane 0.

```
( CAM-A )                              : 1D-RANDOM-WALK
                POISSON-CLOCK IF       \ sense Poisson clock
                   OPPOSITE ELSE       \  and accordingly swap
                     CENTER THEN       \  or stay as you are
                         >PLN0 ;
```

Putting it all together. The following is a summary of the complete recipe

```
NEW-EXPERIMENT
CAM-B
        : CHANGE-LATTICE                   CENTER NOT >PLN2 ;

CAM-A N/VONN &/CENTERS
        : STIR                          ... >PLN1 ;
        : LEFT/RITE                    &CENTER ;
        : OPPOSITE        LEFT/RITE { EAST  WEST  } ;
        : OPPOSITE'       LEFT/RITE { EAST' WEST' } ;
        : POISSON-CLOCK     CENTER' OPPOSITE' XOR ;
        : 1D-RANDOM-WALK                ... >PLN0 ;

MAKE-TABLE CHANGE-LATTICE
MAKE-TABLE STIR
MAKE-TABLE 1D-RANDOM-WALK
```

Phew!

We'll start the experiment by filling the middle third of each row with ink and the rest with water (Figure 10.2a): water and ink will steadily diffuse into each other (b), eventually leading to an even mixture (c).

We have succeeded in constructing a microscopic model of *diffusion* that is remarkably realistic and robust. If we define ρ as the *density* of ink particles over a relatively large area of the array, this quantity will evolve in a continuous way as a function of space and time. Unlike the diffusion equation

$$\frac{d\rho}{dt} = \frac{d^2\rho}{dx^2},$$
(10.2)

which is an extreme macroscopic approximation, our model captures important physical details such as the impenetrability of bodies and the finite speed of propagation of information.[5] On the other hand, as we study it on a larger and larger scale, our model converges to (10.2); this explains why the diffusion equation is after all a legitimate modeling tool in the appropriate macroscopic context.

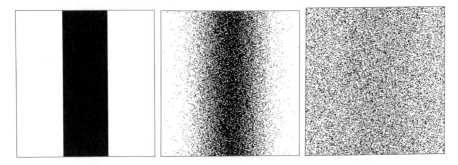

Figure 10.2: Initially separated (a), ink and water diffuse into each other (b), eventually producing a uniform mixture (c).

If we consider now a single copy of the one-dimensional ink/water system, we can make CAM display a spacetime trace of its evolution, as explained in Section 9.7 (the NOW line can be drawn on plane 3). If we start this experiment with a tight cluster of particles somewhere near the middle of the NOW line, we'll be able to see each particle of the cluster follow a separate zig-zag path, as in Figure 10.1b. The diffusion rate is half of that of Figure 10.1a, since the Poisson clock is ticking on average once every other step.

If we stop the Poisson clock during the experiment,[6] the diffusion rate goes to zero as expected (Figure 10.3a). What will happen if we make the clock invariably tick at *every* step?[7] (of course, such a synchronous clock hardly deserves the "Poisson" name any longer). The result is shown in Figure 10.3b: the swap operations are now perfectly coordinated, and the row of swappers turns into a bucket brigade. Particles fly right or left at a uniform speed! This type of particle-transport mechanism will be used in a number of gas models to be introduced later.

---

[5] The diffusion equation predicts that in an arbitrarily short time *some* ink will be found at an arbitrarily large distance from its starting point—which is physically unrealistic.

[6] For instance by putting all 0's in plane 1.

[7] Filling plane 1 with 1's won't do, since STIR will still return all 0's; filling it with alternating stripes of 0's and 1's *will*—with the given definition of STIR. But of course these are kludges, and it would be better to load a new rule where the clock is not sensed at all.

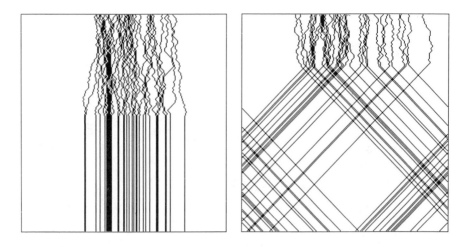

Figure 10.3: (a) When the Poisson clock is stopped, particles stop diffusing. (b) With a clock pulse at every step, a particle keeps moving always in the same direction—right or left depending on where it started.

Chapter 11

Pseudo-neighbors

> I have always wanted to have a neighbor just like you! I've always wanted to live in a neighborhood with you!
>
> [Mr. Rogers]

In the previous chapter, certain pieces of equipment needed for an experiment were actually simulated in the cellular automaton as part of the experiment itself. Besides the random-number generator used for the Poisson clock, we synthesized the following features:

- A striped pattern, used to partition the array into two-cell blocks.

- A mechanism for switching between this pattern and the complementary one on successive time steps—so as to alternately use two different block partitions.

- A cell neighborhood whose make-up—'CENTER, WEST' or 'CENTER, EAST'—changes according to the cell's position in a block, and a *relative* naming scheme by which the other element of a block always appears under the same neighbor name— OPPOSITE —independently of whether it happens to be, in *absolute* terms, the west or the east neighbor of the selected cell.[1]

Since they are useful in quite general situations, CAM provides several resources of this kind directly *in hardware*; in this way the bit planes and the

---

[1] The look-up table is still physically connected to both neighbor lines, but the effect is to multiplex these two lines into a single "virtual" line carrying the right information at the right moment.

look-up tables can be better utilized, and the programming itself is simplified. Spatial and temporal information useful for constructing block partitions and for other purposes is available in the form of *pseudo-neighbors*—i.e., signals that can be sensed directly by the look-up tables but whose source is not the contents of a cell. In the next chapter we shall see that some of these signals are also available *indirectly*, in a form that is even more effective for certain purposes, through the neighbors of the Margolus neighborhood.

11.1 Spatial phases

Each cell position in the 256×256 array that makes up a CAM cellular automaton is uniquely identified by its row and column address (we shall assume that both rows and columns are numbered from 0 trough 255). If the rule could sense this address in its entirety it could specify a different behavior for every cell ("If your address is $\langle 3,7 \rangle$ do this, if it is $\langle 0,95 \rangle$ do that, etc."). Leaving aside the practical difficulty of providing 16 more inputs for the look-up table ($256 \times 256 = 2^{16}$), this approach would represent a gross violation of the spatial-uniformity policy that characterizes cellular automata; for example, in this situation what sense would it make to say "Now run the *same* rule on a 1000×1000 array"?

On the other hand, it is sometimes convenient—as we've seen—to use rules that can avail themselves of a small amount of spatial "texture.[2]" For this reason, in CAM the least significant bit of a cell's column address is broadcast (either directly or in complemented form, as the user wishes[3]) as an internal signal called HORZ—the *horizontal phase*; similarly, the least-significant bit of the row address (or its complement) is broadcast as the signal VERT—the *vertical phase*. One way to "tune in" to these broadcasts is to select the minor neighborhood &/HV (cf. Section 7.3.2), where they appear respectively as &HORZ and &VERT. Thus, the value of &HORZ will alternate between 0 and 1 as one moves along a *row* of the array; since all of the rows are in-phase, this yields a pattern of vertical stripes:

$$\cdots 010101010 \cdots$$
$$\cdots 010101010 \cdots \quad ;$$
$$\cdots 010101010 \cdots$$

similarly, &VERT will alternate along a *column*, yielding horizontal stripes:

$$\cdots 000000000 \cdots$$
$$\cdots 111111111 \cdots \quad .$$
$$\cdots 000000000 \cdots$$

---

[2]A crystal of NaCl is still *uniform* in spite of the alternating arrangement of Na and Cl atoms on each row; to qualify as 'uniform', what counts is that the arrangement is periodic.
[3]See Section 11.2.

By XOR'ing the neighbors **&HORZ** and **&VERT** one obtains a checkerboard pattern

$$\begin{array}{c}\ldots 010101010 \ldots \\ \ldots 101010101 \ldots \\ \ldots 010101010 \ldots\end{array}\quad ;$$

on the other hand, the joint version **&HV** of these two neighbors, which is a four-state variable, yields the following two-dimensional periodic pattern

$$\begin{array}{c}\ldots 010101010 \ldots \\ \ldots 232323232 \ldots \\ \ldots 010101010 \ldots \\ \ldots 232323232 \ldots\end{array}\quad ,$$

where the block $\begin{smallmatrix}01\\23\end{smallmatrix}$ is indefinitely repeated both horizontally and vertically.

11.2   Temporal phases, and phase control

Although in writing a rule it is convenient to visualize a neighbor word, say NORTH, as returning the current state of a certain cell, it is important to remember that these words are only used by the host software in *compiling* a table; their role is exhausted once this table has been shipped to CAM. Thus, NORTH does not answer the real-time question "What is the current state, in CAM, of this cell's north neighbor?"—its value is only meaningful during table generation.

Once CAM is operating, the table's input lines are connected to live hardware signals that are in one-to-one correspondence with the neighbor words used in compiling the table. The signals corresponding to ordinary neighbors, such as **CENTER**, **NORTH**, etc., come from the bit-planes; who supplies the signals corresponding to the pseudo-neighbors?

As mentioned in the previous section, the signals corresponding to the spatial phases **&HORZ** and **&VERT** are generated internally by CAM's horizontal and vertical counters—which know each cell's row and column address. The remaining phase signals, corresponding to the pseudo-neighbors **&PHASE** and **&PHASE'** mentioned in Section 7.3.2 (as well as **PHASE** and **PHASE'** to be introduced in Section 12.5) are driven directly by the host computer—which before every step can independently set each one of them to either 0 or 1. If the signal corresponding to **&PHASE**, say, is set to 1, during the step itself the neighbor **&PHASE** will be seen to have the value 1 by *all* cells, and thus will appear in the simulation as a space-independent—but possibly time-dependent[4]—parameter.

---

[4]We are referring, of course, to *cellular-automaton time*, which advances in a discrete fashion step after step. The fact that in CAM's internal implementation cells are updated *sequentially* is irrelevant here: this internal time is hidden from view, as explained at the beginning of Chapter 7.

Defining a rule that makes reference to a pseudo-neighbor word such as
&PHASE is of course pointless if the corresponding hardware signal is not
driven by the host computer through the desired sequence of values, step
after step, *during* the experiment itself. Thus, alongside the neighbor term
PHASE there exists a command of the form

$$\langle \text{value} \rangle \ \text{IS} \ \texttt{<\&PHASE>},$$

to be used for placing a specific value on the corresponding signal line. Appropriate contexts for giving this kind of command are discussed in the rest
of this chapter; for reference, here we shall list the available options and the
argument range for each.

RANGE	COMMAND	REMARKS
0 1	IS <&PHASE>	signal seen by &PHASE
0 1	IS <&PHASE'>	signal seen by &PHASE'
0 1 2 3	IS <&PHASES>	joint setting of the above
0 1	IS <ORG-H>	origin of HORZ signal
0 1	IS <ORG-V>	origin of VERT signal
0 1 2 3	IS <ORG-HV>	joint setting of the above
0 1	IS <PHASE>	signal seen by PHASE
0 1	IS <PHASE'>	signal seen by PHASE'
0 1 2 3	IS <PHASES>	joint setting of the above

$$(11.1)$$

A spatial-phase signal such as HORZ of course does take—during the same
step—different values at different sites of the array; that is, for each cell this
value depends on the *position* of the cell itself, which is fixed, rather than
on the experimenter's whim at a certain *moment*. However, at each step
the experimenter may choose for HORZ either the pattern $010101\cdots$—which
starts with a 0 at the *origin* of the array—or the complementary pattern
$101010\cdots$—which starts with a 1. The choice of the value at the origin
is thus a *time-dependent* variable, listed in the above table as <ORG-H>; its
default value is 0. Similar considerations apply to VERT. These two signals
can be set jointly, by assigning a value between 0 and 3 to the variable
<ORG-HV> (as shown above). The ordering of the two bits within this joint
variable is <ORG-HV> = <ORG-H> $+2\times$ <ORG-V>.

11.3   A two-phase rule

In Chapter 9 we saw how a suitable rule can make the *state of a cell* go through
a multi-phase cycle. As an illustration of the use of pseudo-neighbors, here
we'll describe a simple experiment where *the rule itself* changes from step to
step in a cyclic way.

We want to synthesize a "composite" rule called `BORDER/HOLLOW` that works on bit-plane 0 as follows

- At even steps, grow a border of $\boxed{1}$'s around any cell that is in state $\boxed{1}$.

- At odd steps, hollow out any solid areas by turning into a $\boxed{0}$ any cell that is completely surrounded by $\boxed{1}$'s.

To know whether the time is "even" or "odd," the rule looks at the pseudo-neighbor `&PHASE`; the value of this parameter will be made to alternate between 0 and 1 on successive steps when the experiment is actually running. The whole experiment is constructed as follows.

1. We start a clean slate by saying

```
NEW-EXPERIMENT
```

This initializes the whole machine—hardware and software—to a well-defined default state. Options will remain dormant until explicitly activated.

2. Then we make the appropriate neighborhood declarations and separately write down the two "pieces" of the rule:

```
N/MOORE &/PHASES   \ in this minor neighborhood
                   \   &PHASE and &PHASE' are visible

                            : BORDER ( -- newstate)
    CENTER NORTH SOUTH WEST EAST
    N.WEST N.EAST S.WEST S.EAST
       OR OR OR OR OR OR OR OR ;
                            : HOLLOW ( -- newstate)
       NORTH SOUTH WEST EAST
    N.WEST N.EAST S.WEST S.EAST
    AND AND AND AND AND AND AND IF
                      0 ELSE
                 CENTER THEN ;
```

3. Out of these two pieces we make a single, phase-sensitive rule, and ship it to the look-up table by passing it as an argument to `MAKE-TABLE`:

```
                            : BORDER/HOLLOW
    &PHASE { BORDER HOLLOW } >PLN0 ;

    MAKE-TABLE BORDER/HOLLOW
```

4. At this point, we define a run-cycle descriptor, i.e., a Forth word that specifies to what value the signal corresponding to &PHASE should be set before each step. This word, which we have called EVEN/ODD, is passed as an argument to the command MAKE-CYCLE (much as a table descriptor is given as an argument to the command MAKE-TABLE). The possible ingredients of a run cycle are discussed in Section 11.5; here the matter is straightforward:

```
                              : EVEN/ODD
        0 IS <&PHASE>  STEP
        1 IS <&PHASE>  STEP ;
```

```
MAKE-CYCLE EVEN/ODD
```

We are now ready to run. The cellular automaton will alternate one step of BORDER with one step of HOLLOW. The result is essentially one of iterated spatial derivatives; that is, the first two-step cycle will extract the outlines of any solid region of $\boxed{1}$'s present in the initial configuration; the second cycle will draw outlines of the outlines, and so on, eventually filling the space with complex animated doodles (Figure 11.1).

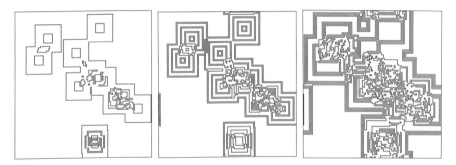

Figure 11.1: Successive stages of the BORDER/HOLLOW rule.

11.4   Incremental phase control

In the previous example, the value of <&PHASE> was explicitly set to 0 or 1 on alternate steps of the run cycle. Since phase variables can be read as well as written, instead of specifying the new value of a phase in *absolute* terms one could specify it in *relative* terms, i.e., with respect to the phase's value at the previous step.

For example, for a two-valued variable such as <&PHASE>, one can just *complement* its value at every step. (With this incremental approach, initialization of the phase variable at the beginning of a run, if required, must

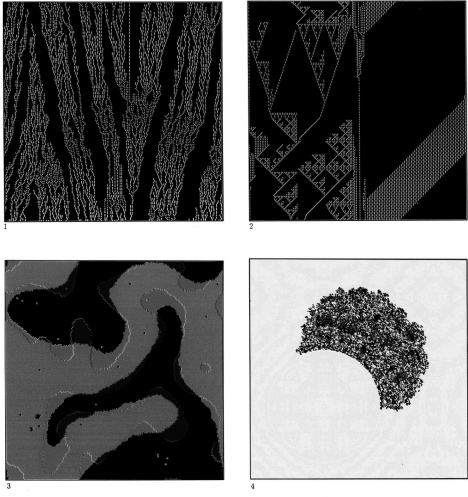

Plates 1, 2: Several hundred steps into the evolution of the HGLASS rule (Section 4.1), started respectively from a random configuration and a small area of zeros.

Plate 3: Surface tension (Section 5.4). The green areas are bays that have been filled over a few hundred steps; the blue, capes that have been eroded.

Plate 4: Differential evolution (Section 9.2). We compare in real time the evolution of two copies of the same system, started from initial states that differ by just one bit. The area where the two evolutions no longer agree, displayed in color, rapidly expands but can't penetrate the circular barrier.

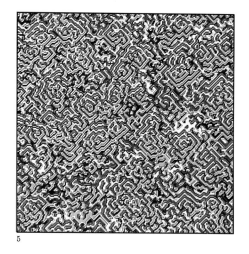

5

6

7

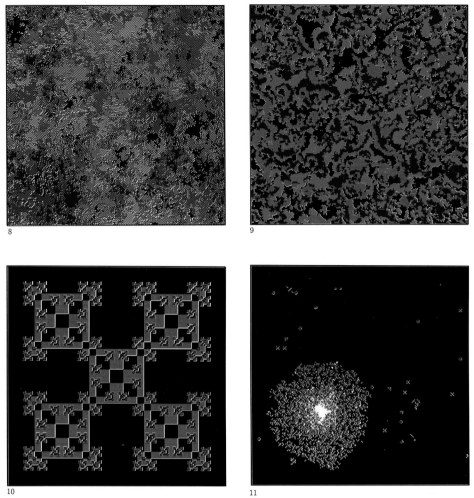

Plates 5, 6, 7 (facing page): Phase waves in excitable media with latency, using different excitation parameters (Section 9.3); the system of Plate 7 (where a small detail is shown magnified) provides a model for the Zhabotinsky reaction.

Plate 8: Random spread of four competing populations (Section 9.4) provides a model of genetic drift.

Plate 9: Another drift model, where the competition is regulated by a cyclic ranking (Section 9.6). Similar mechanisms can be used to provide timing signals that allow an asynchronous system to perform deterministic computation.

Plates 10, 11: Fractals (Section 12.8.1) and self-organization (Section 12.8.2) in reversible systems.

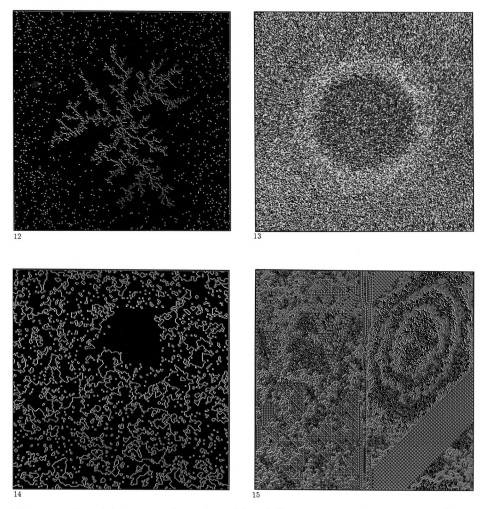

Plate 12: Dendritic crystal produced by diffusion-limited aggregation (Section 15.7) started from a one-cell seed.

Plate 13: Sound wave in a lattice gas (section 16.1). Notice that the propagation pattern is circular even though the individual gas particles can only move horizontally or vertically.

Plate 14: Ising spin model, using bond energy (rather than spin orientation) as the state variable (Section 17.7).

Plate 15: A reversible second-order rule (TIME-TUNNEL, Section 6.3), started from the configuration of Plate 2. Note how certain features are conserved.

be taken care of by a separate command). The run cycle would be set up as
follows

```
                      : INIT-PHASE
         0 IS <&PHASE> ;
                      : CHANGE-PHASE
 <&PHASE> NOT IS <&PHASE> ;
                      : EVEN/ODD
        STEP  CHANGE-PHASE ;
```

```
MAKE-CYCLE EVEN/ODD
INIT-PHASE
```

Note that commands such as INIT-PHASE and CHANGE-PHASE, defined as
above as separate routines, can be interpolated at an arbitrary moment in
the course of a simulation[5] in order to alter the regular alternation of phase
values otherwise defined by the run cycle. This is one way to achieve time-
reversal in rules where the direction of time is controlled by a phase variable
(cf. Chapters 12 and 14).

11.5 The run cycle

If one were dealing with a cellular automata machine where the only relevant
data were the contents of the bit-planes and that of the look-up table, then
to run an experiment one would just say, "This is the rule, this is the initial
configuration—go!" In fact, many simple experiments can be run on CAM in
just this fashion, as shown in the previous chapters.

On the other hand, in a composite rule such as that of Section 11.3 a
complete cycle may consist of several steps, each performed in a different
environment. Many of the resources of CAM may usefully be made to play
different roles at different points of the cycle: besides controlling the phases,
one might want to change the color map, service the event counter, or even
switch from one neighborhood to another.

Here we shall discuss the main iteration loop that runs a cellular automaton on CAM. This consists of a skeleton to which different kinds of "decora-
tions" can be attached in order to create a specific run-cycle environment.

The command STEP tells CAM to perform a step. What kind of action
the step will take is determined by the contents of the look-up tables and by
the state of other signals—such as the pseudo-neighbors—which collectively
make up the *dynamical parameters* of the machine; these parameters can be
modified between one step and the next.[6] Besides using these parameters as

---

[5]E.g., by typing them at the keyboard or associating them with a control-panel key.

[6]It is also possible to modify between one step and the next the contents of the bit-
planes, which collectively make up the *state variables* of the system. The CAM hardware

an "input," the step itself may return an "output"—for example a value in
the event counter.

Thus, to run an experiment one must (a) initially set all of the relevant
dynamical parameters, (b) specify what changes (if any) are to be made to
certain parameters before each step,[7] and (c) specify what data (if any) should
be monitored or collected after each step.

In essence, the "order of the day" for an experiment could be written as
follows

:   AGENDA

⟨service operations⟩
STEP
⟨service operations⟩
STEP

. . .

⟨service operations⟩
STEP
⟨service operations⟩ ;

(of course, repetitive sections could be embedded in iteration statements),
and in fact this way of running CAM is useful for "canned" demos and other
specialized applications.

If we execute **AGENDA**, the machine will run at full speed (unless ⟨service
operations⟩ itself provides a delay); if we want to suspend the simulation we'll
have to abort the program—and it will be difficult to know where we were and
how to resume in an orderly way. Of course, we could intersperse throughout
the program explicit instructions to sense control-panel keys, synchronize
with an external clock, stop at certain points, etc. However, all of these
timing options are usually better kept separate from the essential issues of a
simulation—that is, *what* to do and *in what order*.

In CAM, this separation between timing and sequencing is achieved by
letting a program such as **AGENDA** run as a *coroutine* of the main control
program—which will activate the coroutine whenever desired. A coroutine
used in this way will be called a *run cycle*. The main program will pass control
to the run cycle when it wants the next step to be executed, the run cycle
will pass control back to the main program when the step has been started
and parameters for the next step have been set up. Both the main program

---

provides in between steps a brief time-window in which the host can "talk" to CAM without
disrupting the execution of the steps. There is enough time in this window to update all the
dynamical parameters—which are few; in the little extra time that remains one can read
or alter on-the-fly a few bytes of plane or table data. More extensive manipulations would
exceed the window width, and force CAM to suspend the simulation for one or more steps.
At the cost of slowing down the simulation, both plane and table data can be modified at
will between steps.

[7]When several CAM modules are used together, parameters for each of them can be
modified independently between steps.

and the run cycle always continue where they left off each time control passes to them.

The grammar is the following. We tell CAM that the word AGENDA (for example) is to be the current run cycle by the declaration

MAKE-CYCLE AGENDA

In the run cycle, occurrences of the word STEP have a special significance; as soon as it is declared as the run cycle, AGENDA will start running and continue until the first occurrence of STEP is found. Right before executing that word, AGENDA will go to sleep: the machine's parameters are all set up for the first step, but the step itself hasn't been performed yet.

The main program will have responsibility for generating the "ticks" of the simulation clock. Ticks may come fast or slow; they may be suspended, resumed, sent in groups of two, etc., as desired. At each "tick," the command NEXT-STEP is issued; this command wakes up AGENDA, which executes the pending STEP and keeps running until it finds the next occurrence of the word STEP—at which point it goes back to sleep. Now the first step has been performed, and the machine is already set up for the next one—and so on.

When AGENDA reaches the end of its code, it goes back to the beginning: there is no need for an explicit iteration statement to run the cycle over and over.[8]

For example, for all the cellular automata introduced so far[9] it would be sufficient to say

MAKE-CYCLE STEP

That is, since no parameters are changed between steps, the task to be executed at every tick of the clock consists of just STEP.

The bare word STEP is the default run cycle; thus, applications that do not need a custom run cycle need not even be aware of the existence of this scheduling mechanism.

11.6 Alternating spatial textures

Textures that can be created in one or two dimensions with the help of the spatial phases (such as block partitions, stripes, or checkerboards) are particularly useful when a regular alternation of phase values is added to the *time* dimension.

---

[8]The command FINISH-CYCLE will continue execution of the current cycle until the end of its code, and then put it to sleep. This is useful when during an interactive session one wants to switch in an orderly way from a given run cycle to a different one.

[9]Except, of course, the ad hoc example of Section 11.3.

One example was provided by the random-walk experiment of Section 10.1, where we used bit-plane 2 to provide a pattern of vertical stripes that was complemented at every step. To achieve the same result using a spatial-phase pseudo-neighbor, one would select the minor neighborhood &/HV (rather than &/CENTERS) and use the following definition for the block marker LEFT/RITE used in that example

```
              : LEFT/RITE
      &HORZ  ;
```

An appropriate run cycle (cf. table (11.1) and Section 11.4) would be

```
                : ALT-STRIPES
  STEP   <ORG-H> NOT IS <ORG-H> ;
```

If it is important to start the cycle with a definite choice of pattern, the run cycle can be defined as follows (cf. Section 11.4):

```
                : ALT-STRIPES
      0 IS <ORG-H>  STEP
      1 IS <ORG-H>  STEP ;
```

Note that in order to gain access to the two pseudo-neighbor lines of &/HV one has to relinquish the two neighbor lines of &/CENTERS . In the next section we'll show how one can "have one's cake and eat it too."

At any rate, even though these particular trade-offs are specific to CAM, they reflect a real contention for resources, and thus are illustrative of the trade-offs that one would have to consider in other high-performance simulation contexts.

A standard technique in the simulation of lattice models of physical systems is to update at one step the cells lying on the "black" sublattice of a checkerboard, and at the next step those belonging to the "white" sublattice (cf. Section 17.3). The intuitive reasons for this are provided by the examples of Sections 9.5 and 10.1; indeed, the two approaches based on "alternating partitions" and "alternating sublattices" are in a sense dual aspects of the same approach, as explained in Section 17.7.

Chapter 12

The Margolus neighborhood

> Do unto others as you would have others do unto you.
>
> [The golden rule]

In this chapter we shall discuss the resources offered by CAM in support of the *Margolus neighborhood*, a cell-interconnection scheme that is useful in physical modeling, particularly when microscopic reversibility is an issue. The conceptual motivations for the Margolus neighborhood and typical applications will be given in Part III; here we shall be concerned principally with its functional aspects—what it is and how it is used.

12.1 Block rules

Following the precedent of Section 10.2, let us introduce a new style of cellular automaton, called a *partitioning cellular automaton*:[1]

1. The array of cells is partitioned into a collection of finite, disjoint and uniformly arranged pieces called *blocks*.

2. A *block rule* is given that looks at the contents of a block and updates the whole block (rather than a single cell as in an ordinary cellular automaton); an example is given by table (12.1) below. The same rule is applied to every block. Note that blocks do not overlap, and no information is exchanged between adjacent blocks.

---

[1] We are not changing the rules in the middle of the game! At the cost of using more states and neighbors, a system of this kind can always be rewritten as an ordinary cellular automaton.

3. The partition is changed from one step to the next, so as to have some overlap between the blocks used at one step and those used at the next one.

Point 3 is essential: if we used the same partition at every step the cellular automaton would be effectively subdivided into a collection of independent subsystems.

In this book we shall use only the simplest partitioning scheme, namely:

• The array of cells is subdivided into blocks of size 2×2.

• Steps in which the blocks are aligned with the *even* grid of the "graph paper" alternate with steps that use the *odd* grid, as shown in Figure 12.1.

This partitioning scheme is called the *Margolus neighborhood*, and is directly supported by CAM.

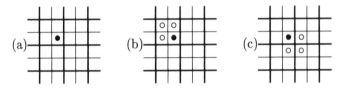

Figure 12.1: The 2×2 blocks of the Margolus neighborhood; consecutive steps alternate between the even grid (thick lines) and the odd grid (thin lines). Depending on which grid is used, the cell marked in (a) will have as neighborhood either an even-aligned block (b) or an odd-aligned block (c).

Notice that the Margolus neighborhood makes use of only *two* partitions (namely the even grid and the odd grid). In general, it is understood that the different partitions used step after step by the rule of a partitioning cellular automaton should be *finite* in number and reused in a cyclic way, so as to retain *uniformity* of space and time.[2]

12.2 Particles in motion

To give a simple example of use of the Margolus neighborhood, let's model a stylized gas consisting of particles moving at uniform speed with *no inter-*

---

[2]Cellular automata can be seen as dynamical systems whose laws are *periodic* in space and time. In an ordinary cellular automaton, one temporal cycle corresponds to one step of the rule, and along either axis one spatial cycle corresponds to one cell. Partitioning cellular automata, though defined on the same spacetime grid, have laws that are periodic with a *coarser* pitch. Specifically, with the Margolus neighborhood it takes two steps to complete a cycle along the time axis (one step will use the even grid, the other the odd grid), and it takes two cells (the length of a 2×2 block) to span a cycle along either spatial axis.

actions. Cells can be in one of two possible states; i.e., a cell can be empty (' ') or contain a particle ('•'). The rule is the following

- SWAP-ON-DIAG   In every 2×2 block of the current partition, swap the contents of each cell with that of the cell diagonally opposite to it.

Such a block rule can be given explicitly, by listing for each possible state of a block the corresponding new state; the full table consists of 16 entries:

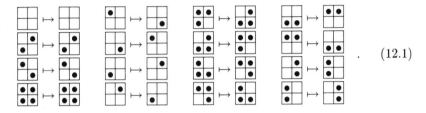

(12.1)

Since the present rule is rotation-invariant, several entries of (12.1), such as, for instance,

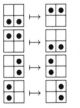

,

coincide up to a rotation; for clarity and brevity, it will be convenient to use a compressed form of table (12.1) in which each equivalence class under rotation is represented by a single entry, so that only six rather than sixteen entries are needed:

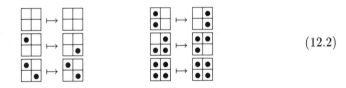

(12.2)

It will be instructive to analyze in detail the behavior of this rule.

- Observe that the prescription of table (12.2) is consistent with the following intuitive interpretation: a particle lying in a given corner of the block it currently occupies will move to the diagonally opposite corner of the same block.

- Recall that the make-up of the blocks alternates in time between the even grid and the odd grid.

- Look at an isolated particle. For the first step choose, say, the even grid (solid lines), and consider a particle lying in the upper-left corner of its block (Figure 12.2a); the rule will make the particle move to the lower-right corner, in a down-right diagonal motion.

- At the next step use the odd grid; here the particle will *again* find itself in the upper-left corner of a block, and the rule will again drag it in a down-right motion.

- Continue like this, alternating the two partitions. Each particle will move on a diagonal at a uniform rate; which of the four possible directions it will follow is determined by its initial position.

- When two particles meet head-on they exchange places on the diagonal as a matter of routine (SWAP-ON-DIAG swaps anything it finds— particles or vacuum—without even looking at it!) and continue on their courses; particles traveling on intersecting diagonals go by without noticing one another (Figure 12.2b).

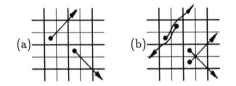

Figure 12.2: SWAP-ON-DIAG: (a) Uniform motion of a particle (here and in the following figures the particle is shown at the beginning of an *even* step—where the relevant blocks are those delimited by thick lines). (b) Particles go "through" one another without interacting.

The resulting dynamics is rather trivial: since particles do not interact with one another, each particle constitutes an isolated system. However, the particle-transport mechanism presented here is the main ingredient in a number of rules (introduced starting in the next section) of interest for computation and for physical modeling.

12.3   Collisions

Having provided a simple mechanism for uniform motion, we shall now complement it with a collision mechanism that will maintain as far as possible the analogy with physics.

In a stylized gas such as that described in the previous section, one may think of the particles as having *mass* and consequently *kinetic energy*. Since all particles are identical and travel at the same speed, they all have the same energy; thus, energy conservation is equivalent to conservation of particles— and of course particles are conserved by a "swapping" rule such as SWAP-ON-DIAG. Momentum is also trivially conserved, since particles have uniform motion.

If one wants to introduce collisions that conserve momentum as well as energy, inspection of look-up table (12.2) will show that only one modification is possible.[3] Namely, the third entry of the table, where two particles traveling in opposite directions along a diagonal meet head-on, can be changed so that the particles instead of proceeding undisturbed will leave in opposite directions along the *other* diagonal (in either case, the total momentum is zero before and after the interaction):

$$\boxed{} \mapsto \boxed{} . \tag{12.3}$$

The table for this rule, called HPP-GAS, is thus

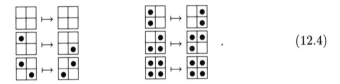

$$\tag{12.4}$$

Figure 12.3 illustrates the behavior of this rule.

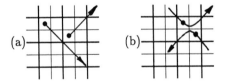

Figure 12.3: HPP-GAS: (a) Uniform motion of an isolated particle. (b) Particles that collide head-on leave along the opposite diagonal.

A remark is in order. Let's call a and b the two particles undergoing a collision, and assume that all particles are identical. Then, because of the symmetry of the output, it does not make sense to ask which of the two outgoing particles is a and which is b; one may imagine, if one wishes, that the collision annihilates the original particles and creates a brand new pair.

---

[3]Observe that the first and the last entries cannot be changed because of energy conservation. The second entry, which describes the free motion of a particle, characterizes the family of gases we are interested in now; altering this entry (which is possible only at the cost of breaking one more symmetry at the microscopic level) leads to a different family of gases, discussed in Section 12.7.

Despite the fact that its particles are restricted to a discrete set of positions and move at a fixed speed in one of four possible directions, the *macroscopic* properties of HPP-GAS are in many respects identical to those of physical gases. This important result will be discussed in Chapter 16, devoted to fluid dynamics.

12.4   How to turn a block rule into a cell rule

A *block rule* such as that of table (12.2) specifies the new state of every cell of a given block (let's label them UL, UR, LL, LR for "upper-left," "upper-right," "lower-left," and "lower-right") as a function of the current state of the same four cells; in formulas,

$$
\begin{aligned}
\text{UL}_{new} &= f_{\text{UL}}(\text{UL}, \text{UR}, \text{LL}, \text{LR}),\\
\text{UR}_{new} &= f_{\text{UR}}(\text{UL}, \text{UR}, \text{LL}, \text{LR}),\\
\text{LL}_{new} &= f_{\text{LL}}(\text{UL}, \text{UR}, \text{LL}, \text{LR}),\\
\text{LR}_{new} &= f_{\text{LR}}(\text{UL}, \text{UR}, \text{LL}, \text{LR}).
\end{aligned}
\qquad (12.5)
$$

In CAM, however, the rule must be given in the form of a recipe for updating a *single* cell, rather than a whole block; to simulate the effects of a block rule we must use a "position-smart" recipe that in essence would instruct a single cell as follows

1. If in the current grid you happen to be the UL cell of your block, then use the first expression of (12.5); if you are the UR cell, use the second expression, and so on.

2. Having determined where you are in the block—and consequently which of the four expressions to use—find out where the other block neighbors are with respect to you. For example, if you are a UL cell, then the UR argument in that expression coincides with your EAST neighbor, the LL with your SOUTH neighbor, and the LR with your S.EAST neighbor; of course, since you are a UL cell, the UL argument is nothing but yourself—i.e., the neighbor called CENTER.

   In other words, the first expression of (12.5) applies *only* to UL cells, and for them it is equivalent to

   $$\text{CENTER}_{new} = f_{\text{UL}}(\text{CENTER}, \text{EAST}, \text{SOUTH}, \text{S.EAST}).$$

All this sounds rather complex; however, the situation is greatly simplified by special hardware provisions and matching software support. The *Margolus neighborhood* declaration (in any of its "flavors" N/MARG N/MARG-HV and N/MARG-PH) activates, among others, a set of neighbor words that is particularly appropriate for rules that are rotation-invariant.[4] With respect to any

---

[4]See Section 12.5 for a complete list of Margolus neighbors.

of the four cells, treated as the current CENTER of attention—and which may happen to be in any of the four block positions—the other three cells of the block will be called CW, CCW, and OPP (from your corner of the block, the other three corners can be reached by moving *clockwise, counter-clockwise,* or diagonally *opposite*), as shown here (the star indicates the CENTER cell):

UL	UR		*	CW		CCW	*		CW	OPP		OPP	CCW
LL	LR		CCW	OPP		OPP	CW		*	CCW		CW	*

$$(12.6)$$

With this *relative* labeling, the SWAP-ON-DIAG rule of table (12.2) becomes simply

```
                  : SWAP-ON-DIAG
      OPP >PLNO ;
```

that is, the new state of any given cell is the current state of its opposite neighbor, OPP. Note that OPP "knows" which grid is in use at the present step and where in its block the given cell is located.

Similarly, the HPP-GAS rule of table (12.4) can be expressed as follows

```
                  : COLLISION ( -- f|t )
      CENTER OPP =
         CW CCW  = AND
      CENTER CW <> AND ;
                  : HPP-GAS
  COLLISION IF CW ELSE OPP THEN
                  >PLNO ;
```

where we have modified the above SWAP-ON-DIAG rule by inserting an IF clause that takes care of the "collision" entry.[5]

The simplicity of the code for SWAP-ON-DIAG and HPP-GAS above derives, of course, from the rotational invariance of these rules and from the fact that the relative block neighbors CENTER, CW, OPP, and CCW refer to block elements in a way that is indifferent to rotations. Thus, four expressions analogous to those of (12.5) can be condensed into a single expression of the form

$$\text{CENTER}_{new} = f(\text{CENTER}, \text{CW}, \text{CCW}, \text{OPP}),$$

and the issue of selecting one of four expressions according to the position in the block (cf. point 1 above) is avoided. Moreover, the work of point 2 is automatically performed by these "position smart" neighbor words.

---

[5]In COLLISION, we check that each diagonal is either full or empty, and then that if one is full the other is empty. In HPP-GAS, if a collision occurs we rotate the whole block counter-clockwise by replacing each cell by its CW neighbor.

An advantage of using a 2×2 block rule is that each bit-plane contributes only four bits of input to the look-up table. Thus, in order to see a whole block's contents for *both* planes 0 and 1 the look-up table need only use eight probes, rather than the eighteen required for a 3×3 neighborhood.

Having been exposed in Sections 9.1 and 10.1 to the cumbersome techniques needed for "programming" particle dynamics in ordinary cellular automata, the reader will not fail to appreciate the clarity of description and the economy of means that can be achieved with this alternative approach. The issue is not merely one of compact *notation*; in CAM, the *implementation* is essentially isomorphic to the conceptual model, and its simplicity translates directly into simulation efficiency.

12.5   The Margolus neighbors

As already mentioned, in CAM the Margolus neighborhood is supported by special hardware; this leads to a more efficient utilization of the look-up tables and gives one access to a wider range of experiments.

As noted in Section 11.1, the two spatial phases &HORZ and &VERT jointly provide the information necessary to partition the array of cells into a grid of 2×2 blocks; in fact, one can define a *block* as a set of four adjacent cells for which the values of the joint spatial phase &HV are arranged as follows

01
23

The two different groupings of cells into blocks corresponding to the even and the odd grid are obtained by alternating between 0 and 3 the value taken by &HV at the origin of the array (this is done by manipulating <ORG-HV> as explained in Section 12.6).

In principle, then, one could define the relative block neighbors of the previous section in terms of the usual cell neighbors NORTH, N.EAST, etc. provided by the Moore neighborhood. For example, CW, CCW, and OPP are functionally equivalent to

```
                                  : CW
    &HV { EAST SOUTH NORTH WEST } ;
                                  : CCW
    &HV { SOUTH WEST EAST NORTH } ;
                                  : OPP
&HV { S.EAST S.WEST N.EAST N.WEST } ;
```

In other words, the rule table could be programmed so as to multiplex eight ordinary neighbors into three block-neighbors, under control of the spatial phases (the fourth block neighbor is CENTER, and can be used directly). However, in order to synthesize four block-neighbors in this way one would have to use 11 of the 12 table inputs (nine spatial neighbors plus two spatial phases), leaving little room for any additional features.

In CAM the above multiplexing is done directly by the hardware, so that CW, CCW, and OPP—as well as CENTER—correspond to actual signals on the board; this is done for plane 1 as well as for plane 0. These eight signals (four for each plane) are connected to eight inputs of the look-up table by the *Margolus neighborhood* major assignment, as shown in table (7.2). This assignment comes in three slightly different "flavors," namely N/MARG, which yields the neighbors

$$\begin{array}{llll} \texttt{CENTER} & \texttt{CW} & \texttt{CCW} & \texttt{OPP} \\ \texttt{CENTER'} & \texttt{CW'} & \texttt{CCW'} & \texttt{OPP'} \end{array} \quad,$$

N/MARG-HV, which yields the neighbors

$$\begin{array}{lllll} \texttt{CENTER} & \texttt{CW} & \texttt{CCW} & \texttt{OPP} & \texttt{HORZ} \\ \texttt{CENTER'} & \texttt{CW'} & \texttt{CCW'} & \texttt{OPP'} & \texttt{VERT} \end{array} \quad,$$

and N/MARG-PH, which yields

$$\begin{array}{lllll} \texttt{CENTER} & \texttt{CW} & \texttt{CCW} & \texttt{OPP} & \texttt{PHASE} \\ \texttt{CENTER'} & \texttt{CW'} & \texttt{CCW'} & \texttt{OPP'} & \texttt{PHASE'} \end{array} \quad.$$

The N/MARG assignment leaves two inputs available for user supplied neighbors on the user connector—see Section 7.3.1. The other two flavors of this neighborhood fill out the ten inputs of a major assignment with pseudo-neighbors. In particular, PHASE and PHASE' correspond to two additional host-controlled phase signals, analogous to &PHASE and &PHASE' (which are offered by the minor assignment &/PHASES) but *distinct* from them; they are available only in the N/MARG-PH neighborhood. On the other hand, the HORZ and VERT pseudo-neighbors offered by the major assignment N/MARG-HV refer to the *same* internal signals as &HORZ and &VERT (which are offered by the minor assignment &/HV).[6] Note that in the neighborhood selected by the assignment

N/MARG-PH &/PHASES

the spatial phases HORZ and VERT do not appear at all as inputs to the look-up tables; this does not prevent CW, CCW, etc. from working properly, since these block-neighbors are synthesized by the hardware by tapping the spatial-phase information from the signals HORZ and VERT, whether or not these are routed to the look-up tables.

The *absolute* block-neighbors UL, UR, LL, and LR return the values of the four cells of a block according to their absolute position within a block (cf.

---

[6]Thus, there is no point in accompanying the major assignment N/MARG-HV by the minor assignment &/HV.

Section 12.4), no matter where the cell that requests them is located in the block. They are not directly provided by the CAM hardware; however, they can be defined in terms of the relative block-neighbors CENTER, CW, CCW and OPP *and* the two spatial phases. Since all this information is available to the look-up tables in the N/MARG-HV neighborhood, when this neighborhood is selected the software makes the neighbor words UL, UR, etc. available for use within a rule definition.

In conclusion, the following neighbor words are available in the three versions of the Margolus neighborhood

N/MARG		
CENTER	CENTER'	CENTERS
CW	CW'	CWS
CCW	CCW'	CCWS
OPP	OPP'	OPPS

N/MARG-PH		
CENTER	CENTER'	CENTERS
CW	CW'	CWS
CCW	CCW'	CCWS
OPP	OPP'	OPPS
PHASE	PHASE'	PHASES

N/MARG-HV					
CENTER	CENTER'	CENTERS	UL	UL'	ULS
CW	CW'	CWS	UR	UR'	URS
CCW	CCW'	CCWS	LL	LL'	LLS
OPP	OPP'	OPPS	LR	LR'	LRS
HORZ	VERT	HV			

12.6   Even/odd grid selection

In Section 11.3 we discussed how to synthesize a two-phase rule. The time-phase was toggled between 0 and 1 by the host computer according to an appropriate run schedule, and this value was made available to the rule in the form of a pseudo-neighbor, &PHASE.

In the Margolus neighborhood we have a similar situation; however, the value of the time-phase (say, 0 for a step using the even grid, and 1 for the odd grid) is not directly communicated to the rule; the rule is affected by it only indirectly, through the the block neighbors' "position smart" behavior, which is aware of which grid is in use.

As noted before, the block neighbors OPP, CW, etc. know their relative positions in a block by sensing the internal spatial-phase signals HORZ and VERT. The value of HORZ alternates *in space* between 0 and 1 as one moves horizontally through the array, and that of VERT, vertically. Which of the two grids is in use at a given step is determined simply by the joint value that this pair of signals takes at the origin of the array: a value of ⟨0, 0⟩ corresponds to the even grid, and ⟨1, 1⟩ to the odd grid. Thus, to switch between even and odd grids one must alternate *in time*—i.e., step after step—between 0 and 1 the values of <ORG-H> and <ORG-V>, as explained in Section 11.2; this is taken care of by the following run cycle

```
                         : ALT-GRID
         0 IS <ORG-HV>  STEP
         3 IS <ORG-HV>  STEP ;
```

12.7 A phase-sensitive gas

In the above examples the same recipe was used for both even and odd steps; however, if the same time-phase that is used for selecting one of the two grids is also explicitly made available to the tables as a pseudo-neighbor, then it becomes possible to "sense" this phase from within the rule and use different recipes for different values of the phase. Thus, the dynamics of a cellular automaton using the Margolus neighborhood can be "modulated" by the time-phase not only implicitly, through the even/odd grid alternation, but also explicitly through the rule itself. An appropriate run cycle for this would be the following

```
                           : ALT-GRID-PH
  0 IS <ORG-HV>  0 IS <PHASE>  STEP
  3 IS <ORG-HV>  1 IS <PHASE>  STEP ;
```

Here we shall describe an alternative particle transport mechanism in which particles move horizontally and vertically—rather than diagonally as in Section 12.2. Having both kinds of mechanisms available is sometimes convenient (see Chapter 15.6).

We shall use the N/MARG-PH neighborhood and the ALT-GRID-PH run cycle defined above. In analogy with Section 12.2, we shall construct first a mechanism for making particles travel at a uniform rate, without interactions. This time the particles will move along the rows and columns of the array. The block rule is the following

- ROT-CW/CCW   On an even step (PHASE=0), rotate *clockwise* the entire contents of the block; on an odd step (PHASE=1), rotate it *counterclockwise*.

In other words, use one of the following two tables depending on the value of PHASE:

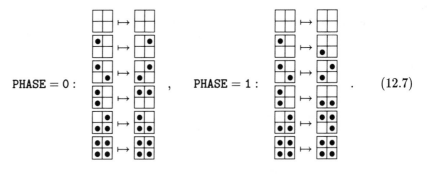

$$\text{PHASE} = 0: \qquad , \qquad \text{PHASE} = 1: \qquad . \qquad (12.7)$$

In CAM Forth, the rule is simply

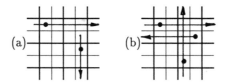

```
: ROT-CW/CCW
PHASE { CCW CW } >PLN0 ;
```

In fact, to rotate the whole block clockwise it is sufficient to ask each cell to make a copy of its CCW neighbor (cf. Section 5.1); to rotate it counterclockwise, a copy of the CW neighbor. The sense of rotation is selected by the value of PHASE.

Figure 12.4: ROT-CW/CCW: (a) Uniform motion of a particle. (b) Particles pass by one another without interacting.

Let's examine the behavior of this rule in detail.

- Look at an isolated particle. For the first step choose, say, the even grid, and consider a cell lying in the upper-left corner of its block (Figure 12.4a); by rotating the block a quarter-turn clockwise, the rule will make the particle move to the upper-right corner.

- At the next step use the odd grid; here the particle will find itself in the lower-left corner of a block, and the counterclockwise rotation of the block will move it to the lower-right corner.

- We have completed one cycle of two steps, and the particle has moved two positions to the right. At the next step, we will again be in the situation we began with.

- Continue like this, alternating the two grids. Each particle will move horizontally or vertically at a uniform rate; which of the four possible directions it will follow is determined by its initial position.

- As in the case of the SWAP-ON-DIAG rule, particles that meet head-on or at 90° continue on their courses without noticing one another; the rule moves anything it finds—particles or vacuum—without even looking at it!

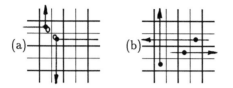

Figure 12.5: TM-GAS (a) Particles that collide within a block bounce at a 90° angle; the little loop is a reminder that they stay in the same place for one step. (b) Collisions do not occur for particles that fly past one another on adjacent blocks, or for particles that travel orthogonally.

To introduce momentum-conserving collisions, again only one modification is possible in our tables (12.7); namely, the third entry of both tables (where two particles traveling in opposite directions have just entered the same block and are about to pass by one another) can be changed so that instead of proceeding undisturbed the two particles will come out in opposite directions along the *other* axis of the array (i.e., if they were proceeding horizontally they will continue vertically after the collision, and vice versa). The new entry is

$$\boxed{\;\begin{smallmatrix}\bullet\;\\\;\bullet\end{smallmatrix}\;} \mapsto \boxed{\;\begin{smallmatrix}\bullet\;\\\;\bullet\end{smallmatrix}\;} \;,\qquad\qquad (12.8)$$

that is, when two particles collide the corresponding block is not rotated at all. In CAM Forth the rule is

```
              : TM-GAS
    COLLISION IF
      CENTER ELSE
PHASE { CCW CW } THEN >PLNO ;
```

where we have modified the ROT-CW/CCW rule by inserting an IF-clause that takes care of the "collision" entry; the COLLISION condition is the same as for HPP-GAS (Section 12.3), but the outcome of a collision is different. The behavior of this rule is illustrated in Figure 12.5.

Note that in TM-GAS two particles that pass each other on adjacent rows or columns do not necessarily collide—if the wrong grid is in effect at the moment of closest approach, the particles will be in separate blocks and will not see each other at all.

12.8   Examples

In this section we shall give a few examples of interesting rules that can be obtained using the Margolus-neighborhood scheme. The major examples (including the cellular automaton model of computation for which this technique was originally invented) are given in Part III—devoted to physical modeling.

12.8.1   Fractals

A rule which generates some simple fractals (cf. [34]) is the following

```
                                  : FORGET-ME-NOT
        CW CCW OPP XOR XOR >PLN0
                   CENTER >PLN1 ;
```

(here and in the following Margolus-neighborhood rules, we imply use of a run cycle that will provide the required grid alternation). Plate 10 illustrates the behavior of this rule starting from a small square of 1's in the center of the screen (the ECHO in plane 1 is just to add some color).

Curiously enough, there is a second-order rule which exhibits similar behavior while using the *Moore* neighborhood, namely

```
N/MOORE
                                  : ME-NEITHER
        N.EAST N.WEST S.EAST S.WEST
                   XOR XOR XOR
                CENTER' XOR >PLN0
                   CENTER >PLN1 ;
```

Indeed, there are some formal connections between reversible rules obtained by means of the Margolus neighborhood techniques and those obtained using the second-order technique (cf. Sections 14.2, 14.3, and 17.7).

If you rotate the last *rule* by 45° as follows

```
                                  : NOR-ME
        NORTH SOUTH WEST EAST
                   XOR XOR XOR
                CENTER' XOR >PLN0
                   CENTER >PLN1 ;
```

you'll again get essentially the same behavior, provided that the initial *configuration* is also rotated by 45° (i.e., start with a diamond rather than a square).

12.8.2   Critters

The FORGET-ME-NOT rule of the previous section is reversible, and can be made to run backwards by simply having it use the same grid twice in succession and then resuming the alternation (as explained in more detail in

Section 14.5). This works because in this rule the transformation applied to a single block coincides with its inverse. Most of the reversible block-rules we shall deal with in this book, including that used by the **HPP-GAS** rule of Section 12.3, have this property; here, however, we'd like to present a rather interesting reversible rule which does not. The rule is the following

```
                          : -CENTER
               CENTER 1 XOR ;

                          : -OPP
               OPP 1 XOR ;
                          : CRITTERS
       CENTER OPP CW CCW + + +
   { -CENTER -CENTER CENTER
              -OPP -CENTER } >PLNO ;
```

That is, a block is complemented unless it contains exactly two $\boxed{1}$'s, in which case it is left unchanged. A block containing three $\boxed{1}$'s is rotated through 180° in addition to being complemented. The inverse rule is

```
                     : CRITTERS*
     CENTER OPP CW CCW + + +
     { -CENTER -OPP CENTER
           -CENTER -CENTER } >PLNO ;
```

Since **CRITTERS** rotates and complements a block with *three* $\boxed{1}$'s in it, the inverse rule must rotate through −180° and complement a block with *one* $\boxed{1}$ in it.

Since the block transformation performed by **CRITTERS** is not its own inverse, to make the system go backwards in time it is not sufficient to retrace backwards the sequence of grid alternations: one must also use the inverse transformation, namely **CRITTERS***. However, we can use **CRITTERS** itself and still see the system proceed on a backwards trajectory—provided we wear "complementing glasses." In fact, this rule is time-reversal invariant (cf. Section 14.1) under the operation of *complementation*: each state of the "inverse" run obtained by complementing the final state and then using **CRITTERS** is just the complement of the corresponding state in the true inverse run, obtained by leaving the final state as is and using **CRITTERS***.

CRITTERS produces a variety of structure and a liveliness reminiscent of **LIFE** (Fig. 12.6a and Plate 11). Since it is invertible, it cannot produce structure from randomness (this is, in simple words, the second law of thermodynamics); however, if we start from a very nonuniform initial state (such as a blob of randomness on a background of $\boxed{0}$'s) we'll see a rich evolution. Small "critters" race horizontally and vertically; when they collide they may bounce back or execute a right-angle turn; occasionally they stick together—at least until freed by being hit again—or even pile up to form complicated little pieces of circuitry.

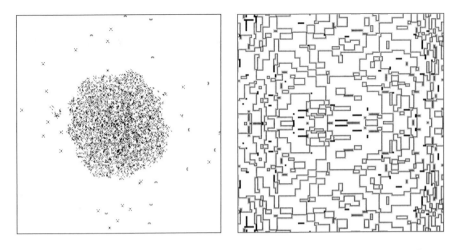

Figure 12.6: (a) "Critters" swarm out of an amorphous lump of matter. (b) A TRON choreography.

Since areas of all 0's or 1's are complemented at every step, the screen will display an annoying flicker; to eliminate it, you may want to use a run cycle which brings in a different color map at even and at odd steps

```
                                        : EVEN-MAP
         0 >RED              0 >GREEN
     ALPHA >BLUE         ALPHA >INTEN ;
                                        : ODD-MAP
         0 >RED              0 >GREEN
     ALPHA NOT >BLUE   ALPHA NOT >INTEN ;
                                        : CRITTER-CYCLE
   MAKE-CMAP EVEN-MAP  0 IS <ORG-HV>  STEP
   MAKE-CMAP  ODD-MAP  3 IS <ORG-HV>  STEP ;
```

MAKE-CYCLE CRITTER-CYCLE

Observe that the color map is a small table of data (only 16 items), and thus can be changed between steps without slowing down the simulation.

12.8.3   Asynchronous computation

A rule with a rather pretty evolution is

```
                        : TRON
    CENTER CW CCW OPP + + +
       { 1 U U U 0 } >PLN0 ;
```

(where U is an abbreviation for CENTER, as before). This rule complements the state of a block if all four elements are the same; otherwise it leaves things unchanged. A rich choreography of line patterns will arise from simple straight-edge shapes on a background of $\boxed{0}$'s (Figure 12.6b).

This rule also happens to provide bit patterns that can be used as "phases" for driving the evolution of an asynchronous cellular automaton, in analogy with Section 9.6—but with a simpler scheme permitted by the Margolus-neighbor discipline (also cf. [37]). Briefly, suppose we run *any* rule that uses the Margolus neighborhood (for example, FORGET-ME-NOT) on plane 0, and the TRON rule on plane 1 (changing CENTER to CENTER', etc., of course). CAM-B will provide a Poisson clock suitable for the Margolus neighborhood, as explained in Section 15.7; that is, the *same* bit of randomness is supplied to all four cells of a block.

```
N/MARG-PH &/CENTERS
                                    : ASYNC-CYCLE
      0 IS <ORG-HV> 0 IS <PHASE> STEP      \ alternate both grid
      3 IS <ORG-HV> 1 IS <PHASE> STEP ;    \   and phase
                                    : RAND
                         &CENTER' ;        \ asynchronous clock
                                    : GO?
          PHASE CENTER' = PHASE  CW' =
          PHASE    CCW' = PHASE OPP' =
                    AND AND AND       \ Can I update?
                    RAND 0<> AND ;    \ Must I try?
                                    : ASYNC
                    GO? IF            \ If I do it,
              FORGET-ME-NOT           \   here's the new data
         CENTER' NOT >PLN1 ELSE       \   and the new status
            CENTERS >PLNA THEN ;      \ else nothing changes
```

The random stimulus will be a signal to try to update a block (rather than a single cell as in Section 9.6). Even blocks are only allowed to run the rule if all four synchronization bits on plane 1 are $\boxed{0}$'s; odd blocks, only if they are all $\boxed{1}$'s. The information about which grid is in use is carried by PHASE. If a block is *prodded* to update by the asynchronous clock and *permitted* to update by the synchronization pattern in plane 1, then we run the rule on that block *and* complement the block on plane 1 (this is our way to tell the synchronization mechanism that we are done with the update step for that block); otherwise we leave the block (both planes 0 and 1) unchanged. Note that if we run this rule deterministically (i.e., if RAND always returns a $\boxed{1}$) then the evolution of the phase bits in plane 1 is simply that prescribed by TRON.

Let's start off with plane 1 filled with $\boxed{0}$'s: all nodes of the asynchronous network start in-phase, for simplicity. The computation in plane 0 will proceed with hills and valleys of time—places that have been updated more often than their neighbors, or less often—but with a limited slope and no breaks. This activity couldn't be recognized as the computation we had in mind (namely FORGET-ME-NOT) if the pattern on plane 1 didn't keep track of

who's ahead of whom; in other words, the bit-pattern in plane 1 is a contour
map of those time hills and valleys.

If at some point we change the definition of RAND to be a constant of 1
(for example, by changing the rule on CAM-B to the identity rule and filling
plane 2 with 1's), then the hills and valleys will flatten out, and you'll see
that indeed the synchronization is correct: we will get a pattern on CAM-A
where all cells have been updated exactly as if FORGET-ME-NOT had been
running synchronously all along.

12.8.4 Digital logic

Here we give a simple rule that allows conventional digital logic to be simulated in a straightforward manner. Of course, any rule that can simulate
general digital logic elements can simulate digital computers. A proof that a
rule such as LIFE can simulate such logic is something of a *tour de force*—a
bit like showing that one can make a computer out of the collisions of billiard
balls! A more humble approach is to design a rule expressly to be able to do
logic—then the proof is rather simple.

Our rule will work as follows. On plane 1 we'll draw lines one-cell thick
that go from place to place; these will be our wires. On plane 0 we'll put
particles that follow these wires and interact at certain junctions; these will
be our signals.

```
NEW-EXPERIMENT  N/MARG
                              : ALT-GRID
              EVEN-GRID STEP       \ alternating-grid rule
              ODD-GRID STEP ;
                              : #WIRES ( -- 0..4)
    CENTER' CW' CCW' OPP' + + + ;   \ no. of wires in block
                              : SIGNALS
          OPP' IF OPP THEN         \ signals follow wires
          CW'  IF CW  THEN
          CCW' IF CCW THEN ;
                              : CONTROLS
      OPP' 0= IF OPP THEN         \ AND? OR? for 3WIRE
      CW'  0= IF CW  THEN
      CCW' 0= IF CCW THEN ;
                              : 1WIRE ( -- 0|1 )
          OPP CW CCW OR OR ;       \ source of ones nearby?
                              : 2WIRE ( -- 0|1 )
      SIGNALS  CW' CCW' OR IF      \ check for NOT  (SIGNALS
              OPP XOR THEN ;       \   gives one output here)
                              : 3WIRE
              CONTROLS IF
          SIGNALS AND ELSE         \ SIGNALS produces 2 values
          SIGNALS  OR THEN ;       \   when there are 3 wires.
```

```
                                : LOGIC
                    CENTER' IF
                      #WIRES
        { O 1WIRE 2WIRE 3WIRE OPP }
                            ELSE
                CENTER THEN   >PLNO
                    CENTER'   >PLN1 ;
```

```
MAKE-TABLE LOGIC
MAKE-CYCLE ALT-GRID
```

With this rule, signals follow wires; which way they go depends on which grid you start with. In a block that contains two pieces of wire with a signal on one of them, the signal moves onto the other piece of wire (Figure 12.7a). Thus signals can move horizontally, vertically, or diagonally—they just follow the wires.

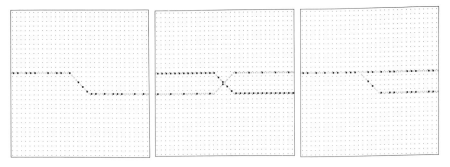

Figure 12.7: Signal propagation, cross-over, and fanout.

If you want to make two signals cross (Figure 12.7b), just cross their wires: the signals will pass through without looking at one another (make sure to cross the wires in the middle of a block, so that the block contains four pieces of wire).

If you need fanout (Figure 12.7c) just split the wire: a copy of a signal will follow both pieces (make sure to split the wire in the middle of a block, so that the block contains three pieces of wire).

To perform logic, a signal sitting *next* to a straight segment of wire (but not *on* it) will be frozen in place, and will cause signals going by in the wire to be complemented (Figure 12.8a). Such a signal sitting next to a fork in a wire (Figure. 12.8b) will turn this fork into an AND gate—each of the three branches will always be the AND of the other two inputs.

Finally, to illustrate the circuit compactness that is possible with this rule, we show in Figure 12.8c a binary half-adder.

A rule such as this could be used as the basis of a VLSI chip that implements *soft circuitry*. You need only download the initial pattern of wires

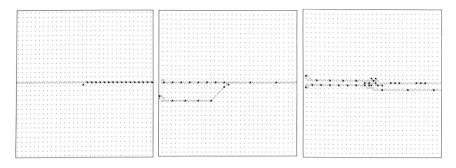

Figure 12.8: NOT (a) and AND (b) gates. (c) A complete half-adder.

and gates to a parallel implementation of this rule contained in such a chip—transducers on the chip could continually transform a few inputs and outputs between their cell-value format within the chip, and voltage levels on the pins. An unclocked, asynchronous implementation using the technique of the previous section might be made to run quite fast.[7]

---

[7] Brian Silverman and Warren Robinett have both invented cellular automata rules that might be suitable for soft circuitry. Roger Banks' rules, one of which was discussed in Section 5.5, might also be suitable.

Part III

Physical modeling

Chapter 13

Symptoms vs causes

> Entia non sunt multiplicanda praeter necessi-
> tatem.
>
> [Occam's "razor"]

The part which we are entering now, devoted to *physical modeling*, is conceptually the central one of this book. In spite of their wide interdisciplinary appeal, cellular automata would have remained at the level of a parlor game if they had not been shown to be capable of playing a serious role in the modeling of physics—a role analogous and to a certain extent complementary to that of differential equations.

Much of the recent progress in this direction comes from the interplay of two factors. On the technological side, there are computers available now that can carry out the directives of a cellular-automaton model in a reasonably efficient way. On the conceptual side, we are learning how to construct discrete, distributed models which capture essential aspects of physical causality—such as microscopic reversibility.

13.1 Fine-grained models of physics

Science is concerned with explaining things. Many of the systems that we are interested in do not come with descriptive manuals and schematics, and cannot easily be inspected or taken apart without disturbing their behavior. We say we "understand" a complex system when we can build, out of simple components that we already understand well, a model that behaves in a similar way.

If the assortment of components at our disposal is too lavish, it is often too easy to arrive at models that display the expected phenomenology just because the outward symptoms themselves, rather than some deeper internal reasons, have been directly programmed in, as the special effects in an arcade game.

Science has little use for models that slavishly obey all of our wishes. We want models that talk back to us, models that have a mind of their own. We want to get out of our models more than we have put in. A reasonable way to start is to put in *as little as possible.*

The simpler the primitives used to describe a complex system, the greater is the computational burden required for obtaining explicit, detailed predictions from a model.[1] For this reason, the development of mathematics in a certain period of time reflects to a much greater extent than many would suspect the nature of the computational resources available at that time. In the past three centuries, enormous emphasis has been given to (1) models that are defined and well-behaved in a *continuum*, (2) models that are *linear*, and (3) models entailing a small number of *lumped* variables. This emphasis does not reflect a preference of nature, but rather the fact that the human brain, aided only by pencil and paper, performs best when it handles a small number of symbolic tokens having substantial conceptual depth (e.g., real numbers, differential operators); in this context, one tends to concentrate effort on problems that are likely to yield a symbolic, closed-form solution.

The advent of digital computers has shifted the region of optimum performance. While much progress can still be made in the above more traditional areas, the horizon has dramatically expanded in the complementary areas, namely (1') *discrete* models, (2') *nonlinear* models, and (3') models entailing a large number of *distributed* variables. Such models give more emphasis to the handling of a large number of tokens of a simple nature (e.g., Boolean variables and logic functions)—a task at which computers are particularly efficient.

Cellular automata attempt to explore the logical limit of this approach. They reduce the number of primitive ingredients that can go into a model to *one*—namely a "unit cell" governed by a simple rule and coupled to identical cells by a uniform interconnection pattern. The challenge is to choose the rule and the pattern so that everything we want from the model, over a wide range of scales, will follow from this one choice.

Whether this approach will work depends, of course, on what it is that we are trying to model. Physicists have for centuries used the working hypothesis that "the world is basically simple—only there is so much of it!" If this is true,

---

[1]For example, chemistry is in principle reducible to quantum mechanics, but only the structures of the simplest atoms have been computed in full detail on that basis; for more complex substances, one must make recourse to approximations, empirical shortcuts, or higher-level phenomenological theories.

cellular automata and cellular automata machines may represent a useful tool in trying to understand and describe nature.

Chapter 14

Reversibility

> Now, if we run our picture of the universe
> backward several billion years, we get a object
> resembling Donald Duck. There is obviously
> a fallacy here somewhere.
>
> [S. Harrison]

As far as we know, reversibility is a universal characteristic of physical law. In particular, it is a precondition for the second law of thermodynamics to hold,[1] and is a sufficient condition for the existence of conserved quantities.[2]

In cellular automata, certain basic features of the physical laws—such as *uniformity* and *locality*—are directly built-in; on the other hand, *reversibility* does not come automatically: it has to be programmed in. Until quite recently no one knew how to do that in a systematic way, and it was even suspected that one could introduce reversibility only at the cost of losing other properties (such as computation- and construction-universality) that are essential for general-purpose modeling.

It turns out that it is possible to construct nontrivial cellular automata that display *exact* reversibility (in this respect, they suffer from none of the approximations that are so common in conventional numerical simulations).

---

[1] For locally-interacting systems having a finite amount of information per site, such as cellular automata, reversibility is *equivalent* to the second law of thermodynamics.

[2] In physics, a reversible system having n degrees of freedom possesses $2n - 1$ conserved quantities, some of which (e.g., energy, momentum, etc.) are of special significance because of their connection with fundamental symmetries of the physical laws[33]. The arguments that lead to these conservation laws can be generalized to cellular automata: the key idea is that a given state "encodes" all of the information necessary to identify the particular dynamical trajectory it lies on, and, if the system is reversible, none of this information is lost in the course of its evolution.

Thus, one can arrive at models that, though perhaps drastically stylized in other respects, make no compromises in the representation of this fundamental aspect of a physical process.

14.1   Invertible cellular automata

A cellular automaton is a *deterministic* system, i.e., for every possible state of the whole cellular automaton the rule specifies one and only one successor. Can we run a cellular automaton "in reverse?" That is, given a rule, can we construct a new rule that will force the system to retrace its steps backwards in time? It is clear that this is possible in general only if the system defined by the original rule is also *backward-deterministic*, i.e., if for every possible configuration of the cellular automaton there exists one and only one predecessor.

A system that is deterministic in both directions of time is called *invertible*, and the rule that makes it go backward in time is called the *inverse* rule—with respect to the original, or *direct* rule. (The term 'invertible', preferred by mathematicians, is equivalent to the term 'microscopically reversible' or, simply, 'reversible', as used by physicists in the present context.)

Note that, except for trivial cases, the inverse rule—when it exists—is *different* from the direct one. For example, after watching for a while a picture being dragged upwards by the `SHIFT-NORTH` rule of Section 5.1, we can view the whole process in reverse by switching to the inverse rule

```
          : SHIFT-SOUTH
     NORTH >PLNO ;
```

which is clearly different from `SHIFT-NORTH`.

However, in special cases it is possible to achieve materially the same "time-reversal" effect by running the *same* rule as in the forward time direction, but using as an initial state for the backward run one that is obtained from the final state of the forward run by a prescribed simple transformation—a "transliteration" procedure.

A dynamical law having this property is said to be *time reversal invariant under the specified state transformation*, or simply *time reversal invariant* when the operator is understood.[3] Thus, "time-reversal invariance" is a stronger property than just "reversibility."

The theory of invertible cellular automata has many open problems[58]; in particular, no general decision procedure is known for determining whether a given rule has an inverse (and this question may well be undecidable). However, given two rules it is always possible, in principle, to decide whether

---

[3]In Newtonian mechanics, for example, the time-reversal procedure consists of reversing the momenta of all particles.

they are the inverses of one another. With the techniques presented below for constructing invertible cellular automata, the direct rule always comes accompanied by its inverse, so that there is never any doubt concerning its invertibility—either in principle or in practice.

14.2   Second-order technique

The first general method we shall consider for arriving at cellular automata that are invertible involves constructing second-order systems that are time-reversal invariant. An example of this technique was given in Section 6.2, of which the present discussion is a natural continuation.

To paraphrase Zeno, if we cut a single frame out of the movie of a flying bullet, we have no way of knowing what the bullet is doing. However, if we are given two consecutive frames, then we can figure out the bullet's trajectory. That is, from these two frames, interpreted as the bullet's "past" and "present" positions, we can construct a third frame giving the bullet's "future" position; this procedure can be iterated. The laws of Newtonian mechanics are such that, if for some reason the two frames got exchanged, we would end up figuring the bullet's trajectory *in reverse*.

The following general approach for constructing cellular automata that work in an analogous way was suggested by Ed Fredkin of MIT.

Let us start with a dynamical system in which the sequence of configurations the system goes through is given by iterating a relation of the form

$$c^{t+1} = \tau c^t, \tag{14.1}$$

where for the moment one can think of the configurations c's as, say, real numbers. τ is the *dynamical law* of the system, i.e., the function that takes the current configuration c^t as an argument and returns the next configuration, c^{t+1}. In general, (14.1) gives rise to a noninvertible dynamics.

Now, let's consider a new system, defined by the relation

$$c^{t+1} = \tau c^t - c^{t-1}. \tag{14.2}$$

This is an example of *second-order* system—where the "next" configuration c^{t+1} is a function of both the "current" configuration c^t and the "past" one, c^{t-1} (thus, it takes a *pair* of consecutive configurations to completely determine the forward trajectory). In general, second-order relations also give rise to noninvertible dynamics. However, a second-order relation of the specific form (14.2) guarantees the invertibility of the dynamics for an *arbitrary* τ. In fact, by solving (14.2) with respect to c^{t-1}, one obtains the relation

$$c^{t-1} = \tau c^t - c^{t+1}; \tag{14.3}$$

that is, a pair of consecutive configurations suffice to determine in a unique way also the *backward* trajectory.

Note that in this case a single configuration isn't enough to allow one to continue the trajectory. A complete specification of the system's dynamical *state* is now represented by an *ordered pair* of configurations, of the form $\langle a, b \rangle$ (in (14.1), a configuration by itself was a *state* of the system).[4]

The fact that for a system defined by (14.2) a reverse trajectory exists and is unique means that the system is *invertible*; the fact that its inverse behavior can be calculated by applying the direct dynamics to suitably defined time-reversed states means that the system is invariant under such a time-reversal operation. Here, time-reversal is defined as the operation that swaps the two configurations that make up a state; i.e., $\langle c_\beta, c_\alpha \rangle$ is changed by time-reversal into $\langle c_\alpha, c_\beta \rangle$.

The above considerations can immediately be extended to cellular automata. In equation (14.1), let the c's be configurations of a cellular automaton, and τ an arbitrary cellular-automaton rule. If our cells have n states $(0, 1, \ldots, n-1)$ the '$-$' in (14.2) can be taken mod n, and the second-order rule becomes

- For each cell, apply the original rule τ to the cell's "present" neighborhood.

- Before releasing this result as the cell's "future" state, subtract the cell's "past" state.[5]

Second-order reversible rules can be constructed using operations other than subtraction in an equation like (14.2). You can even let the decision of which operation to use depend on the neighbors at time t. In the most general second-order reversible rule, the neighborhood at time t is used to select a permutation on the state set $\{0, 1, \ldots, n-1\}$. The cell applies this permutation to its previous state to construct its next state[62].

In the examples of Chapter 6, the two consecutive frames that jointly specify the system's state are stored in bit-planes 0 ("present") and 1 ("past"). At each step, we construct the "future" configuration from planes 0 and 1 and put it in plane 0, while the current contents of plane 0 is moved to plane 1. In this way, planes 0 and 1 always contain the two most recent frames.

In CAM one can easily deal with four-state cells by storing the present in CAM-A (planes 0 and 1) and the past in CAM-B (planes 2 and 3). The coupling between present and past is made possible by the neighborhood assignments

---

[4]One can have a system whose state is a pair of configurations and is *not* second-order. The fact that the dynamics is a *second-order* one is expressed by the constraint that a state $\langle a, b \rangle$ can be followed by another state $\langle c, d \rangle$ only if $b = c$.

[5]In the examples of Sections 6.2–6.3, the cells had just two states, and 'n mod 2' could be written as XOR.

```
CAM-A &/CENTERS
CAM-B &/CENTERS
```

whereby CAM-A can see the past in CAM-B and use it for computing the future, while CAM-B can see the present in CAM-A and save it for one more step as the past.

14.3   Alternating sublattices

Let us denote by $c_{i,j}^t$ the state at time t of the cell located at coordinates i, j. A special situation arises when only the four neighbors *north*, *south*, *west*, and *east* enter as arguments of τ, so that equation (14.2) becomes

$$c_{i,j}^{t+1} = \tau(c_{i,j-1}^t, c_{i,j+1}^t, c_{i-1,j}^t, c_{i+1,j}^t) - c_{i,j}^{t-1}.$$

This relation connects only spacetime sites for which $i + j + t$ has the same parity, i.e., sites that all belong to the same sublattice (black or white) of a spacetime checkerboard. Thus, the system consists of two *independent* subsystems—one running on the black sublattice and one on the white—having identical dynamical properties.

In this situation it is reasonable, for clarity and efficiency, to try to simulate only one of the two subsystems. But then the past state of a cell can be stored in the *other* sublattice, rather than in a second bit-plane. At one step the even sites (i.e., where $i + j$ is even) represent the *present* and the odd sites the *past*. During the step itself, the past is modified by τ and turned into the *future*. At the next step the roles are reversed.

Note that at each step we *look* at only one sublattice, and use this information to *change* the state only of the other. When we want go back in time, the arrangement is such that the same information that was used to make a change is now available to "undo" the change. (To be reversible, the change must of course be a *permutation* of the cell state.)

Thus, alternating sublattices can be seen as a specialization of the second-order technique for achieving reversibility. This approach (which has a long tradition in numerical analysis) will be used for the Ising spin models of Chapter 17.

14.4   Guarded-context technique

In the alternating sublattice approach, the spatial *position* of a cell is used to determine whether the cell can be updated at a given step without risk of *information loss* (that is, indeed, what invertibility is about). It is possible to devise rules where information sufficient for this purpose is encoded in the *state* of the cells; that is, the *context* represented by the collective state of the neighbors is used to guard against irreversible changes. Only cells which find themselves in a distinguished position in a special neighborhood pattern may change their state.

This technique, which is discussed in [55,62] is cumbersome to use and is mentioned here only for completeness.

14.5   Partitioning technique

The invertibility of second-order systems such as those discussed in the previous section comes as a bit of a surprise. Note that in (14.2) the function τ could be chosen arbitrarily; if the c's are real numbers, τ might involve, say, squaring and rounding off—operations that "throw away" information. Yet the resulting dynamics is invertible, that is to say, *information-lossless*. One is left with the feeling that a feat of mathematical magic was performed.

We will now discuss a method for producing invertible rules in a much more deliberate and obvious way—i.e., *partitioning cellular automata*, some examples of which were considered in Chapters 10 and 12.

In a conventional cellular automaton, the machinery that in one step produces a new configuration from the current one can be thought of as an array of *logical gates*, one per cell, uniformly extending in space and time. As sketched in Figure 14.1a (where, for clarity, only one spatial dimension is represented), each gate has several inputs lines, corresponding to the cell's neighbors, but only one output line—at which the new state of the cell will appear. In general, the function computed by a gate of this kind cannot be an invertible one: since only a fraction of the information available at the inputs can appear at the output, some information will be *lost*.[6] It is true that some of each gate's input information is also seen by neighboring gates— and so there is a chance that what was lost here may have been preserved in some form elsewhere. However, it takes a very clever conspiracy to insure that no information is ever lost anywhere during the operation of the cellular automaton.

For the above reasons, almost any rule that one may write down yields a *noninvertible* cellular automaton (in fact, until a few years ago only a handful of invertible rules were known, and even these were utterly trivial[58]).

In partitioning cellular automata, on the other hand, owing to a special discipline for the information flow, there is an immediate connection between the invertibility of the overall dynamical system and the invertibility of the individual gates that make up the array. Thus, invertibility can be directly

---

[6]This loss of information cannot be ascribed to what the function does for a *specific* input assignment; rather, one has to consider all possible input assignments, and see whether the input-output correspondence is such that from the output one can always reconstruct the input.

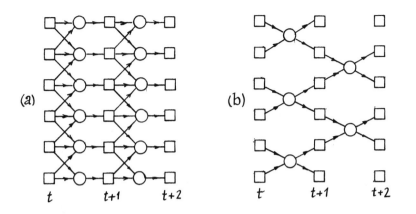

Figure 14.1: (a) In a conventional cellular automaton, a gate is associated with each *cell* and has many inputs but only one output. (b) In a partitioning cellular automaton, a gate is associated with each *block* and has as many outputs as inputs.

programmed in. This is illustrated using the Margolus neighborhood (cf. Chapter 12)—one of the simplest partitioning schemes.

In this neighborhood, the rule uses as inputs the four cells of a block and returns as outputs the new states of *all four cells* of the same block. Thus, the cellular-automaton's machinery can be represented as as uniform array of gates each having *as many outputs as inputs* (Figure 14.1b), where none of the inputs are shared with adjacent gates. In this situation, each gate oversees the information flow for a whole four-cell block, and has total control over it. If the individual gate is invertible, the global process is invertible as well; if the gate loses information, none of its neighbors will be able to make up for its losses, and the process is certainly noninvertible.

A rule for the Margolus neighborhood will be invertible if and only if it establishes a one-to-one correspondence between the old and the new state of an individual block. In other words, if in the first column of the look-up table that defines the rule we list all the possible states of a block, then in order for the rule to be invertible the second column must be a permutation of the first, as in the following example (note that each of the sixteen states of the left column appears somewhere in the right column):

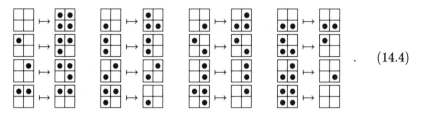

$$. \qquad (14.4)$$

It is easy to verify that the full table for the HPP-GAS rule (cf. Section 12.4—where the table is given in an abbreviated form since the rule is rotation-invariant) has this property, and thus HPP-GAS is an invertible cellular automaton.

In the applications discussed in later chapters we shall make heavy use of this block-updating technique. The stimulus for its development was provided by the study of reversible models of computation, and indeed its first application was a cellular-automaton realization of "billiard-ball" computers (cf. Chapter 18).

Having constructed an invertible rule with this partitioning technique and having run it for a number of steps, how do we go backward in time? Clearly, by performing the inverse steps in the reverse order. Suppose, for definiteness, that we were using the rule of table (14.4) and that the last step had been done on the odd grid. Then the first step of the reverse process will *again* use the odd grid (we want to "undo" what has just been done to each block), and will use the rule obtained from table (14.4) by reversing the direction of the arrows, i.e., by looking up the argument in the *second* column and finding the result in the *first*. This new table, in fact, defines a permutation that is the inverse of the original one. We will keep using the inverse rule throughout the backward run, alternating even and odd grids as before. With a rule such as HPP-GAS (cf. Section 12.3), which happens to be its own inverse, all one has to do to start going backwards is use the same grid twice in a row, and then resume the alternating pattern.

This discussion can easily be generalized to more dimensions, more states per cell, and more complex alternations of partitioning schemes and rules.[7] The key considerations can be summarized as follows.

A cellular automaton can be thought of as a distributed mechanism whose evolution is governed by a system of coupled equations; the number of equations equals that of cells. The problem of assigning these equations in such a way that the system is *globally* invertible is very hard in general (the difficulty is analogous to that encountered in studying the invertibility of large

---

[7]Cf. the TM-GAS rule of Section 12.7, where two different versions of the same basic recipe are used for even and odd steps.

matrices), but becomes easier if the interconnection pattern obeys a suitable discipline. Specifically, if during a given step the mechanism is effectively partitioned into a collection of small independent regions, then the step as a whole is invertible if and only if its action with respect to each individual region is invertible. The latter is a *local* property, and thus is easy to enforce.

Of course, if the partition were to remain the same at all steps, the individual regions would be permanently isolated from one another. However, by cycling through different partition schemes on successive steps, communication between regions is again made possible.

In this way, not only does one guarantee invertibility: one automatically obtains the inverse law as well. Namely,

- To undo a step, undo the transformation of each individual region.

- To undo the overall time-evolution, undo the individual steps, from the last to the first.

14.6 Reversibility and randomness

If we fill the cells of our screen with randomly-chosen binary values and then evolve it according to the LIFE rule, we see a complex web of structure and activity (Chapter 3) with various levels of organization. If instead of LIFE we follow some invertible time evolution, we invariably find that at each step the system looks just as random as when we started; in physical terms, the entropy will not decrease (but it may—and in general will—increase, unless it is already as large as possible).

This property of reversible systems can be derived by a simple counting argument: since *most* configurations look random, only a very few random configurations can be mapped in any given number of steps into the *few* simple-looking configurations—if the mapping is an invertible one. That is, there is no way to establish a one-to-one correspondence between a large set and a small set.

One shouldn't conclude that reversible cellular automata are less interesting than irreversible ones. It's just that, in these systems as in physics, nothing particularly interesting can occur if we start from a maximally disordered state.

Chapter 15

Diffusion and equilibrium

> When the atoms are traveling straight down
> through empty space by their own weight,
> at quite indeterminate times and places they
> swerve ever so little from their course.
>
> [Lucretius]

As a preliminary to discussing models of fluid mechanics and other physical
phenomena of a fundamentally statistical-mechanical nature, in this chapter
we shall present simple models of diffusion and equilibrium.

15.1 Noise-driven diffusion

In Section 10 we presented a simple model of the one-dimensional random
walk. The system consisted of a single particle, which at every step would
move right or left depending on the outcome of a coin toss. The model
couldn't deal with more than one particle: two particles might have tried to
occupy the same spot.

We also discussed a physically more realistic model. At every step the
system was partitioned into two-cell blocks, and the contents of each block
was shuffled at random. In this simple case, the shuffle could have only one
of two outcomes, that is, (1) leave the two cells of the block as they are or
(2) swap their contents. The partition was changed at every step, so that
information could travel from place to place.

The tools we had to synthesize in order to enforce the partitioning discipline are useful in a much more general context, and for this reason they
are provided in CAM as primitive resources—in the Margolus neighborhood.

Here we shall tackle first the analogous problem of diffusion in *two dimensions*, making direct use of these resources.

Two-dimensional shuffle. In a Margolus-neighborhood block, the cell to be updated, called *center*, is automatically associated with its block neighbors, called, relative to the cell itself, *clockwise*, *opposite*, and *counter-clockwise*. The contents of such a block can be shuffled in 4! different ways; for our purposes, a choice of two distinct shuffles will be sufficient, namely (1) *rotate* the block's contents one-quarter turn *clockwise* or (2) rotate it *counterclockwise*. As a reminder, the rule that would rotate all blocks of plane 0 clockwise is simply

```
                 : CLOCKWISE
          CCW >PLN0 ;
```

(cf. Section 12.7).

In the present diffusion model, the decision to rotate a block in one or the other direction will depend on the outcome of a coin toss, represented by a "noisy neighbor" RAND, and the diffusion rule will be the following:

```
                 : 2D-BROWNIAN
          RAND { CCW CW } >PLN0 ;
```

Of course, the run cycle ALT-GRID of Section 12.6 will be in force, in order to alternate between the two grids on successive steps.

A coin toss for each block. In CAM, the above rule is applied individually to each cell of the array, and in particular to the four cells of each block; the value returned by RAND may change from block to block and from step to step, but at each step must be the *same* for the four cells of a block. Therefore, the random-number generator in plane 1 must be told to let all four cells see the same result.

In analogy with Section 10.2, the stirrer in plane 1 will be

```
                 : MARG-STIR
          CENTER' CW' OPP' CCW'
            AND XOR XOR >PLN1 ;
```

This provides a random bit for each cell, and thus four bits for each block.[1] These four bits are combined in a symmetrical way into a single random bit by

```
                 : RAND ( -- 0|1)
          CENTER' CW' OPP' CCW'
                XOR XOR XOR ;
```

so that the result will be the same when seen from any cell of the same block (cf. table (12.6)). As usual, plane 1 will be filled with a random seed.

---

[1]As mentioned in Section 8.4, higher-quality randomness can be obtained from a hardware random-number generator, or from another CAM module.

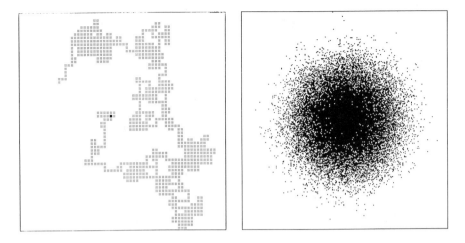

Figure 15.1: (a) Tangled path of a particle in a two-dimensional random walk (magnified view). (b) Gradual diffusion of a dense cluster of particles.

We are ready to run. A single particle placed in plane 0 will move about in a jerky fashion, describing a tangled, unpredictable path (as in Figure 15.1a, where plane 2 was used to record a trace of the particle). A dense cluster of particles placed in the middle of the screen will slowly diffuse in all directions, as in Figure 15.1b; compare this result with that of Figure 9.3a, which was obtained with a more naive approach. There are two remarkable things about this behavior:

- Over a region, say, twenty cells across, the distribution of particles is quite uniform; from a certain distance, where the individual particles can no longer be clearly distinguished, the effect is that of a half-tone picture: different concentrations of particles appear as different shades of gray. This becomes even more apparent in the brief time-exposure of 15.2a (the blurring of time-averaging being in this case equivalent to that of space-averaging.) It makes sense to associate with each point **r** of the picture the *density* $\rho(\mathbf{r})$ of the surrounding area; as the scale of observation is made coarser, this density becomes a continuous function of **r**: *real numbers* emerge out of *bits*.

If we study ρ as a function of *time*, in the same macroscopic limit we'll see that $\rho(\mathbf{r}, t)$ becomes a continuous function of t as well as of **r**. At this point, one may wonder whether the evolution of $\rho(\mathbf{r}, t)$ can be described by a differential equation. Indeed, by choosing a sufficiently coarse scale, ρ will be found to obey as closely as desired the so-called *heat* equation

$$\frac{\partial \rho}{\partial t} = \nabla^2 \rho.$$

The sequence of time-exposures in Figure 15.2 attempts to convey some of the flavor of this continuous behavior.

• At each step a particle can go up, down, right, or left with probability 1/4 for each of the four directions;[2] intermediate directions are not allowed. Thus, on a microscopic level the rule is certainly not *isotropic*: if one could see only the particle one would nonetheless be able to infer the orientation of the lattice's axes. However, on a macroscopic level all directions are equally likely, and the diffusion pattern is exactly circular. This is in striking contrast with the cellular-automaton rules we've presented so far—in which the orientation of the lattice leaves its signature on the evolution no matter how coarse a scale one uses.

One might object that the "footprint" of this rule's light-cone is a *diamond*—like that of Figure 5.1b: after a time t the probability for the particle to be in any given place within this diamond will be different from zero, while it will be exactly zero outside the diamond. As t increases the diamond will grow proportionally in size, always maintaining the same *shape*; won't this shape be recognizable by the macroscopic observer? It turns out that, as $t \to \infty$, the probability that a particle will be found at a distance much larger that $\sqrt{t}$ from its original position becomes negligible: the probability distribution spreads *much more slowly* that the light cone, and the overwhelming bulk of it remains circularly symmetric (cf. Figure 15.6)—even though the remotest, vanishingly thin edges of it do reach out to the diamond's perimeter.

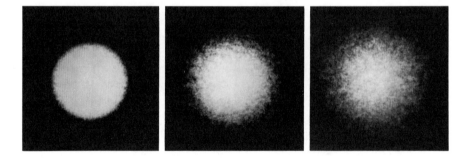

Figure 15.2: Gradual evolution in time of the particle density ρ.

In conclusion, in this system a symmetry emerges, on a macroscopic scale, that was not present at the microscopic level: not only the *pitch*, but also the *orientation* of the lattice is forgotten. The first of these features is common to practically all lattice models (and thus is in no way remarkable) while the

---

[2]For the sake of the present argument, one can ignore the fine-grained correlations that arise from the partitioning into blocks.

second seems to be very rare, and is particularly desirable in the context of physical modeling—since on any known scale physics is isotropic.

15.2 Expansion and thermalization

In the previous example, the random-number generator could be thought of as a source of *thermal agitation*. In this interpretation, one step of the cellular-automaton model corresponds to a physical time-interval long enough for real molecules to go through innumerable collisions on a finer scale than that represented in the model, so that the direction of a molecule at the end of the interval is totally unrelated to that at the beginning: the molecule has had enough time to "forget," as it were, where it was going. In this idealization the path of an ink particle is completely determined by the noise.

We shall now consider the opposite idealization: namely (a) no external noise is present, (b) particles travel in a vacuum, and thus (c) any deviations from a rectilinear path are due solely to the effect of collisions with other particles.

A rule appropriate for this situation is TM-GAS, which was presented in Section 12.7. Here particles travel horizontally or vertically; two particles traveling in opposite directions on two adjacent rows or columns may undergo a glancing collision, in which case both particles make a right-angle turn, leaving in opposite directions. (Most of the considerations of this section apply as well to the HPP-GAS rule of Section 12.3, where, however, particles travel in diagonal directions.) Uniform motion was achieved by making the contents of a Margolus-neighborhood block rotate clockwise or counter-clockwise on alternating steps—in an invariable, predetermined sequence rather than at the whim of a noise generator (cf. end of Section 10.2 for analogous behavior in one dimension). Collisions were achieved by replacing a rotation step by a "no change" step whenever two particles occupied opposite corners of a block. We recall the rule here

```
                  : TM-GAS
         COLLISION IF
         CENTER ELSE
  PHASE { CCW CW } THEN
             >PLNO ;
```

For our first experiment we shall put this gas in a "bottle." The outlines of this container (Figure 15.3a) will be drawn on bit-plane 1. Collisions between particles and the container's wall will be taken care of by modifying the rule as follows. If any portion of the wall falls inside a given block, then no rotation of the block's contents is performed at that step—just as in the case of particle-to-particle collision. The reader may verify that with this provision particles do indeed bounce off a wall.[3] The rule is the following

```
                          : WALL ( -- 0|1)
        CENTER' CW' OPP' CCW'
                OR OR OR ;
                          : TM-GAS/WALLS
        COLLISION WALL OR IF
                CENTER ELSE
        PHASE { CCW CW } THEN
                >PLN0
            CENTER' >PLN1 ;    \ walls don't move
```

Here too we'll start with a dense cloud of particles in the middle; the rest of the container will be empty ((a) in Figure 15.3). This time the cloud will expand very rapidly. The leading particles travel in a vacuum, all at the same speed, and thus proceed on straight lines all the way to the walls (b). As they bounce off the walls they start disrupting the paths of the particles that come after them (c); this disruption rapidly extends in scope (d), and after a while the original cloud will have diffused through all the available space (e). Eventually the container will be filled with rarefied gas in a state of thermodynamic equilibrium (f).

Observe that the initial expansion pattern is strongly *anisotropic*. This should not come as a surprise: in a vacuum, the peculiar kinematic constraints of this lattice gas (only one speed and four directions) are directly reflected in the shape of the expansion pattern. The situation is different if we dump in a second scoop of gas: the new particles start colliding with the old ones before reaching the container's walls, and their paths get randomized sooner.

Let us dump in more and more gas until a good fraction of the cells are occupied. At equilibrium, the mean free path of a particle is now only a few cells (cf. Section 15.4) and the individual particle will follow a tangled path very similar to that of the previous experiment. Thermal agitation is now driven by *the totality of the remaining gas particles* rather than an external noise source.

The fact that the system as a self-contained whole is perfectly deterministic makes little difference to the individual particle—which is still swimming in a sea of noise (cf. Sections 17.3–17.5). In this light, the issue of whether a cellular-automaton rule is *deterministic* or *stochastic* is a moot one; Lucretius' *clinamen* is conceptually superfluous.[4]

---

[3]Reflections off the walls will not be *specular*—but of course, on the scale of a molecule, walls cannot be imagined as being "smooth" or having a definite orientation.

[4]In his book *On the nature of things*, the Roman poet Lucretius (1st century BC) gives an unabashedly reductionistic—and surprisingly modern-sounding—account of the natural world. The *clinamen* was an ever-so-slight random swerving of atoms from their straight paths, which the author felt he had to introduce—with some reluctance—in order to make his model do what he believed it should but otherwise couldn't.

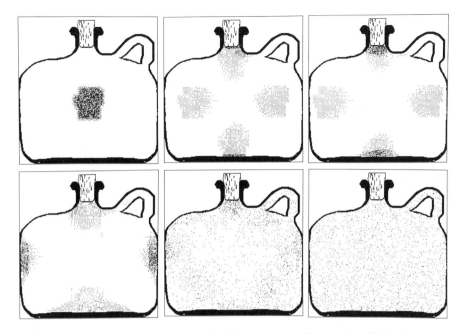

Figure 15.3: Expansion of a TM-GAS cloud in a vacuum. Repeated collisions between particles and with container's walls eventually lead to thorough thermalization.

15.3 Self-diffusion

In the previous experiment we used a container of rather irregular shape in order to destroy possible symmetries in the initial conditions—which in an absolutely isolated gas may otherwise linger for a long time (try the same experiment using all of CAM's array as a boundaryless toroidal universe). Once the gas has reached equilibrium we can forget about the container. Here we shall fill the whole array with gas already at equilibrium; a uniformly random configuration of a certain density will do.

We shall take the liberty of painting some of the particles red and some green (respectively black and grey on the printed page, as in Figure 15.4) without altering the particles' distribution. This is easily done by identifying a red particle by means of a marker in plane 1 and letting the marker accompany the particle on its journey (we'll leave the code for this variant of the rule as an exercise for the reader). In this way, the array will contain three kinds of cells, namely red particles, green particles, and empty cells.

For a color-blind observer nothing has changed, and the gas is still at equilibrium; however, a color-sensitive observer will see red and green gases diffuse into each other (Figure 15.4) until this newly-introduced degree of freedom reaches equilibrium (in the form of a yellow mixture). Color does not affect the dynamics, and for this reason helps us understand that even in an "uncolored" gas *self-diffusion* is a real phenomenon; the rate of self-diffusion is one of the transport parameters that characterize the response of a gas to perturbations of equilibrium (cf. Chapter 16).

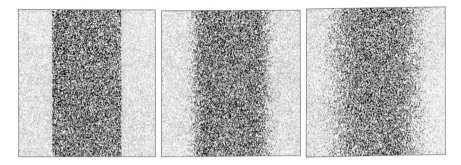

Figure 15.4: Self diffusion of two gases having different colors but identical dynamical properties.

15.4   Mean free path

For the sake of illustration, let's compute the mean free path of a particle as a function of the particle density, in TM-GAS. From a particle's viewpoint, at any moment the remaining three cells of its block will be occupied with probabilities given by the following table (where a solid circle denotes the particle under consideration, and ρ is the particle density)

$$\begin{array}{llll}
& (1-\rho)^3 & & \rho^2(1-\rho) \\
& \rho(1-\rho)^2 & & \rho^2(1-\rho) \\
& \rho(1-\rho)^2 & & \rho^2(1-\rho) \\
& \rho(1-\rho)^2 & & \rho^3
\end{array} \qquad (15.1)$$

According to the fourth entry of this table, the probability of a collision (and by this we mean a *binary* collision—the only kind that can deflect a particle's trajectory in TM-GAS) is $p = \rho(1-\rho)^2$. One can easily express the probability of a certain sequence of collisions; for instance, the probability that in seven steps the particle will collide at, say, the second and the seventh steps is

$$qpqqqqp = q^5 p^2$$

(where $q = 1 - p$), and a *free path* of length i (i.e., free flight for i steps followed by a collision at the $(i + 1)$-th step) will occur with probability $q^i p$.

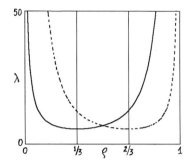

Figure 15.5: The solid line plots the mean free path λ as a function of the particle density ρ, in TM-GAS; the dashed curve plots the mean free path for the "holes."

The *mean free path*, i.e., the weighted sum of all possible free-path lengths is thus

$$
\begin{aligned}
\lambda &= 0p + 1qp + 2qqp + 3qqqp + \cdots \qquad (15.2)\\
&= qp(1 + 2q + 3q^2 + \cdots)\\
&= \frac{qp}{(1-q)^2} = \frac{q}{p}.
\end{aligned}
$$

We could have arrived at the same result by a more intuitive argument. If a particle has a probability p to collide at any step, then on average it will spend a time $1/p$ from one collision to the next (mean free *time*); since for one unit of this time the particle is "stuck" (in TM-GAS, no travel occurs during a collision step) the mean free *path* is $1/p - 1 = q/p$.

Figure 15.5 plots the particle's mean free path λ as a function of the particle density ρ. This curve has a minimum of $\lambda = 23/4$ (≈ 6) for $\rho = 1/3$. For small values of ρ, particles travel almost freely in a vacuum; at high densities, they slide almost freely past one another (since encounters of more than two particles inhibit collisions).

Since the rule is symmetric between particles and vacuum (1's and 0's), "holes" in a sea of particles behave much as particles in a sea of vacuum.

15.5 A tour de force

Here we shall describe an experiment of a kind that in ordinary circumstances one would think twice about before undertaking—and that instead can be approached very light-heartedly with a cellular automata machine.

When diffusion is driven by an external random source each segment of a particle's path is completely independent of the previous one: the noise is absolutely fresh at every step. However, correlations may arise when a particle's path is determined by collisions with other particles; intuitively, some of the effects of one collision may "come around" to affect the same particle. Since any deviations from an ideal random walk are expected to be slight, a long accumulation of statistical data is necessary.

In the present experiment the path of one gas particle starting at the origin of coordinates is followed for a fixed number t of steps—say, a few thousand. The particle's path is recorded, and in particular the particle's final position is noted. The procedure is repeated a large number n of times, each time with a different initial arrangement of particles. Each run entails, of course, simulating the entire gas system, consisting of tens of thousands of particles. Various kinds of statistical analyses can then be performed on the collected data.

This experiment was conducted at MIT by Andrea Califano. One result is the numerical determination of the probability distribution $P(x, y; t)$; this is shown in Figure 15.6 for $t = 1024$ steps. For any value of x, y the height of the plot represents the actual number of runs on which the particle ended at x, y: thus, the total number of runs equals the *volume* of the "Gaussian mountain" in the figure. Given the wide dynamic range, in order to have a reasonable resolution for the lower values of P it is necessary to make a very large number n of runs—about half a million in this case. Thus, the plot of Figure 15.6 corresponds to a computation involving a total of $256 \times 256 \times 1024 \times 500,000$ (≈ 30 trillion) cell updates!

Who is going to record the position of the selected particle step after step? If we paint the particle red, the eye can follow its trajectory on the screen with relative ease; however, the coordinates of this particle do not explicitly appear anywhere in the simulation: we just have an array of cells of which some happen to be green, one red, and the rest empty. We could instruct the host computer to stop the simulation after every step, read the contents of the array, and look for the cell that contains the red particle, but this would be grossly inefficient. The technique that was actually used is the following.

Assume we start with PHASE = 0 and with the particle in the upper-left corner of a block of the Margolus neighborhood. If the COLLISION condition is true the particle will not move during the first step; otherwise it will move to the right (since the whole block rotates clockwise). In this situation, in order to know the position of the particle at the end of the first step we don't have to look at the whole array; we only need to be given *one bit* of information, namely whether the particle collided or not. At the next step we know that PHASE = 1, and from the bit collected from the previous step we know the particle's position within a block at the beginning of the current step. Again, a single bit of information will allow us to determine the particle's new position at the end of this step. As long as we are only concerned with that particle, the entire history of a thousand-step simulation can unequivocally be compressed into a a string of a thousand bits. The host computer can easily process one bit per step—even as CAM is updating hundreds of thousands of bits during the same time interval.

As explained in a little more detail in Section 17.6, alongside the look-up table that computes a cell's new state (*transition function*), an auxiliary look-up table fed with the same neighborhood data is programmed to compute the following values (*output function*):

> 1, If the cell contains a red particle and this particle is undergoing a collision.
>
> 0, Otherwise.

This value is fed to the event counter, which accumulates cell events on-the-fly; since only one red cell is present, the total count at the end of each step will be 0 or 1; this is all the information that we need, and it can be read off the event counter at the end of each step without disturbing the simulation.

For many analysis purposes this string of bits can be processed in real-time as it comes out of the machine. However, the string itself captures all of the relevant data of the experiment in such a compact form that storage on, say, a disk file presents no problems. In this way the same string can be used for many different analysis purposes. For example

- By "integrating" the string of an individual run one can reconstruct the end-position of the particle in that run, and thus accumulate one more volume element for a histogram like that of Figure 15.6.

- The string can be compared to that produced by an ideal random-number generator.

- The string can be correlated with a delayed version of itself; this is probably the most relevant piece of analysis in an experiment of the present kind.

Techniques for computing autocorrelations involving the whole contents of the bit-planes—rather that a single bit extracted in the above fashion—will be discussed in Section 16.6.

15.6 A tuneable noise source

Lattice gases such as HPP-GAS and TM-GAS provide convenient noise sources for experiments on a cellular automata machine. Their most useful feature is that, since the initial number of $\boxed{1}$'s is conserved by these rules, the probability p of finding a $\boxed{1}$ at any site is constant and is adjustable in fine increments over a wide range. To obtain a different probability it is not necessary to load

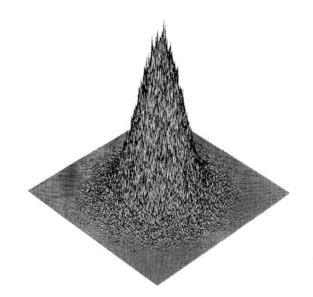

Figure 15.6: Histogram of $P(x, y; t)$—the probability that a particle of TM-GAS will be found at x, y at time t—as determined by a long series of simulation runs on CAM.

a new "'stirring" or "sampling" rule: one can just add or remove particles from a bit-plane.

Moreover, the equilibrium properties of these gases are well characterized. The spontaneous equalization of density and pressure observed in Section 15.2 is analogous to that of a viscous fluid and obeys similar laws (cf. Section 16.2). The mean free path, which is related to how vigorous is the randomization process, is less than a dozen cells over most of the density range (cf. Figure 15.5). Local correlations do exist, of course, since information cannot diffuse faster that one cell per step, but they are fairly short-term and well-understood (cf. Section 16.6).

The availability of two distinct gases, in one of which particles travel on rows and columns (TM-GAS) and in the other on diagonals (HPP-GAS), is also very useful. For example, a rule based mostly on horizontal and vertical exchanges of information (e.g., one that uses the von Neumann neighborhood) is least likely to be affected by the correlations of a diagonally moving gas.

The two gases can be run on different bit-planes and used as a combined noise source, for instance by AND'ing or XOR'ing them. One advantage is that two noise sources based on different mechanisms compensate to a certain extent for one another's limitations. The other advantage is that, by taking the product of the probabilities p and p' supplied by the two bit-planes, one can synthesize a much lower probability pp' without using gases of too low a density (which would yield a long mean free path and thus sluggish shuffling).

Finally, local correlations can be virtually eliminated by using an additional CAM module. In fact, CAM's architecture allows one at any moment to offset the spatial origin of one module with respect to the other in any direction and by any amount simply by changing the contents of a register. This makes "action at a distance" possible, and in particular permits global (rather than just local) scrambling of data. One would run a lattice-gas noise generator on the second module, and shift the origin of this module by a random amount both vertically and horizontally at every step; the random numbers for this shift are only required at the low rate of one or two per step, and are easily provided by the host computer using any of a number of well-known algorithms.

This method was used for the experiment of Figure 17.6, where a good-quality random-number generator was needed to simulate an ideal heat bath.

15.7 Diffusion-limited aggregation

Diffusion-limited aggregation occurs when diffusing particles stick to and progressively enlarge an initial seed represented by a fixed object. The seed typically grows in an irregular dendritic shape resembling frost on a window, as we shall see in a moment. Diffusion-limited aggregation is a reasonable model of physical growth processes (frost, for one), in which dendritic growth occurs because the material needed for growth must diffuse from outside, or some growth byproduct (such as heat) must escape[69,51,53].

The following is a variant of a rule suggested by Charles Bennett. In CAM-A, plane 0 will contain the diffusing particles, as in 2D-BROWNIAN of Section 15.1, and plane 1 will contain the initial seed and accumulate the growing dendrite. Both planes use the Margolus neighborhood. The diffusion is driven by a noise generator in CAM-B.

The growth mechanism is very simple; the presence of the dendrite is detected just as the container's wall in Section 15.2. If a portion of dendrite appears anywhere in a block, any diffusing particles contained in this block will "stick" to the dendrite, i.e., are transferred from plane 0 to plane 1— where they remain without moving. The effect is much like that of flypaper.

```
CAM-A N/MARG &/CENTERS
                            : RAND ( -- 0|1)
              &CENTER' ;      \ noise comes from CAM-B
                            : WALL ( -- 0|1)
      CENTER' CW' OPP' CCW'    \ sense wall
              OR OR OR ;
                            : DENDRITE
          WALL IF            \ Particles: If on wall,
```

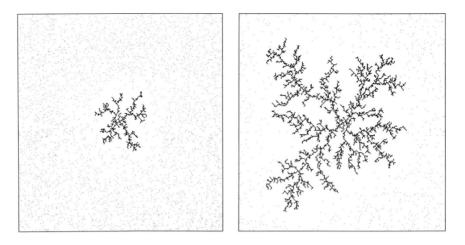

Figure 15.7: Dendritic growth by diffusion-limited aggregation. The process was
started from a one-cell seed in the middle, and with a 10% density of diffusing
particles.

```
                     0 ELSE               \   stick to it
           RAND { CW CCW } THEN >PLN0     \   else keep going
                    WALL IF               \ Dendrite: If wall,
         CENTER' CENTER OR ELSE           \   catch any particles
                CENTER' THEN >PLN1 ;      \   else no change
```

Since the connection between CAM-A and CAM-B is only through the center
cell, a little ingenuity is needed to provide in CAM-B a random-number generator suitable for the Margolus neighborhood in CAM-A. The casual reader
may skip the following description.

```
CAM-B N/MARG-HV
                                 : STIR/SAMPLE/DELAY
       UL  UR  XOR                       \ Take data from both
       LL  LR  AND XOR                   \   planes, shuffle,
       UL' LL' AND                       \   and return same outcome
       UR' LR' XOR XOR XOR >PLN2         \   to all four cells
                CENTER >PLN3 ;           \ One-step delay line
```

We noted in Section 15.1 that all four cells of a block must see the same random
outcome in order to take concerted action; there, RAND XOR'ed the four block
neighbors to produce such a block-position-invariant outcome. Here, since CAM-
A cannot see the four block neighbors in CAM-B, such an invariant outcome is
computed within CAM-B and *stored* in plane 2. However, a problem arises; that
is, this result is available only one step later, when the machine is using the *other*
partition. To have it in the correct phase, we delay the result one more step by
copying it from plane 2 to plane 3, where CAM-A will eventually see it through
&CENTER'.

To give a reasonably random result, the function that is to produce the position-invariant outcome for plane 2 cannot consist only of XOR's; a nonlinear component such as AND is required as well. This destroys the rotational symmetry of the function, and forces us to use the absolute block neighbors UL, UR, etc. (cf. Section 12.5).

To initialize the random-number generator, put a random pattern on plane 2 and run 2 steps. This fills the one-step "delay line" with valid data, and you can now proceed to initialize the planes of CAM-A.

Figure 15.7 shows an early and a late stage in dendritic growth obtained with this rule, starting with a particle density of ≈10% (see also Plate 12). The shape is a branched cluster; branches form because the progressive depletion of particle density in the interior bays of the existing cluster inhibits growth there. Branch tips get to "pick first," as it were, and only a few of the diffusing particles make it to the space between the branches.

For higher densities of the diffusing particles the shape of the aggregation cluster is more globular; for lower densities, more dendritic. In the low-density limit, diffusion-limited aggregation produces patterns having a well-defined fractal dimension; in two-dimensional models the fractal dimension is ≈1.7 (see [53], page 121).

Chapter 16

Fluid dynamics

This chapter deals with the modeling of fluid dynamics by reduction to microscopic laws (in a somewhat idealized form).

In a very large system, even relatively small portions of the system still contain a large number of parts, and thus can be meaningfully subjected to a macroscopic analysis. An interesting situation arises when equilibrium has established itself on a certain scale but not yet on a larger scale, so that the system as a whole is not at equilibrium. In this situation, the macroscopic parameters gradually change from place to place;[1] moreover, at each place these parameters may gradually change also *in time*—such macroscopic evolution being of course driven by the spatial gradients of the macroscopic quantities involved.

A system of this kind can be visualized as a collection of local equilibria that smoothly merge into one another and smoothly evolve in time; the various macroscopic quantities *flow* in a continuous way.

16.1 Sound waves

We shall continue here the series of experiments started in Chapter 15. Under a rule such as TM-GAS, particles (represented by $\boxed{1}$'s in a vacuum of $\boxed{0}$'s) travel in straight lines and collide with one another; these collisions are momentum-conserving. Collisions lead to a gradual randomization of the particles' paths, and eventually the gas attains equilibrium.

What happens if we suddenly disturb this equilibrium? Let's start, for definiteness, with a configuration having density $\rho = 1/2$, and let's replace a

---

[1]Changes are gradual because any two samples that overlap to a substantial extent must have almost identical parameters.

small volume of this gas by a tightly-packed cloud of particles (Figure 16.1a). The cloud will immediately start expanding, compressing the surrounding gas; the momentum of this outward rush is such that at a certain moment the center of the disturbance will be left depleted of particles (b). In turn, the compressed ring will expand outwards and inwards as well, thus creating a new pressure peak at the center. Alternating compressions and rarefactions propagate outwards as a *sound wave* (c). The overall effect is much like that of a bucket of water dumped into a pond.

Plate 13 shows the same phenomenon at a higher resolution, using a four bit-plane version of HPP-GAS described in Section 16.5.

There are a number of remarkable facts about the above behavior:

- On a time scale comparable with the size of the disturbance, the gas be-haves as an *elastic medium*; motion is underdamped. The extra density at the center does not just slowly *leak* out; it *rushes* out; in attempting to equalize its pressure, the gas overshoots its mark, and overshoots again when it tries to correct the first attempt.

- Although the microscopic laws are strongly anisotropic—there are privi-leged directions of motion (cf. Figure 15.3b)—the sound wave is *circular*. Much as in the diffusion of Section 15.1, here too the collective behavior of the particles displays a symmetry that is not present in the behavior of the individual particle.

- The speed v of sound in this medium is substantially less than that of the particles; namely, using the latter as a unit, $v = 1/\sqrt{2}$ (cf. Section 16.7). This speed is independent of the direction, the wave-length, and, as it turns out, also of the density of the lattice gas. Thus, a well-characterized mechanical property emerges at the macroscopic level which has no counterpart at the microscopic level.

Figure 16.1: Circular wave produced by a localized disturbance.

16.2 Hydrodynamics

Sound waves are only one aspect of the phenomenology of fluids, and actually one of minor interest in hydrodynamics; we shall return to them at the end of this chapter for experiments in wave optics (Section 16.7).

Hydrodynamics is chiefly interested in situations where different parts of a fluid move with respect to one another and with respect to solid obstacles at velocities that are much smaller than that of sound. In this limit, and neglecting external forces such as gravity, any density differences equalize themselves in a negligible time and the fluid can be treated as *incompressible*. Even when these simplifications apply, the phenomenology of fluids can be enormously varied. Depending on the speed of the main flow, the size and shape of the obstacles, and the viscosity of the fluid one can have laminar flow, vortices, turbulence, etc. (cf. [65] for a rich collection of illustrations).

In this context, the relevant variable is the *velocity* $\mathbf{V}$ (a vector) of flow at different points, and the relevant parameter is the *viscosity* ν of the fluid. The behavior of the fluid is governed by the *Navier-Stokes* equation

$$\frac{\partial \mathbf{V}}{\partial t} + (\mathbf{V}\nabla)\mathbf{V} = -\frac{1}{\rho}\nabla p + \nu \nabla^2 \mathbf{V}, \qquad (16.1)$$

where p is the pressure and ρ is the (constant) density. This is is a *nonlinear* differential equation, and, except for special cases, one must make recourse to numerical methods in order to find its solution for given initial and boundary conditions. Much computer time all over the world is devoted to the simulation of hydrodynamical problems.

It turns out that, on a macroscopic scale, the gases described by a cellular-automaton rule such as HPP-GAS or TM-GAS obey the Navier-Stokes equation approximately[23]; and a similar rule on a hexagonal lattice, namely FHP-GAS, discussed in Section 16.5, obeys this equation *exactly*[18]. Many researchers have recently become interested in such models of fluid dynamics, which have a number of attractive conceptual features and show considerable practical promise[28].

Reasonably detailed simulation of fluid dynamics problems requires a very large amount of computational resources. Figure 16.2 shows a simulation of flow past an obstacle conducted by Salem and Wolfram[50] (similar experiments were also conducted by d'Humières et al[14] at about the same time). This experiment was run on a Connection Machine, which was programmed as a cellular automaton with an array of $\approx 5000 \times 5000$ bits; the rule is a variant of FHP-GAS; the arrows show the magnitude and direction of the flow. To draw the arrows, the array was divided into regions of approximately 25,000 bits each; a computer program outside of the simulation proper explicitly counted the number of particles going in different directions in each region.

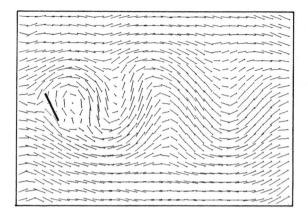

Figure 16.2: Flow past an obstacle (from Salem and Wolfram).

16.3 Tracing the flow

With a single CAM module one can barely begin to see the significant aspects
of hydrodynamic flow—though with more modules or with the "scooping"
technique mentioned at the end of this section a substantial range of possibilities opens up. Much larger cellular automata machines are needed for experiments on a significant scale. However, the basic concepts and techniques
can be explored quite independently of the size of the available machinery.

The equilibrium state for TM-GAS obtained by filling the array with a certain density (say 50%) of particles at random does not exhibit, at a macroscopic level, any net flow: the fluid is stationary. To make the fluid slowly
drift in one direction we have to increase the fraction of particles going in
that direction and decrease the fraction going in the opposite direction. In
the absence of obstacles, the momentum thus introduced will be conserved.

Let us call ρ_N, ρ_S, ρ_W, and ρ_E the "concentrations" of particles going in
the four cardinal compass directions, so that

$$\rho = \rho_N + \rho_S + \rho_W + \rho_E \qquad (16.2)$$

where ρ is the total density. In a drifting gas at equilibrium, even though
these concentrations are different, each concentration must be, in the long
run, *constant*; each population must be replenished at the same rate as it is
depleted by collisions.

On collision, a north/south pair will produce a west/east pair and vice
versa; we can symbolically denote these two "reactions" by

$$N + S \rightarrow W + E \quad , \quad W + E \rightarrow N + S.$$

The rate of each reaction is proportional to the product of the concentrations of the colliding species; thus, the corresponding rates are

$$\rho_N \rho_S \quad , \quad \rho_W \rho_E. \tag{16.3}$$

At equilibrium the two reaction rates must balance; therefore, the equilibrium concentrations must obey the relation

$$\rho_N \rho_S = \rho_W \rho_E, \tag{16.4}$$

which, together with (16.2), completely characterizes the equilibrium state. For small drift velocities, one may use the linear approximation

$$\rho_N + \rho_S = \rho_W + \rho_E,$$

where the geometric averages of (16.4) have been replaced by arithmetic averages.

Thus, if we construct an initial configuration where the density of north- or south-going particles is $\rho/4$, east $(1 + 2\epsilon)\rho/4$, and west $(1 - 2\epsilon)\rho/4$, the gas will be close to equilibrium, and as a whole will drift rightwards at a speed ϵ. Such a configuration, with $\rho = 1/2$ and $\epsilon = 1/10$ is shown in Figure 16.3a. Since the density is uniform, there are no macroscopic symptoms that the gas is in motion; intuitively, we are looking at a clear stream with no distinguishing marks that we can follow. To make the streamlines visible one could use the approach of Figure 16.2—which however requires a large amount of nonlocal processing. Here we'll try an approach that more closely mimics what is possible in a physical experiment.

The idea is to place some discrete *tracers* in the flow, and follow their trajectories. For this purpose we shall mark a few of the particles, as in Section 15.3; the motion of each particle will of course have a random component (Brownian motion) but superposed on this there will be a slight rightward bias. Figure 16.3b shows the drift of marked particles emitted by a "smokestack." It is clear that on this scale the drift is barely noticeable, swamped as it is by the random component of the motion.

However, as the scale of the simulation is increased—so that the markers can be followed for a longer time t—the coherent component of the motion grows as t while the random component grows only as $\sqrt{t}$; as the relative weight of the random component decreases, well-defined streamlines begin to appear. Figure 16.3c shows the same experiment performed on an array of 1024×1024.

Scooping. In spite of the fact that it uses an array sixteen times as large as that of CAM, the experiment of Figure 16.3c was still performed using a single CAM module. The basic idea is to keep the large array stored in the memory of the host computer; you take a small "scoop" of this array, give it

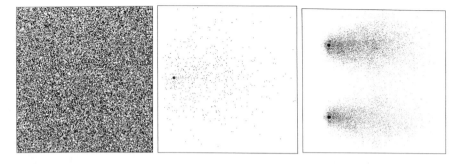

Figure 16.3: (a) The direction of drift is invisible if the fluid has uniform density. (b) Markers ejected by a smokestack diffuse in the fluid. (c) On a larger-scale simulation, the streamlines start becoming visible.

to CAM to process for, say, a dozen steps, and store the result back into the array; you then move to the next scoop, and so on.[2] When a pass over the whole array has been completed (the whole array has now evolved a dozen steps) a new pass is made, continuing like this as long as desired.

Using this technique, CAM can update an array of arbitrary size with a slowdown of less than a factor of two in time per cell-update.

16.4   Flow past an obstacle

Flow past an obstacle is achieved by making the walls of the obstacle reflect the gas particles, for example as in Section 15.2. Sources and sinks can be introduced as well. Obstacles, sources, and sinks are "programmed" by just *drawing* them on auxiliary bit planes; they can be positioned in an arbitrary way and given arbitrary shapes. Different amounts of friction with the walls are not programmed by introducing an ad hoc "coefficient of friction" in certain equations; they are achieved altering the texture of the wall—which can be made pitted or spongy. It will be up to the individual particle to find its way in and out of these pits; its momentum will be altered to a greater or lesser extent by the collisions, and friction will spontaneously emerge as the collective result of these detours.

Note that boundary conditions can be made as complex as desired *without making the simulation in any way harder to program or more expensive to carry out*. Moreover, since macroscopic quantities appear only as averages taken over explicitly represented microscopic configurations, numerical insta-

---

[2]Since the scoop within CAM does not receive edge information from the adjacent scoops, which are still in the host computer, after twelve steps the edge of the scoop will contain useless data for a thickness of twelve cells. This portion is thrown away; thus, each scooping operation updates a portion of the array that is a little smaller than the scoop itself.

bilities and diverging solutions are ruled out. When "things are what they seem," we can safely let them "do what they must."

16.5 Other lattice gases

A number of conceptual and practical variations can be played on the lattice-gas theme. Here we shall briefly present the FHP approach[18], but first we'll take a second look at the HPP gas introduced in Chapter 12.

The HPP gas was originally formulated as follows[23]. Consider an orthogonal lattice consisting of sites connected by north, south, west, and east links. There are four kinds of particles, one for each direction, and a site can be occupied by at most one particle of each kind (thus, there can be up to four particles per site). The updating is done with a two-step cycle. At step 0 each particle moves along a link from its current site to the adjacent site corresponding to its direction; at step 1 particles get shuffled within each site in a way analogous to table (12.4). That is, if there are at that site exactly two particles which have come in from opposite directions, say north and south, then they are replaced by a west/east pair; otherwise nothing changes.

This approach can be implemented directly on CAM. The four bit-planes correspond to the four kinds of particles, so that all four bits of a cell are used. At step 0 ("move") each plane is made to shift one step in the appropriate direction, while at step 1 ("collide") the contents of the four center bits is examined and the appropriate swaps are performed. On CAM it is possible to combine the two steps into one by using a custom neighborhood. That is, some neighbor and phase signals are routed to the tables externally via the user connector rather than internally (cf. Sections 7.5, 9.7). The *shift* step by itself involves collecting one compass neighbor from each plane and depositing it in the center position of the same plane; but once we have these four bits as arguments to the look-up table, before depositing them we might as well program the table to shuffle them as prescribed by the *collide* step. Figure 16.4 shows circular wave propagation in this more dense realization of the HPP model. This sort of scheme is an example of partitioning the state-set of each cell (each bit of the state of a cell is used as a neighbor by exactly one other cell) rather than using block-partitions.

It must be noted that this realization of the HPP gas uses CAM less efficiently than that which uses the Margolus neighborhood; the particles belong to two decoupled spacetime sublattices, each evolving independently of the other (cf. Section 14.3). Instead of a system containing N particles one ends up simulating two separate systems containing $N/2$ particles each. With the Margolus neighborhood version, only one sublattice is represented and simulated.

Although the smaller number of bits used at each cell by the Margolus neighborhood implementation was a disadvantage when we wanted to produce pictures with more particles visible in a 256 × 256 window (compare Figures 16.1 and 16.4) it will be an advantage in the next section when we want to simultaneously run two copies of the same system on different bit-planes, in order to compare corresponding sites.

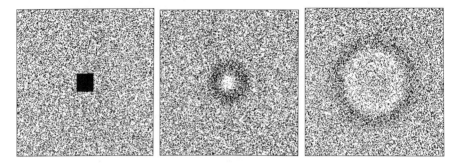

Figure 16.4: Wave propagation in a denser realization of the HPP gas model. To enhance contrast, only sites that contain three or four particles are shown.

As we mentioned earlier, the behavior of the HPP model departs from the Navier-Stokes equation; even at a macroscopic level the viscosity is anisotropic—a "ghost" of the lattice. This blemish is removed by the FHP model[18], which uses *six* kinds of particles; i.e., there are six directions of travel, with a 60° angle from one to the next. The lattice is a hexagonal one, and each site can contain up to six particles (one of each kind). As in the HPP and TM models, collisions are defined so as to conserve energy (number of particles) and momentum.

A simple version of the FHP rule has a collision occur whenever the momentum at a site is zero. If there is no collision, all particles go straight. If there is a collision, all particles at that site are deflected 60° clockwise (or counterclockwise) from the path they were following.[3]

The FHP model can be implemented on CAM using the Margolus neighborhood on two planes. One axis of the lattice has to be imagined tilted at 30° from the vertical, as shown in Figure 16.5. Each block represents one site; of the eight bits of the block (four per plane) six are used for the particles; the remaining two are "spares" and can be used, for example, to define obstacles or other space-dependent properties of the medium (cf. Section 16.7). The FHP-GAS rule, which we won't write here in detail, uses a two-step cycle, as in the above HPP model; one step is used for moving the particles along the links, and one to carry out the shuffle entailed by a collision.

---

[3]In the original FHP rule, four-particle collisions were ignored, and this is the version we used for Figure 16.6. During a single step, we used the same direction of rotation for all deflections, and the two possible rotations were alternated on successive steps.

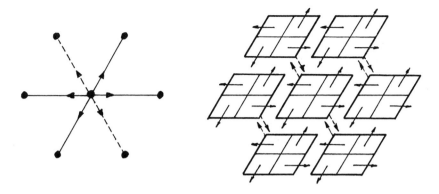

Figure 16.5: For the **FHP-GAS** rule, the blocks of the Margolus neighborhood are conceptually arranged in a hexagonal pattern. Each block implements a site. Solid links refer to particles in plane 0, dashed ones to particles in plane 1.

An embedding similar to that of Figure 16.5 allows an ordinary (non-partitioned) hexagonal neighborhood to be implemented on CAM: simply write rules for the N/MOORE neighborhood which don't use, say, N.EAST and S.WEST (try the rules of Section 6.4 on this hexagonal neighborhood). By using a custom neighborhood and two CAM machines, one can similarly implement the FHP model with 6 particles at each site: use separate bit-planes for each of the six velocities, and alternate steps which shuffle the particles at each site (collisions) with steps which shift the bit-planes (movement). Just as in the HPP example above, these two steps can be combined by using a neighborhood in which each cell is connected to the south-going plane of the cell above it, the north-going plane of the cell below, etc. Unlike the N/MARG implementation we described first, this realization would avoid wasting half of its time on data-shifting steps. It would however be more awkward to use for the autocorrelation experiments of the next section.

16.6 Autocorrelations

The velocity time-autocorrelation function answers the following question: Consider the microscopic velocity of the fluid at a certain place; how *different* is this velocity likely to be some time t later? Similar questions can be asked for quantities other than velocity, or for space- rather than time-correlations. Autocorrelations represent an important tool, both theoretically and experimentally, for establishing connections between macroscopic and microscopic properties of a system.

Conceptually, the measurement of autocorrelations entails dealing with two copies of the same system, one offset with respect to the other by a

certain space or time amount (or both).[4] In many cases of interest the amount
of correlation decreases rather steeply as the offset is increased, and soon
becomes swamped by statistical noise; a large amount of data is required to
filter out this noise. In this context, it is desirable to measure the correlation
at every point of the array and average over the whole array; a further average
of these results is taken over the course of a long simulation run.

The differential-measurement technique discussed in Section 9.2 can be
extended to the study of autocorrelations. Instead of comparing in real-time
the histories of two copies of a system started from slightly different initial
configurations, here one uses the *same* initial configuration—but one copy of
the system is started t steps later. (A similar approach is used for space-
autocorrelations.)

In a lattice gas such as HPP-GAS or TM-GAS, each cell of a Margolus-
neighborhood block is reserved for a particle having a certain direction of
motion (Sections 12.2, 12.7). The velocity at that point can be defined as
1 if the cell contains a particle and 0 if the cell is empty. The velocity
autocorrelation between two homologous cells[5] is defined as the *product* of
the corresponding velocities. Thus, if one copy of the system is run on plane
0 and the other on plane 1, one can program the intensity output of the color
map to return the product of these two planes, cell by cell

```
                              : AUTOCORR-MAP
        ALPHA ALPHA' AND >INTEN        \ Product of C, C'
                          ...          \ Other colors as desired
                          ... ;        \  for visual display
```

Here we used 'AND' rather than '*' (the result is identical; cf. Section A.14) to
stress that the product of two bits is a one-bit value.

As explained in Section 7.7, the intensity output of the color map is fed to
the event counter—which will thus integrate at each step the autocorrelation
over the whole array. The responsibility for averaging these counts over a
large number of steps—a trivial task—is left to the host computer.

Theoretical arguments suggest that for simple lattice gases in one, two, or
more dimensions the velocity time-autocorrelation function $\nu(t)$ should be a
power of t (at least asymptotically, as $t \to \infty$). The exponent of this power,
which in a log-log plot of $\nu(t)$ is simply the slope of the curve, is expected to
approach -1 for large t in a truly 2-dimensional model.

Figure 16.6 shows the measured values of $\nu(t)$ for the three lattice gases

---

[4]When the simulation costs are overwhelming one may prefer to run a single copy of
the system, record its history, and then study it. As noted in Section 9.2, this approach
may be very burdensome.

[5]I.e., a given cell and the corresponding cell under a time or space shift.

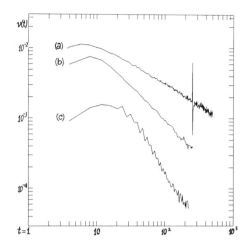

Figure 16.6: Time-correlation function $\nu(t)$ for HPP-GAS (a), TM-GAS (b), and FHP-GAS (c).

mentioned in this book, namely HPP-GAS, TM-GAS, and FHP-GAS.[6] These experiments, discussed in [36], were conducted at MIT by us and Gérard Vichniac, using a single CAM module. Each of the data points plotted represents the accumulation of a billion or more comparisons—the whole experiment entailed accumulating about 3/4 of a trillion comparisons, and took about two and a half days to run.

Experiments of this kind take good advantage of CAM's bit-serial, plane-parallel internal architecture (cf. beginning of Chapter 7 and Section B.5). At each step the two bit-planes containing the two copies of the system under study are scanned serially, in lock step. A single AND function straddled across the two bit-streams monitors the local correlations on-the-fly (this is what AUTOCORR-MAP accomplishes) and feeds them to the event counter (which in this implementation is simply a serial counter) where they accumulate in the course of a step. At this stage, out of a simulation stream involving, say, a hundred-thousand bits per step, the relevant information, consisting of just a few bits (the contents of the counter), has already been extracted, and any further processing is trivial.

---

[6]For our implementation of FHP-GAS, one copy of the system occupies planes 0 and 1 (see Figure 16.5) while a second copy of the system is run on CAM-B. Two steps are used to compare the two corresponding pairs of planes—since update/translate also takes two steps, these comparisons can be done without slowing down the simulation.

16.7   Wave optics

A theoretical analysis[23] shows that, for small perturbations from equilibrium, the elastic properties of lattice gases of the present kind are *linear*. In this situation, the propagation of a disturbance is governed, at a macroscopic level, by the familiar *wave equation*

$$\frac{d^2\rho}{dt^2} = \frac{1}{v^2}\nabla^2\rho$$

We can thus consider using the lattice gas as an "ether" and study phenomena of wave interference, reflection, diffraction, and refraction. The experiments of Section 16.1 show that a good approximation of this behavior can be attained on a scale smaller than that required for the study of flow.

Here we shall use the HPP-GAS rule. In addition to waves traveling at the speed of sound this rule also supports "solitons" traveling at the speed of light. These solitons, which in one orientation consist simply of alternating vertical stripes superposed on the random medium, behave much like sound pulses but undergo less scattering and allow one to operate with shorter wavelengths.

Reflection on a mirror is achieved by treating the mirror as a solid wall; the interaction of HPP-GAS with a wall can be achieved in analogy with what was done for TM-GAS in Section 15.2. Figure 16.7 shows the reflection of a plane-wave pulse by a spherical mirror.

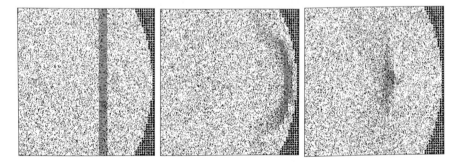

Figure 16.7: A plane pulse traveling towards a concave mirror (a) is shown right after the reflection (b) and approaching the focal point (c).

Reflection was easy. How about refraction? can we make a *lens*? What we need is a medium with a higher refractive index than the "ether;" i.e., in this medium signals should travel at reduced speed.

We'll draw the lens in plane 1, and we'll modify the rule so that cell-blocks of "lens material" will be updated at half the rate as "ether" blocks. This will slow down the particles by a factor of 2, yielding a proportionately higher refractive index for the lens. The rule is the following

```
N/MARG-PH
                                : LENS ( -- 0|1)
            CENTER' CW' OPP' CCW'     \ is some of the lens
                      OR OR OR ;      \    within the block?
                                : REFRACT
            LENS PHASE AND IF       \ when within lens
                   CENTER ELSE      \    mark time on PHASE=1
                COLLISION IF        \ otherwise behave
                       CW ELSE      \    like the ordinary
                      OPP THEN      \       HPP-GAS
                          THEN
                          >PLN0
                  CENTER' >PLN1 ;   \ the lens stays put
                                : 0011-CYCLE
        0 IS  <PHASE>
        0 IS <ORG-HV>  STEP         \ Two steps of PHASE=0:
        3 IS <ORG-HV>  STEP         \    everyone works
        1 IS  <PHASE>
        0 IS <ORG-HV>  STEP         \ Two steps of PHASE=1:
        3 IS <ORG-HV>  STEP ;       \    only ether works
MAKE-TABLE REFRACT
MAKE-CYCLE 0011-CYCLE
```

Recall that `HPP-GAS` performs one step using the even grid and one using the odd grid. We want to slow down the activity within the lens, but without separating the two elements of the step pair (this pairing of steps is an essential aspect of the rule). Within the lens, a pair of active steps will be followed by a pair of idle steps, and so on in alternation. `PHASE` is used for distinguishing between active and idle steps. Everything else is as in the plain `HPP-GAS` rule; the definition of `COLLISION` was given in 12.4 and is not repeated here.

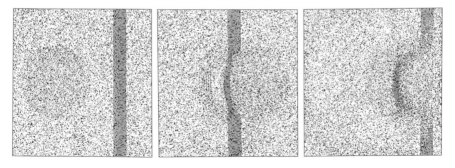

Figure 16.8: Refraction and reflection patterns produced by a spherical lens.

The experiment is shown in Figure 16.8. The part of the wave that enters the lens first is slowed down first; this bends the wave-front and makes the wave converge. Since we are using a circular lens the converging rays show *spherical aberration*: instead of a sharply defined focal point they produce a *caustic*—the pattern one sees when light is reflected on the inside of a cup filled with milk.

Notice that there is also a weak reflected wave. This is not an artifact of the model; in a *reversible* medium, theory predicts reflections whenever there is a sharp discontinuity in the index of refraction, i.e., in the speed of propagation of information. *If information arrives faster than it can proceed onward, some of it must be reflected since none can be lost.*

Chapter 17

Collective phenomena

> Every individual endeavors to employ his capital so that its produce may be of greatest value. He generally neither intends to promote the public interest, nor knows how much he is promoting it. He intends only his own security, only his own gain. And he is in this led by an *invisible hand* to promote an end which was no part of his intention. By pursuing his own interest he frequently promotes that of society more effectually than when he really intends to promote it.
>
> [Adam Smith]

It is a common occurrence in nature for a large number of similar elements (e.g. molecules, animals) to interact in such a way as to exhibit large-scale phenomena not present in the individual elements. An example we have already discussed is that of gases: molecules that individually obey rather simple collision laws give rise to collective behavior that can be quite varied and complex, including sound waves, vortices, and turbulence.

What is interesting from a modeling viewpoint is that substantially the same macroscopic behavior can be obtained starting from "individuals" that are much simpler than real molecules, namely, the cells of a cellular automaton. Only certain features (such as, in this case, conservation of particles and of momentum) manage to make their effects felt all the way up to the macroscopic level; the others become irrelevant on a sufficiently large scale.

In this chapter we show how cellular automata can be used to simulate other collective phenomena such as magnetization, and to study the phase

transitions that occur at critical values of certain parameters. This phenomenology was originally observed in physics, but analogous effects have
been described in other fields, such as biology and economics, where the interacting individuals may be much more complicated than gas molecules. As
was the case with gases, the essential aspects of these collective phenomena
can generally be reproduced by cellular automata because they possess the
essential feature of locality of interaction among a large number of similar
individuals.

17.1 Critical parameters and phase transitions

In an ideal gas, the equilibrium state corresponding to given global constraints
(total energy, momentum, etc.) is *unique* and *undifferentiated*; that is, (a) essentially all initial states compatible with those constraints eventually evolve
into the same macroscopic state, and (b) in the absence of external fields,
samples of the system taken at different places or times all look the same.

In brief, equilibrium in ideal gases is a rather undistinguished business. Is
this the case for equilibrium in general?

Intuitively, many of the properties of matter are the outcome of a contest
between attractive forces, which tend to induce an orderly local structure, and
heat, which tends to break up this order. A number of distinctive phenomena
occur near the so-called *critical temperature*, where the tendency to achieve
more local order and the disordering effect of heat are in balance, with no
long-term winner.[1]

The phenomenology of collective phenomena is extremely varied. Other
parameters may interact with temperature in establishing critical sets of values, around which smooth changes in some variables lead to strikingly sudden
(and interesting, if only for that reason) modifications of structure.

17.2 Ising systems

As a paradigm for systems having a richer equilibrium phenomenology than
that of ideal gases we shall consider *Ising* systems—a class of models that were
originally introduced in the study of magnetic materials. We shall retain here
some of the suggestive terminology that comes from that physical context.

Spins.   The "individuals" of an Ising system are *spins* (which can be
naively visualized as little magnets) arranged in a regular array. Unlike gas
particles, these spins occupy *fixed positions*: the only thing that is left variable

---

[1]In a classical "ideal gas" there are no attractive forces: disorder distributes itself as
evenly as possible, and there is no critical temperature.

is a spin's *orientation* in space. We shall further restrict our attention to the case in which a spin is permitted only two orientations, conventionally denoted by *up* (↑) and *down* (↓). (One can imagine the "up/down" axis oriented perpendicularly to the plane of the array). For a one-dimensional array, a possible configuration of the system would be the following

$$\cdots \uparrow\uparrow\downarrow\uparrow\downarrow\uparrow\downarrow\downarrow\uparrow\downarrow\downarrow\downarrow\downarrow\uparrow\uparrow\downarrow \cdots$$

Two spins will be called *parallel* if they point in the same direction (↑↑), *anti-parallel* if they point in opposite directions (↑↓).

Familiarity with ordinary magnets suggests that spins may exert on one another forces depending on their mutual orientation and distance and on the nature of the intervening medium. In the case of Ising systems the analogy is retained; however the details of the coupling (which in the original physical situation involves quantum-mechanical effects) will be assigned on the basis of rather abstract considerations, and only *immediately adjacent* spins will interact (no long-range forces).

Coupling energy. Let us consider the very simple case of a spin system in which the forces between neighboring spins tend to *align* them. The *bond* between two spins can be visualized as a spring which is at rest when the spins are parallel, and under tension when they are anti-parallel. Each spring under tension stores one unit of energy. In the following configuration, where the energy of each coupling is explicitly indicated by a 0 or a 1,

$$\begin{array}{ccccc} a & b & c & d & e \end{array}$$
$$\cdots \uparrow\!0\!\uparrow\!0\!\uparrow\!1\!\downarrow\!1\!\uparrow\!1\!\downarrow\!0\!\downarrow \cdots, \tag{17.1}$$

spin *a* is aligned with both of its neighbors. If you try to turn it from ↑ to ↓, so as to obtain the configuration

$$\begin{array}{ccccc} a & b & c & d & e \end{array}$$
$$\cdots \uparrow\!1\!\downarrow\!1\!\uparrow\!1\!\downarrow\!1\!\uparrow\!1\!\downarrow\!0\!\downarrow \cdots, \tag{17.2}$$

you'll have to fight two springs at the same time, one on the right and one on the left, and the system will *gain* two units of energy; similarly, flipping spin *c* in (17.1) would *release* two units of energy. On the other hand, spin *b* in (17.1) is in an *indifferent* energetic situation: if you flip it, as the spring on the right is put under tension the one on the left is released, and the overall energy of the system remains the same.

Energy-conserving transformations. In physics, in the time-evolution of an isolated system energy is *conserved*. In the Ising models presented in the following sections we'll keep faith with this principle no matter what drastic simplifications may be introduced in other respects.

In a real spin system there may be many more "places"—besides the inter-spin bonds—where energy can be stored, and there are a variety of Ising-type models that take this into account, some of which we shall examine later. For the moment, however, let us consider a simple model where the only energy that matters is that of the inter-spin bonds. In this situation, can we write a cellular-automaton rule that makes the system evolve in a nontrivial way while obeying a strict energy-conservation policy?

Suppose for a moment that you update one spin at a time—say, one chosen at random; the two possible outcomes of the updating are "flip" and "no-flip." If you flip the spin, the only bonds that will be modified are those surrounding it. Then, energy conservation will only allow you to flip spins that are in an *indifferent* energetic situation, such as spin b in

$$\begin{array}{ccccc} a & b & c & d & e \end{array}$$
$$\cdots \uparrow_0 \uparrow_0 \uparrow_1 \downarrow_0 \downarrow_1 \uparrow_1 \downarrow \cdots. \qquad (17.3)$$

As soon as b is flipped, spin a—which formerly was "stuck" in place by energetic constraints—becomes a good candidate for flipping:

$$\begin{array}{ccccc} a & b & c & d & e \end{array}$$
$$\cdots \uparrow_0 \uparrow_1 \downarrow_0 \downarrow_0 \downarrow_1 \uparrow_1 \downarrow \cdots. \qquad (17.4)$$

Thus, one change may lead to another, and after a while the system may have evolved by a substantial amount.

Now, suppose that you are in a hurry to make the system evolve as fast as possible. First of all, whenever the spin you happen to choose is not prevented from flipping by energetic considerations, you always flip it. Then, you may get the help of an assistant: you pick a spin and start working on it, while he works on a different one. Of course, both of you flip only energy-indifferent spins. As long as the two of you keep a minimum distance apart, everything goes well; however, suppose you set your eyes on spin c in (17.3) and your assistant on spin d—which happens to be next to it. At either site the energy picture looks favorable to a flip; you each flip your spin—but when you look at the result

$$\begin{array}{ccccc} a & b & c & d & e \end{array}$$
$$\cdots \uparrow_0 \uparrow_0 \uparrow_0 \uparrow_0 \uparrow_0 \uparrow_1 \downarrow \cdots, \qquad (17.5)$$

you realize that the total energy has changed from 3 to 1! A spin is energy-indifferent only under the assumption that when you flip it its neighbors remain in the same orientation. (This situation is analogous to that of "land developers" of Section 9.5.) If one wants to (a) act with a *local* rule, (b) update *in parallel* as many spins as possible, and (c) *conserve energy*, a safe policy is to update all even-numbered spins at one step, all odd-numbered ones at the next step—and so on, back and forth.

Similar considerations apply to the two-dimensional case. Here spins are arranged in an orthogonal lattice, and are connected to their four neighbors by bonds having energy 0 or 1, as in the following diagram

$$
\begin{array}{ccccccc}
\boxed{\downarrow} & 1 & \boxed{\uparrow} & 1 & \boxed{\downarrow} & 0 & \boxed{\downarrow} \\
0 & & 0 & & 0 & & 1 \\
\boxed{\downarrow} & 1 & \boxed{\uparrow} & 1 & \boxed{\downarrow} & 0 & \boxed{\uparrow} \\
0 & & 1 & & 1 & & 1 \\
\boxed{\downarrow} & 0 & \boxed{\downarrow} & 1 & \boxed{\uparrow} & 1 & \boxed{\downarrow}
\end{array}
\qquad (17.6)
$$

For updating, the lattice is divided into two sublattices, much as in an ordinary checkerboard

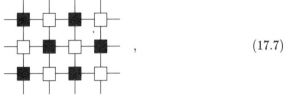

$$(17.7)$$

and the two sublattices are updated in alternation. Note that each bond joins two cells of different colors, so that at each step its energy may be modified only "from one end;" in this way, a purely local accounting scheme is adequate to make sure that energy is conserved.

In what follows, it will be more convenient to denote 'up' by $\boxed{1}$ and 'down' by $\boxed{0}$.

In the following sections we shall use the Ising-spin framework to simulate

• An isolated system, whose energy is strictly conserved.

• A system that exchanges energy with its environment, either

     − *explicitly*, by keeping track of individual transactions, so that the sum of the energies of the system and the environment is conserved, or

     − *implicitly*, by treating the environment as a massive thermal reservoir, or heat bath, which gives and takes energy from the system with certain probabilities but is not itself significantly affected by these exchanges. In the latter case the energy of the system is conserved only in a statistical sense.

The implicit (heat-bath) approach is traditional, having been used for many decades of numerical and theoretical work on the Ising model. The explicit-environment approach was introduced and extensively discussed by Creutz[13]. The isolated system approach (discussed in the next section) though conceptually simplest, has been used in large scale simulations only recently (by Herrmann[26]). It is based on the Q2R rule discovered by Vichniac[66] using CAM, and shown by Pomeau[45] to provide a conservative dynamics for the Ising model.

17.3   Spins only

With CAM, the above Ising system can be realized as follows. The spatial
phases are used to establish the checkerboard pattern (cf. Section 11.6), so
that even- and odd-numbered sites can be updated in alternation. Spins are
in plane 0, with state ☐ denoting "spin up" and ☐, "spin down." In the
currently active sublattice, any spin that can be flipped with no energy gain
or loss (with four neighbors, this corresponds to having exactly two neighbors
of each kind) *will* be flipped. The rule, called SPINS-ONLY, operates in the
following run-cycle context:

```
NEW-EXPERIMENT
N/VONN &/HV
                                    : ACTIVE-SITE ( -- F|T)
                    &HORZ &VERT = ;
                                    : 4SUM  ( -- 0,..,4)
        NORTH SOUTH WEST EAST + + + ;
                                    : U
                            CENTER ;    \ unchanged
                                    : FLIP
                        CENTER NOT ;    \ flipped
                                    : SPINS-ONLY
              ACTIVE-SITE IF
  4SUM { U U FLIP U U } ELSE
                CENTER THEN   >PLNO ;
  MAKE-TABLE SPINS-ONLY
                                    : CHANGE-LATTICE
              <ORG-H> NOT IS <ORG-H> ;
                                    : ALT-LATTICE
                  STEP  CHANGE-LATTICE ;
  MAKE-CYCLE ALT-LATTICE
```

The word ACTIVE-SITE locates those spins that belong to the currently active
checkerboard sublattice (&HORZ = &VERT); the alternation between active sublattices
is brought about by the run-cycle ALT-LATTICE, which complements the "phasing"
of &HORZ at every step. 4SUM counts the number of spin-up neighbors; SPINS-ONLY
uses this count to decide whether to flip a spin or leave it unchanged; the spin will be
flipped if it is in an indifferent energy situation, i.e., if it has exactly two neighbors
of each kind (4SUM =2).

Let's fill the plane at random with half of the spins up and half down
and run the rule: as one might expect, the chaos keeps churning and nothing
significant happens.

Now, let's try with one quarter of the spins up—a somewhat thinner
random soup. Soon this soup coalesces into an "emulsion" of smallish black
and white globs separated by irregular, unsteady boundaries (Figure 17.1a).
After a while, the amounts of black and white will be approximately equal; if

you measure and record step-after-step the fraction u of spins up (this can be done on-the-fly, without interrupting the simulation, as explained in Chapter 7.7), you'll find that this fraction remains close to $1/2$, with small, short-term fluctuations.

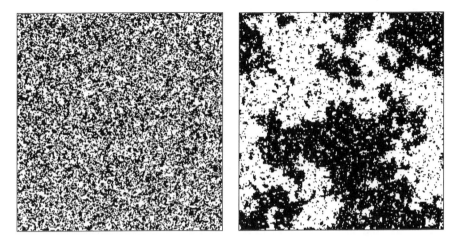

Figure 17.1: Equilibrium configuration (a) above the critical energy and (b) at the critical energy.

Note that the number of $\boxed{1}$'s is definitely *not* conserved. On the other hand, the overall length of the boundary between black and white areas is conserved; in fact, each unit segment of this boundary separates two adjacent spins having opposite orientations—and thus represents one unit of bond energy. For an initial random configuration in which spins up have a probability p, the (expected) energy per site,[2] ϵ, is given by the relation $\epsilon = 4p(1 - p)$, plotted below

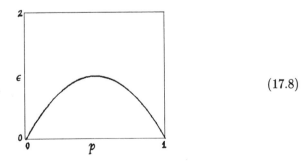

(17.8)

---

[2]It is convenient here to divide the total energy of the array, E, by the number of sites, so that the resulting energy range is independent of the size of the array.

This relation can be used to calibrate in terms of energy the dial of the random-number generator used for constructing the initial configuration.[3]

The dynamics of SPINS-ONLY is reversible, and indeed is equivalent (cf. Section 14.3) to a second-order reversible rule[66]. If you stop the simulation, issue the command CHANGE-LATTICE, and resume, the system will go backwards in time. If the system has run forward for two hours, on the backward run the fraction u of spins up will spend the best part of two hours hovering about $1/2$, in an apparently aimless way, but in the last few seconds it will suddenly drop down to $1/4$—the value you started with.

In place of the fraction u of spins up it is customary in the literature to speak of the *magnetization* of the sample, defined as $\mu = u - (1-u)$ (i.e., the fraction of spins up minus that of spins down). When all of the spins are up $\mu = +1$, while when they are all down $\mu = -1$.

As the initial random fraction of spins up—and correspondingly the energy ϵ—is gradually lowered, the average size of the black and white blobs becomes larger, but the equilibrium distribution of the two colors remains in balance ($\mu = 0$). This trend continues until ϵ reaches a critical value ϵ_{crit} (Figure 17.1b); at that point, μ very suddenly starts departing from zero. As the energy is further decreased below the critical value, μ will settle on one of the two values indicated in Figure 17.2: two distinct equilibrium states are equally possible, one with a white majority, as in Figure 17.3a, and one with a black majority. The curve was obtained experimentally by Charles Bennett, using CAM.

When ϵ is still just slightly below ϵ_{crit}—and thus the two values of μ differ by little—the system may occasionally be observed to swing quite suddenly from one equilibrium state to the other. At lower energies this spontaneous reversal of magnetization becomes virtually impossible.

For the above reason, some attention must be given to preparing symmetric initial conditions if one wants to observe the symmetry-breaking implied by Figure 17.2.[4] One procedure is to prepare a non-equilibrium state having $\epsilon < \epsilon_{\text{crit}}$ but $u = 1/2$. For example, one can fill half of the array with, say, 5% of $\boxed{1}$'s, and the other half with 5% of $\boxed{0}$'s. This balance is precarious: the boundary between the two regions will swing wildly (Figure 17.3b), the regions themselves will break up, and eventually one color will dominate (with equal chances for the two colors).

---

[3] The largest energy achievable with a *random* distribution of spins is $\epsilon = 1$, for $p = 1/2$. However, the largest possible value is $\epsilon = 2$, achieved by a completely *regular* configuration where one of the sublattices contains all $\boxed{1}$'s and the other all $\boxed{0}$'s; in this case, every bond is "excited."

[4] Note that in (17.8) the same value of ϵ can be obtained for two different settings of p. Below the critical point, however, the lower setting of p will result with overwhelming probability in the lower value for u (and similarly for the higher setting).

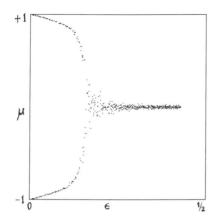

Figure 17.2: Magnetization μ versus energy ϵ. Below the critical value ϵ_{crit}, two distinct values of μ are possible.

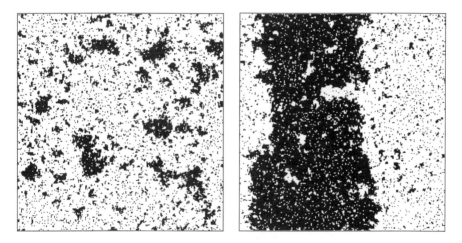

Figure 17.3: (a) One of the two equilibrium states below the critical energy. (b) Approach to equilibrium from a non-equilibrium state.

The sharpness of the critical point depends on the size of the array. Only in the ideal case of an infinitely extended array does this point become perfectly localized.

17.4 Energy banks

For a given spin system, consider the set $\Gamma(E)$ of all configurations having a certain energy E. A question of wide interest in statistical mechanics is how the properties of this set vary as a function of E.

Even for systems having a moderate number N of spins the size of this set is astronomical (since the number of configurations grows exponentially with N); it is clear that one cannot explicitly generate and examine all the configurations of a given energy. However, a relatively small sample of Γ may give a good approximation of the statistical properties of the entire set, provided that the sampling procedure is somehow "fair."

To construct such a sample one could choose new configurations completely at random, calculate their energy, and take only those whose energy equals E; this approach is extremely inefficient and is hardly ever used in practice. The dynamics discussed in the previous section can be seen as a cheaper approach to the same goal: one starts from a configuration of known energy E and by a series of local changes constructs new configurations having the same energy—thus walking more or less at random through the set $\Gamma(E)$. In this way one never has to explicitly calculate the energy of a configuration (only to realize, in the majority of cases, that that configuration was not among the ones sought!): one just "knows" that each new configuration has the same energy E as the initial one. On the other hand, with this timid exploratory approach one may get stuck forever in one "valley" of energy E: there may be no level path around a barrier that separates this valley from another one of equal energy (or existing level paths may be so long and devious that the chances of following one to the end are negligible). Can we set up a bank from which modest amounts of energy can be borrowed to go uphill, later to be returned when going downhill?

In the following Ising model, each cell is equipped with a little "piggy-bank" capable of storing just one coin—worth two energy units (cf. [13]). The spins will be in plane 0 as before, and the banks in plane 1. The instructions for each site are

- If you can flip the spin with no energy gain or loss, do it.

- If flipping would release two energy units and the bank is empty, flip the spin and put the energy in the bank.

- If flipping would require two units of energy and the bank is full, take the energy from the bank and flip the spin.

The new rule, SPINS-BANK, defined below, uses the same run-cycle environment as SPINS-ONLY of the previous example.[5]

---

[5]Plane 1 is now used for the banks rather than for the usual ECHO of plane 0 (cf. Section 3.2), and the colors on the screen will reflect this role. If an ECHO is desired, a plane of CAM-B can be devoted to this function, or an output function can be used to achieve the same effect without tying up a plane.

```
                            : BONDS ( -- 0,..,4)
    NORTH SOUTH WEST EAST + + +
        CENTER IF 4 SWAP - THEN ;
                            : GET
            CENTER' { 0 3 } ;
                            : PUT
            CENTER' { 3 0 } ;
                            : SPINS-BANK
                    CENTERS
                ACTIVE-SITE IF
        BONDS { 0 GET 1 PUT 0 }
                    XOR THEN
                        >PLNA ;
```

With CENTERS, we put the joint state of the spin and its bank on the stack, and then we use the value of the bond energy, namely BONDS, to decide how to alter this state—by XOR'ing it with an appropriate mask. A mask of 0 means no change; 1, complement only the spin bit; and 3, complement both spin and bank. BONDS is just the sum of the four neighbors if the spin bit is ⓪, and its complement relative to 4 if the spin bit is ①. If the bond energy is 0 or 4 we leave everything unchanged. If BONDS =2 we flip the spin without making recourse to the bank. GET and PUT, corresponding respectively to energy values of 1 and 3, check if the bank is available for the desired transaction; if so, they produce a mask that complements both bits of CENTERS (the spin bit, to flip the spin, and the bank bit, to move two units of energy in or out of the bank); otherwise they return a "no change" mask.

We can play with this rule. Start with empty banks and fill the spin plane with, say, 50% of ①'s. Run for a few seconds, until spins and banks are at equilibrium; since some of the initial bond energy is now stored away in the banks, the configuration in the spin plane will look pretty much like that of Figure 17.1a—where we had started with a lower energy. Now clear plane 1, thus wiping away all the savings; the spin configuration will adjust by making more deposits until the two forms of currency (bonds and savings) are again at equilibrium with one another (Figure 17.4a). You can repeat this procedure to bring the system to a state of lower and lower energy.

In the intervals between your interventions, the system's total energy is strictly constant. However, the energy of the spin component is, at equilibrium, only approximately constant; repeated measurements will reveal an energy distribution having some spread about a central value E. The appropriate parameter for describing the equilibrium state of the spin plane is no longer energy, but *temperature*:[6] stealing energy from the banks "cools" the spin system, and adding energy "heats" it. As in the previous model, a phase transition similar to that of Figure 17.2 will occur at a certain critical value

---

[6]In this context, the concept of 'temperature' is well-defined only in the limit of an *infinite* spin system; this term will acquire its strict technical sense even for a *finite* spin system in the model introduced in the next section.

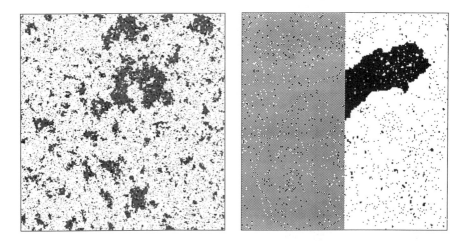

Figure 17.4: (a) Equilibrium state of Ising model with energy banks, a little below the critical point. Spins up are colored dark-gray (bank empty) or black (bank full), while spins down are colored respectively white and light-gray. (b) Checkered phases appear as the temperature goes above the upper critical point; the right half of the configuration is shown XOR'ed with a checkerboard pattern.

(of the energy of the spin/bank system, or of the temperature of the its spin component).

As we have seen, at low temperature the spin system neatly separates into two *phases* (states of matter having a well-defined composition and microscopic texture); in one phase most spins are aligned upwards, in the other, downwards. Regions of one phase are separated from regions of the other phase by boundaries that become more sharply defined and straighter as the temperature decreases (cf. Section 5.4). What will happen if we pump more and more energy into the banks? The result, shown in Figure 17.4b, could have been guessed from the cue of footnote 3. The system again separates into two phases; this time, however, in each phase adjacent spins are *anti-parallel* rather than parallel, and thus the microscopic arrangement is a checkered one; in one of the phases the $\boxed{1}$'s are positioned on the even sublattice, in the other, on the odd sublattice. (Figure 17.4b is a split-screen picture. The left-hand side shows only the spins, arranged in checkerboard domains that only differ by the relative phase of the checkerboard; the right-hand side of the picture is the right half of the same configuration, but was correlated, i.e., XOR'ed, with a checkerboard of a given phase, so as to clearly show the two kinds of domains.) In this spin system, increasing the energy beyond a certain point brings about order rather than disorder![7] The curve that plots the fraction

---

[7]This phenomenon is well known in physics, and has led to the coining the term "negative temperature." One may imagine the temperature axis to be wrapped around, so that

v occupied by either of the two checkered phases runs for a while at the level
1/2 as the temperature is increased but eventually, as more energy is added,
splits into two lines (in analogy with that of Figure 17.2). Thus, alongside a
critical temperature associated with the parallel phases, the system possesses
a second critical temperature associated with the anti-parallel ones.

17.5 Heat bath

In the previous example (spins with banks) one might be tempted to view the
bond energy as *potential* energy, and the energy stored in each bank as *kinetic*
energy associated with the corresponding spin: if a spin has enough kinetic
energy it can use it to climb a potential hill of a certain height. However, this
analogy does not lend itself to useful generalizations; what really matters is
that we have introduced a new energy account in addition to that of inter-
spin bonds, and that the two accounts are coupled in a reversible way so that
they can achieve statistical equilibrium with one another.

The capacity of the banks may be increased,[8] neighboring banks may be
allowed to transfer energy between one another, and transactions may be
subject to more complicated rules (for example, a spin may not be allowed
to perform two bank transactions in a row). As we proceed in this direction,
from the viewpoint of an individual spin the mechanics of the underlying
banking complex becomes too involved to track in detail, and (as in real life)
transactions with the bank take on a probabilistic flavor. The concept of
heat has been invented to deal with energy that presents itself in this random
form.

From a macroscopic point of view one may visualize the array of spins
as laid out on a *thermal substrate* having a heat capacity proportional to
the size of the banks and a thermal conductivity proportional to the ease of
exchanging sums between banks. Near equilibrium, deposits and withdrawals
made by an individual spin average out in the long run, and the banks have
time to equalize their holdings; in this situation, the whole banking complex
can be treated as a monolithic heat reservoir whose willingness to supply
energy is described by a single parameter, namely *temperature.*

From a practical point of view, the heat-bath approach dispenses with
the many variables representing the banks, and replaces them by a random
number generator which decides each banking transaction probabilistically.

---

by increasing the temperature one eventually reaches zero again, passing through negative
temperatures of decreasing absolute value. With this convention, the two ordered textures
(all parallel, all anti-parallel) of the spin lattice both correspond to temperatures that are
close to zero—one positive and the other negative.

[8]With the resources of one CAM module, for example, an easy thing to do is use the
bits of a third plane so that banks can deal with coins worth four—as well as two—energy
units (in this way, isolated ⓵'s and ⓪'s also get a chance to flip).

It is an elementary result of equilibrium statistical mechanics that a heat bath has a well-defined temperature T if and only if, for any energy change ΔE, the probability $P(\Delta E)$ that a request for a loan of size ΔE will be granted and the probability $P(-\Delta E)$ that a deposit of the same amount will be accepted are connected by the relation

$$\frac{P(\Delta E)}{P(-\Delta E)} = e^{-\frac{\Delta E}{kT}},   \tag{17.9}$$

where k is a proportionality constant that defines the units in which temperature is measured.

To set up a CAM experiment appropriate to this situation, observe that, in the spin system we have been considering, a spin flip may only involve one of the following values for the change of energy of the spin system, ΔE

$$-4, -2, 0, +2, +4,$$

(as one can easily verify). Therefore, the corresponding probabilities

$$p_{-4}, p_{-2}, p_0, p_2, p_4$$

must be set up so that

$$\frac{p_4}{p_{-4}} = (\frac{p_2}{p_{-2}})^2, \quad \text{and} \quad \frac{p_2}{p_{-2}} = e^{-\frac{2J}{kT}},$$

where the energy amount associated with a bond has been written as J so as to make the dimensional aspects clearer. Since we are dealing only with ratios, there is some latitude in choosing the probabilities themselves; for simplicity, we shall choose $p_0 = p_2 = p_4 = 1$, so that the final values are

$$p^2, p, 1, 1, 1,   \tag{17.10}$$

with

$$T = \frac{2J}{k \log p}.   \tag{17.11}$$

The last relation allows us to calibrate the setting p of the random number generator in terms of T.

We shall put the spins in plane 0, as usual, and use CAM-B as a random-number generator. In CAM-B, each plane will independently provide 1's with a probability p, so that by AND'ing the two bits one obtains 1's with a probability p^2. Access to CAM-B demands that the minor neighbor assignment for CAM-A be &/CENTERS —and thus cuts us off from access to the spatial phases. To avoid using a custom neighborhood, we shall synthesize the ACTIVE-SITE pseudo-neighbor by initializing plane 1 with with a checkerboard pattern and complementing this plane at every step, much as we did in Section 10.1. The rule for this system is

```
CAM-A N/VONN &/CENTERS
                                    : ACTIVE-SITE ( -- 0|1)
                          CENTER' ;      \ checkerboard
                                    : CHANGE-LATTICE
                    CENTER' NOT >PLN1 ; \ complement chckrbrd
MAKE-TABLE CHANGE-LATTICE
                                    : P  ( -- 0|1)
                         &CENTER ;
                                    : P2 ( -- 0|1)
             &CENTER &CENTER' AND ;
                                    : 4SUM
    NORTH SOUTH WEST EAST + + + ;
                                    : DELTA ( -- 0,..,4)
                       CENTER IF
                       4SUM ELSE
                    4 4SUM - THEN ;
                                    : SPIN-CANON
                          CENTER
                    ACTIVE-SITE IF
             DELTA { P2 P 1 1 }
                        XOR THEN
                            >PLNO ;
MAKE-TABLE SPIN-CANON
```

From the state of the cell and that of its neighbors, **DELTA** computes the value of the energy exchange in a form that is useable by the case statement (i.e., $\Delta E/2 + 2$ rather than ΔE). This value is used by **SPIN-CANON** to select one of the five probability values assigned in (17.10). The bits **P** and **P2**, corresponding to the probabilities p and p^2, are obtained from the random-number generator in CAM-B.

A system such as the **SPIN-CANON** model that exchanges energy freely with an external thermal reservoir is called *canonical*. By contrast a self contained deterministic system such as the **SPINS-ONLY** model of Section 17.3 is called *microcanonical*. The behavior of the two models is nevertheless rather similar, because in the microcanonical model each part of the system exchanges energy with a "thermal reservoir" consisting of the rest of the system. Figure 17.5 shows (a) a typical configuration and (b) a time-exposure just below the critical temperature. Note that, unlike Figure 17.3a, there are no isolated spins that remain stuck in the same direction for a long time: the thermal reservoir is capable of giving or accepting, with an appropriate probability, *any* amount of energy.[9]

In Figure 17.6 we show the magnetization-vs-temperature curve for this system, as determined experimentally by Charles Bennett on a large number

---

[9]Two-bit bankers, capable of loaning the entire energy needed for an isolated spin to flip, allow a system to overcome energy barriers almost as efficiently as with a thermal reservoir[13].

of runs with CAM.[10]

From a practical viewpoint, the introduction of a heat bath is justified by a faster and more thorough equilibration. On the other hand, the explicit banks and the spins-only approach preserve certain aspects of the *dynamics* of a real physical system that are lost with the heat bath approach. "Because the temperature of the system is internally determined, heat flow and thermal conductivity can be studied numerically. It is not clear that these concepts have any meaning in a conventional Monte Carlo simulation."[13]

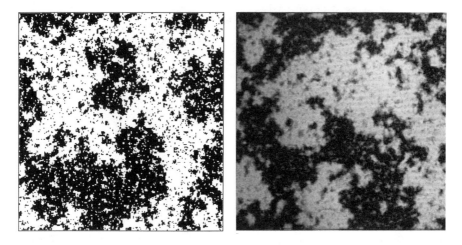

Figure 17.5: (a) Typical spin configuration in the canonical model, near the critical temperature. (b) Time-exposure in the same conditions; no spins remain stuck indefinitely.

17.6   Displaying the energy

So far, energy in the Ising model has played the role of a rather abstract quantity—a *relation* between objects (the spins) rather than an *object* itself.[11] As a preliminary to constructing models in which energy is treated as a state variable on its own account, it will be useful to give it a more material existence by directly displaying it on the screen.

Let's go back to the "spins only" model of Section 17.3, where the only energy involved is that of the inter-spin bonds. This energy sits, so to speak,

---

[10]To minimize correlations in the random-number generator—and thus achieve results that could be directly compared with those in the literature—this experiment used the technique mentioned at the end of Section 15.6.

[11]In the lattice gas models considered before, the energy is purely kinetic and accompanies the particles in a one-to-one correspondence, so that this distinction does not arise.

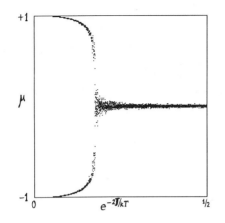

Figure 17.6: Magnetization μ in the canonical-ensemble model, versus the Monte Carlo acceptance probability. Note the sharp transition at the critical temperature T_{crit}.

on the edges between adjacent cells, and these edges are twice as many as the cells, so that we cannot devote a whole pixel to each energy token. A simple solution is to associate with each pixel the total bond energy of the corresponding spin, and represent the five possible values, 0 through 4, by five colors or five levels of gray. Note that each bond will give a contribution to two adjacent pixels, since it "belongs" to two spins, and thus will be somewhat smeared in the picture. We can get a sharper picture if we associate with each pixel only the two bonds to the north and to the west of it, so that each bond appears only in one place on the screen. Let's use this second approach, and choose to represent the three energy levels for a pixel, 0, 1, and 2, respectively by white, gray, and black.

Naturally, we would like to display the energy *while the simulation is running*, so that we can directly view its evolution; therefore we need *two* look-up tables—one to compute the next state of a cell and send it to the bit-planes (*transition function*), and one to compute the cell's bond energy and send it to the monitor (*output function*); both of these tables must see the whole neighborhood. As explained in Section 7.7, computing an output function is one of the intended uses for the auxiliary tables.

The energy of the north and west bonds is computed by the auxiliary table programmed as follows

```
                     : ENERGY-DISPLAY
        NORTH CENTER XOR >AUX0      \ north bond
        WEST CENTER XOR >AUX1 ;     \ west bond
MAKE-TABLE ENERGY-DISPLAY
```

The command SHOW-FUNCTION instructs the color map to take its input data from this table rather than directly from the planes.

If we run the experiment of Figure 17.3a in this fashion, we'll see energy "ropes" wiggling about the screen, as in Figure 17.7; a good deal of the energy is concentrated on the boundaries between spin-up and spin-down domains, while the rest surrounds isolated spins. Not only is energy conserved, but it is conserved on a *local* basis: it cannot increase here and decrease there without passing through the points in between. In other words, it obeys the *continuity equation*, and on the screen one can observe it smoothly *flow* from place to place.

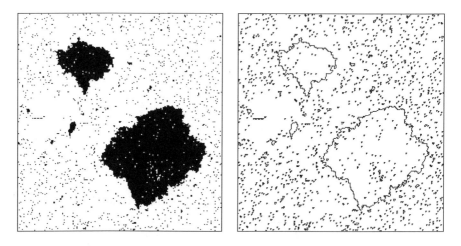

Figure 17.7: (a) A typical spin configuration; (b) the same configuration, but displaying the energy rather than the spins.

Assume, for a moment, that we were displaying on the screen each individual bond, rather than bunching them two per pixel.[12] The energy picture on the screen would still contain less information than the spin plane; that is, knowing the state of the spins one can always calculate the bond energy, but knowing this energy one is left with some uncertainty as to the state of the spins. For example, if you see a sharp energy line here you know that the spins on the two sides of it are pointing in opposite directions; but you can't tell on *which* side the "up" spins are.

On the other hand, the motions through which the energy goes on the screen seem to have a definite logic of their own. The question we are going to ask is, "From a given energy configuration, do we have enough information to determine the *next energy configuration*? Can we give a dynamics for the energy alone?"

---

[12]We could color the north bond red and the west one green, so that yellow would indicate the presence of both.

More formally, if τ is the dynamics of the spins and v the energy function, as in the following diagram

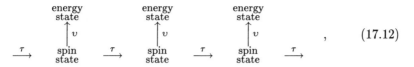

$$(17.12)$$

can we construct a dynamics τ' directly for the energy, obeying the following commutative diagram?

$$(17.13)$$

17.7 Bonds only

For the spins-only model, the answer to the previous question is, Yes! The best way to convince ourselves of this is to make a cellular-automaton model of a spin system in which the energy bonds themselves, rather than the spins, play the role of state-variables.

In this model the contents of each cell corresponds to the state of a bond. In the following diagram the squares represent cells, just as in Figure 12.1, and the spins (which are not explicitly represented in the model) must be imagined sitting at the intersections of two thick lines or two thin lines, in the positions indicated by the small black boxes.

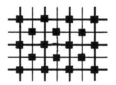

The following diagram illustrates a typical configuration of spin values and bond values in the new layout

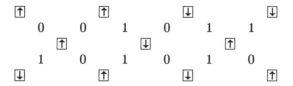

Note that, with respect to the previous model (cf. diagram (17.6)), the axes of the spin lattice have been rotated by 45° and the scale magnified by $\sqrt{2}$.

The area corresponding to a given portion of the system is now twice as large—which is not surprising since there are twice as many bonds as spins.

In this diagram, assuming that it's the turn of the middle row's spins to be updated, after one step the situation will have changed to

$$
\begin{array}{cccccc}
\boxed{\uparrow} & & \boxed{\uparrow} & & \boxed{\downarrow} & & \boxed{\downarrow} \\
0 & 0 & 0 & 1 & 1 & 1 \\
& \boxed{\uparrow} & & \boxed{\uparrow} & & \boxed{\uparrow} \\
1 & 0 & 0 & 1 & 1 & 0 \\
\boxed{\downarrow} & & \boxed{\uparrow} & & \boxed{\downarrow} & & \boxed{\uparrow}
\end{array}
\quad ,
$$

Only the spin at the center of the picture has flipped, since according to the SPINS-ONLY rule a spin flips when its bond energy equals 2.

Note that when this happens, all four bonds surrounding the spin are affected; thus, for the evolution of the bonds we'll need a block rule with four cells to a block. Moreover, the spins on the thick lines are updated in alternation with those on the thin lines (since SPINS-ONLY uses alternating checkerboard sublattices); therefore the alternating block-partitions of the Margolus neighborhood will suit us perfectly.

Denoting a unit of energy by a "particle," the bond-updating rule corresponding to the spin-updating rule SPINS-ONLY is

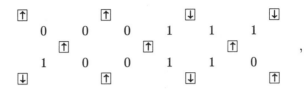

$$
\tag{17.14}
$$

all other entries being "no change." This rule, which we'll call BONDS-ONLY, is illustrated in Plate 14. Besides the scale factor, the structure is of the same kind as that of 17.7b.

By comparing the new model with the old we can gain some insight into the dynamics of an Ising system.

To begin with, if the energy picture is an incomplete one, in the sense that it lacks some of the information, how can it so faithfully track the evolution of the spin picture? How much information is actually missing?

Consider the spin model, and flip *all* the spins: the energy does not change, but neither does the evolution change—the only difference is that black areas are now white and vice versa: the dynamics is invariant under complementation.[13] The decision to interpret the state of a cell as "spin up" or "spin down" is a single binary choice; once that choice is made, the interpretation for all the other cells is completely determined by the values of the

---

[13]In the physical counterpart of an Ising system, this symmetry would be broken by the presence an external magnetic field. The interaction of spins in a field requires, of course, a more complex model.

bonds. The bit corresponding to that choice is the only piece of information that is missing from the energy picture—and its value *does not change in time*: why bother to carry it along all the way through the simulation? This is precisely what the energy model manages to avoid.

In conclusion, the dynamics of the spin system can be "factored" into two components. One consists of a single bit, which is constant; the other component is indistinguishable from the dynamics of the bond-energy system.

Having gained this insight, we may now ask, "If the new model manages to shirk carrying the burden of a 'dead' bit, how come it ends up using twice as much storage as the old model? What is all that extra information doing anyhow?"

Let us consider a configuration of bonds like that of (17.15a), and try to reconstruct a compatible configuration for the surrounding spins.

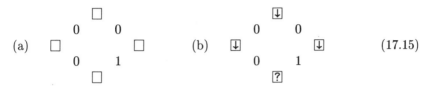

$$\text{(a)} \qquad\qquad \text{(b)} \qquad\qquad (17.15)$$

If we choose ⬇ for the spin at the top of the diagram, as in (17.15b), the two spins adjacent to it must have the same orientation as it, since the corresponding bonds have zero energy; however, the orientation of the last spin (marked ⁇) cannot be assigned in a way that is consistent with the remaining two bonds—one of which suggests ⬇ and the other ⬆ for it.

Thus, many of the possible bond configurations are not compatible with *any* spin configuration,[14] and in this sense are meaningless as initial states for the energy model: in creating an initial configuration for this model, for every ten bonds that we can freely specify there will be ten whose assignment is forced.

In view of this redundancy, does the energy model have any redeeming features? Can we put this redundancy to some good use?

17.8 Spin glasses

Let us retrace our steps back to Section 17.2, where we had considered a row of spins connected by elastic bonds. If two adjacent spins were parallel, the

---

[14]To see what configurations are not legitimate, consider the two 2×2-block partitions (out of the four possible) that are not used by the Margolus neighborhood. The *parity* of the energy of any of these blocks (that is, whether the value of the energy is *even* or *odd*) remains unchanged when a spin—or, for that matter, any number of spins—is flipped. In the energy configuration consisting of all zero's, which is certainly legitimate because it corresponds to all spins parallel, all these blocks have even parity; thus, the legitimate energy configurations are those where *all* these blocks have an even parity.

bond between them was "relaxed;" if they were anti-parallel, the bond was "excited." A bond of this kind is called *ferromagnetic*.

In different physical situations the coupling between spins is better described by *anti-ferromagnetic* bonds, which have the opposite properties—i.e., are relaxed when the spins are *anti-parallel*. The behavior of anti-ferromagnetic spin systems is of course different from that of the ferromagnetic ones. However, in the absence of an external magnetic field the difference between the two systems is trivial: if every other spin of a ferromagnetic system is "read" as if it had the opposite orientation, then its dynamics is identical to that of an anti-ferromagnetic one. With this proviso, the same model will do double duty (cf. the symmetry between parallel phases at low temperatures and anti-parallel phases at high temperatures mentioned at the end of Section 17.4).

There are also systems, called *spin glasses*, that are best modeled assuming that a random fraction of the bonds are of a ferromagnetic nature and the remainder anti-ferromagnetic. Thus, in a spin-glass model the nature of each bond must be explicitly specified, as in the following diagram—where '=' denotes a ferromagnetic bond and '$\neq$' an antiferromagnetic one.

$$
\begin{array}{llllllll}
\boxed{\downarrow} & 1= & \boxed{\uparrow} & 0\neq & \boxed{\downarrow} & 1\neq & \boxed{\downarrow} & \\
0= & & 0= & & 1\neq & & 1= & \\
\boxed{\downarrow} & 1= & \boxed{\uparrow} & 1= & \boxed{\downarrow} & 0= & \boxed{\uparrow} & , \\
0= & & 0\neq & & 1= & & 1= & \\
\boxed{\downarrow} & 1\neq & \boxed{\downarrow} & 1= & \boxed{\uparrow} & 1= & \boxed{\downarrow} &
\end{array}
\qquad (17.16)
$$

The energy of a bond is now a function not only of the orientation of the spins it connects, but also of the type (ferromagnetic or anti-ferromagnetic) of the bond itself.

Spin glasses represent an important paradigm for the study of order and disorder in matter[41], as well as for certain recent approaches to optimization[30,49]. In most simple physical systems the equilibrium state at low temperature, or *ground state*, is essentially unique. Certain Ising systems display two distinct ground states, as we have seen in the previous sections, and that is unusual enough to make them interesting. Spin glasses display a *multitude* of ground states—a property which allows for the nontrivial storage and processing of information.

Since the total number of bonds is twice that of spins, if we want to model a spin-glass system by a cellular automaton in which the state variables correspond to the *spins*, as in Section 17.3, we'll need *three* bits of information per site; that is, the state of the spin and, for instance, the type of the north bond and that of the west bond (cf. beginning of Section 17.6). The information about the bonds can be stored in two extra bit-planes;[15] note that these

---

[15]In CAM, one could use planes 2 and 3 for this purpose, and use a custom neighborhood in order to allow CAM-A to see more than just &CENTERS.

bit-planes would not have to be updated, since the type of an individual bond is a fixed parameter of the model rather than a state variable. We shall not bother the reader with implementation details, except for remarking that the two lattices (one for the spins and one for the bonds) have a slightly different structure and are offset with respect to one another; from an implementation viewpoint this constitutes a minor nuisance.

When we turn our attention to a cellular-automaton model in which cells represent bond states rather than spin states, as was the case in the previous section for Ising systems, we are in for a pleasant surprise. The simple BONDS-ONLY rule of (17.14), which we repeat here

$$
\begin{matrix}
\boxed{} \mapsto \boxed{} \\
\boxed{} \mapsto \boxed{}
\end{matrix}
\tag{17.17}
$$

is perfectly adequate for modeling the new system, and the redundancy that we had noted there—the extra burden of information we were carrying along—is just enough to allow us to represent the effect of bonds of two different types. The problem of (17.15a)—to find an assignment of spins compatible with a given assignment of bonds—always has a solution now that the unknowns are not only spins but also bond types; here is a possible solution

$$
\begin{array}{cccccc}
 & & \square & & & \boxed{\downarrow} & \\
 & 0 & & 0 & & 0= & 0= \\
(a) & \square & & \square & (b) & \boxed{\downarrow} & \boxed{\downarrow} \\
 & 0 & & 1 & & 0= & 1\neq \\
 & & \square & & & \boxed{\downarrow} &
\end{array}
\tag{17.18}
$$

Indeed, there is a *multiplicity* of solutions—but all of them lead to the same dynamics for the energy. As before, the energy model "factors out" some information that is irrelevant to the dynamics; in this case, however, this information is much more than just one bit: it's actually one bit per site. By shedding this burden, the "energy" model manages to capture the dynamics of a spin-glass system by using only *two* bits per site (rather than three as in the "spin" model).[16]

The notation (17.17) clearly shows that in this model energy is treated as an indestructible material particle that can move about subject to certain constraints; energy conservation and reversibility are made obvious.

In conclusion, a certain kind of system may have come to our attention because of its theoretical relevance, and we may be tempted to look upon

---

[16] A transformation that can be applied to a system without affecting its dynamics is called a *gauge* transformation; here, a single "energy" system models a whole class of "spin" systems that are equivalent up to a gauge transformation.

issues of how to concretely model it as being of marginal conceptual importance. However, a careful analysis of implementation methods and trade-offs may lead not only to models that are more compact and efficient, but also to models that provide a better insight into the system itself.

Chapter 18

Ballistic computation

What kind of building blocks must one have available in order to build computers?

Arguments developed by mathematical logic and computer science in the last few decades show that if the issue is just one of feasibility—rather than speed or efficiency—extremely simple hardware, when available in a sufficiently large amount, is capable of performing the most complex computing task that can be performed by *any* hardware at all (cf. Section 5.5). In principle, evolution, life, and intelligence can take place within a world governed by a very simple cellular-automaton rule.

The arguments mentioned above do not worry about whether the primitive mechanisms used in the construction are *reversible*, and in fact today's computers are based on *noninvertible* logic elements. For example, the AND gate, defined by the following input/output table

p	q	p AND q
0	0	0
0	1	0
1	0	0
1	1	1

,

yields an irreversible computation step: when the output is 0 you can't tell for sure what the input was; assuming that the four input combinations occur with equal probabilities, the AND operation *erases* about 1.19 bits of information.

However, the microscopic mechanisms of physics are (as far as we know) strictly reversible; how do people manage, then, to build and operate computers containing irreversible logic elements such as the AND gate? What is actually done is the following. The irreversible behavior of a logic element is *simulated* by a rather large and complex (by microscopic standards) piece of *reversible* machinery. The information that the logical element seems to be erasing is not destroyed after all (this can't happen in physics)—it is just turned into heat and carried elsewhere by an air conditioner; at the same time, a fresh supply of signals is provided by a power supply. All of this is unavoidable as long as we insist on building computers out of irreversible logic (cf. Landauer's seminal paper[32].)

Can one design a computer based on *reversible* logical elements?[4] Can such elements be implemented directly at the level of microscopic physics?[1]

The model of computation presented here is based on reversible mechanisms of the kind considered by classical mechanics (which is not actual physics yet, but a useful idealization of it). We'll also implement this model as a cellular automaton. In this way we'll make two points: (a) that cellular automata can easily model certain aspects of physics, and (b) that, even when requested to obey the constraint of microscopic reversibility, these models are powerful enough to be capable of displaying arbitrarily complex behavior.

18.1   The billiard-ball model of computation

In the course of research concerned with the ultimate physical bases of computation, Edward Fredkin of MIT devised a model of digital computation[17] which explicitly reflects some basic properties of physics—in particular, the reversibility of microscopic processes.

In this two-dimensional model, identical balls of finite diameter travel at constant speed and collide elastically with one another and with flat mirrors. The computation is encoded in the initial condition of the system and performed by the ordinary dynamics of the collisions. A bit of information is represented by the presence or the absence of a ball at a given time and place; wires are represented by the possible ball paths, routed as needed by mirrors; and logic operations are performed where two balls may collide (the presence or absence of a ball on a given path may influence, via a collision, whether a ball will be present or absent on another path).

The "billiard-ball" model of computation is based on an idealized description of a gas which is essentially identical to the model that physicists took historically as the basis of the kinetic theory. A gas is conceived of as a swarm of spheres of finite diameter which collide elastically between themselves and with the container's walls; the mechanics of collisions is governed by short-range repulsive forces. The novelty of the billiard-ball model consists in directing one's attention to the detailed evolution in time of an individual

---

[1]Even if reversibility is no longer an issue, there could be difficulties of some other nature.

microscopic state, rather than of some macroscopic quantities defined on a statistical distribution of states.

This kinetic model is a classical-mechanical system and obeys a continuous dynamics—positions and times, velocities and masses are all real variables. In order to make it perform digital computation, we make use of the fact that integers are just a special case of real numbers: by suitably restricting the system's initial conditions we can make a continuous dynamics perform a digital process. More specifically, we shall (a) assign to the balls (which correspond to gas molecules) very special initial conditions, (b) give to the collection of mirrors (which corresponds to the container's walls) a very special spatial arrangement, and (c) only look at the system at discrete, regularly spaced time intervals. The result is a reversible mechanical system having computation-universal capabilities.

The interested reader may refer to [17,35] for a thorough exposition of the subject. The following brief notes will be sufficient for our present purposes.

Cartesian grid. Each ball will start at a grid point of a two-dimensional Cartesian lattice, moving "along" the grid in one of four directions. All balls travel at the same speed, moving from one grid point to the next in one time unit. The grid spacing is chosen so that balls collide while at grid points. All collisions take place at right-angles, so that one time-step after a collision balls are still on the grid. Fixed mirrors are positioned so that balls hit them while at grid points, and so stay on the grid.

Balls as signals. The presence or the absence of a ball at any grid point can be interpreted as a binary variable associated with that point, taking on a value of 1 or 0 (for "ball" and 'no ball," respectively) at integer times. The correlations between such variables reflect the movements of the balls themselves. In particular, one may speak of binary "signals" traveling in space and interacting with one another.

Collisions as gates. In the billiard-ball model, *every place where a collision might occur may be viewed as a Boolean logic gate.* With reference to Figure 18.1, let p, q denote the presence or the absence, at a given instant, of balls having the indicated position and direction. The variables p and q will be thought of as input signals for a gate residing at the intersection of the two paths; similarly, the variables associated at an appropriate later time (four steps later in the figure) with the indicated four points on the outgoing paths will represent output signals. It is clear that the output variables will have, in the order shown in the figure, the values $pq, \bar{p}q, p\bar{q}$, and pq again. In other words, if there are balls present at *both* inputs, these two balls will collide and follow the outer output paths; if only one input ball is present, this ball will go straight and come out on an inner output path. Of course, with no balls at the inputs there will be no balls at any of the outputs.

Since the interaction gate of Figure 18.1 can realize the AND function and, if one of the inputs is kept constant (a constant stream of balls), also the NOT function, this gate is a universal logic element.

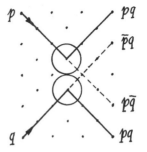

Figure 18.1: The "interaction gate"—a way of performing a logic function by means of ball collisions.

Mirrors as routers. To make circuitry out of gates, one must establish the appropriate interconnections, that is, route balls from one collision locus to another with proper timing. In particular, since we are considering a two-dimensional system, one must provide a way to perform signal crossover. All these requirements are met by introducing mirrors. As shown in Figure 18.2, by letting balls collide with fixed mirrors one can easily deflect the trajectory of a ball, shift it sideways, introduce an arbitrary delay, and guarantee correct crossover (in Figure18.2d, note that when two balls are present the *signals* cross even though the balls don't). Of course, no active precautions need be taken for *trivial* crossover, where the logic or the timing are such that two balls cannot possibly be present at the same moment at the crossover point.

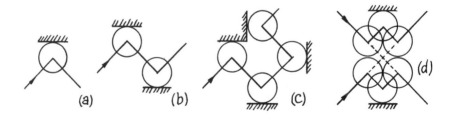

Figure 18.2: Mirrors—indicated by solid dash—can be used (a) to deflect a ball's path, (b) to introduce a sideways shift, (c) to introduce a delay, and (d) to realize nontrivial crossover.

In conclusion, with the above machinery one can synthesize any logic elements and connect them in any desired way. Since a binary signal is encoded in a single ball, and little clearance between ball streams is needed for routing purposes, computations can be pipelined so that all stages of the circuit are kept constantly busy.

With the given constraints on initial conditions, a collection of balls that are on the same vertical line and have the same horizontal velocity component will maintain this alignment as long as they collide only with themselves or with horizontal mirrors. This feature allows one to use easy graphical methods to arrive at the proper geometry and timing for complex collision patterns (cf. Figure 18.3), and makes it easy to maintain the overall synchronization required for efficient pipelining.

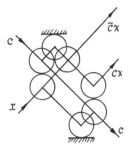

Figure 18.3: A simple realization of the "switch gate" (a two-way demultiplexer).

18.2 A reversible cellular-automaton computer

Once we restrict the initial positions of balls and mirrors to a regular grid, permit only a finite set of velocities, specify the dynamics so that these constraints are preserved at all integral times, and observe the system only at these times, we obtain a discrete dynamical system that can be translated into a cellular automaton.

In this section we shall discuss such a realization. Certain features depart even farther from concrete physics than those of the idealized physical model of the previous section (for instance, here balls will have a "diameter" only along the direction of motion). On the other hand, other features are more realistic; for example, collisions are not instantaneous: since balls have extension in space and no action at a distance is permitted, a collision will affect one part of a ball before another. Intuitively speaking, elasticity of an extended ball cannot be postulated, but must be "synthesized" out of the ball's internal degrees of freedom.

Since the billiard-ball model is basically a gas model, it will come as no surprise that our cellular automaton realization is closely related to the gas models we have discussed in previous chapters.[2] We shall pick up our thread from the SWAP-ON-DIAG rule of Section 12.2, where particles travel with uniform motion along the diagonals of the array without interacting. The HPP-GAS rule, described immediately after (Section 12.3), introduced momentum-conserving collisions; these interactions are not adequate by themselves for our present purposes because (a) they treat the particles as if they were of zero diameter, and (b) they do not provide some "cohesive" effects out of which fixed mirrors can be built (in fact, in order to make a container for HPP-GAS we have to postulate a second kind of "matter," supported by an extra bit plane, as explained in Section 15.2).

Here, we shall also employ interactions that do not conserve momentum. *Note that the "balls" of the billiard-ball model will not be identified directly with the elementary particles of this system; rather, out of these particles we shall construct both balls and mirrors as composite objects.*

The BBM rule[35] utilizes the Margolus neighborhood, and is given by the table

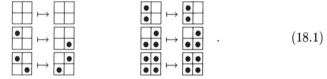

$$(18.1)$$

In this table, the first three entries and the last one are identical to those of HPP-GAS; the other two entries will require a more detailed discussion.

Observe that the contents of a block is modified only if there are one or two particles present. After defining a separate Forth word to take care of the special two-particle case, the BBM rule is easily expressed in CAM Forth

```
                         : 2PART
          CENTER OPP = IF
                   CW ELSE
             CENTER THEN  ;
                         : BBM
     CENTER CW CCW OPP  + + +
  { U OPP 2PART U U }  >PLNO ;
```

where U is an abbreviation for "unchanged" (i.e., CENTER) as in Section 5.2.

Mirrors. We shall now discuss the effect of the fourth entry of table (18.1). When two particles (moving diagonally as in HPP-GAS) collide at right angles, the direction of each is reversed and the particles "bounce back" on their tracks (Figure 18.4). This interaction (which doesn't conserve momentum) allows a group of particles to form a "bound" state. In Figure 18.5a,

---

[2]The Margolus neighborhood was originally developed as a way to "cheat" and produce a simple version of the billiard-ball model as a cellular automaton. It was only later that we developed other uses for it, such as gas models.

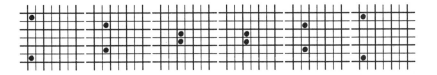

Figure 18.4: Right-angle collision of particles: the particles bounce back on their tracks. Both here and in the following diagram the first step of the sequence uses the blocks of the even grid (thick lines); the second step, the odd grid (thin lines); and so on in alternation.

four particles bounce back-and-forth in a diamond pattern; when this pattern is shrunk to the point that the four particles are in contact (Figure 18.5b) the particles can be interpreted as reversing direction at each step without having a chance to move, and thus are effectively frozen in place. This is the most compact form of a *fixed mirror* (notice that the four particles forming such a frozen group straddle two adjacent blocks). A particle colliding with a mirror will also bounce back on its track, as specified by the fifth entry of table (18.1). Mirrors can be extended by juxtaposition (as, for instance, in Figure 18.7).

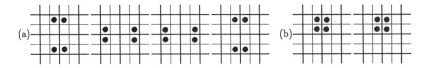

Figure 18.5: Bound states: (a) Four particles bounce back-and-forth in a diamond pattern. (b) In their most closely packed arrangement, the four balls stick together and form a fixed mirror.

Balls. The "balls" of the billiard-ball model are, like mirrors, composite objects, and consist of two particles traveling in the same direction on the same track and separated by a fixed distance. The right-angle collision between two balls (Figure 18.6) involves multiple collisions between the individual particles that make up the balls, utilizing at one time or another all of the first four entries of table (18.1). Note that, as far as the (composite) balls are concerned, such collisions are momentum-conserving.

If one observes the trajectories of two balls whose paths intersect, and compares the case when the balls approach the intersection at the same time (and so will collide) with the case when they approach it at different times (and so will cross it at different moments without colliding), one will notice

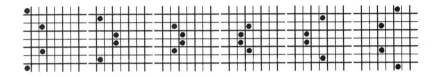

Figure 18.6: Ball-to-ball collision, starting on the odd grid (thin lines).

that the geometry and the timing of the outgoing paths have different characteristics. After a collision, the outgoing paths are not straight-line continuations of the incoming paths (cf. Figure 18.1); moreover, the balls have been delayed by the collision. This is what one would expect from "soft"—though elastic—balls.

Analogous considerations apply to the collisions of balls with mirrors (Figure 18.7). Note that the mirrors act as if they had infinite mass, and with this interpretation the collisions between balls and mirrors are also momentum-conserving.

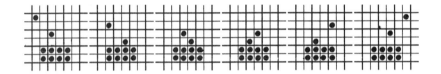

Figure 18.7: Ball-to-mirror collision, starting on the even grid (thick lines).

In conclusion, we have constructed a structure that at the finest level can be interpreted as a gas of pointlike particles with interactions which don't always conserve momentum. At a higher level, and as long as certain constraints in the initial conditions are met, the same structure can be interpreted as a system of finite-diameter balls and fixed mirrors with a dynamics which is surprisingly realistic from a physical viewpoint and is perfectly adequate as a realization of the billiard-ball model of computation. Figure 18.8 represents a digital circuit of a certain complexity, realized with the BBM rule.[3]

---

[3]Since in this realization collisions are "soft," delays have been introduced in certain signal paths to make free-traveling balls keep in step with with balls that have been retarded by a collision. One can get the delays right by noting that the number of steps it takes for a ball to traverse any signal path is exactly equal to the number of cells visited at least once (by a particle) along the path, including extra cells visited during collisions.

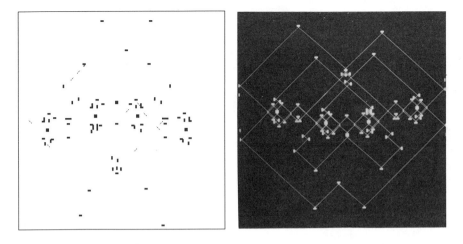

Figure 18.8: BBM-CA circuit: (a) snapshot and (b) time-exposure.

18.3 Some billiard-ball experiments

In this section we'll describe two experiments that can be performed using the BBM cellular automaton and a machine such as CAM.

Unlike irreversible rules such as LIFE, not much will happen if we start BBM from a random initial state: as a gas, a random configuration is an equilibrium system, and no further evolution is expected. However, when **you** run the universe, you can arrange miracles, as in the first experiment.

When a cellular automaton rule is computation-universal, one rule can simulate another. We shouldn't forget that they aren't the same, even if they may at first seem to be; this is illustrated in the second experiment.

18.3.1 A magic gas

Having a reversible computer in hand, one can amuse oneself and surprise one's friends by running it forward and backwards a few times. It would, however, be nice to do something really different. In Figure 18.9a we have what looks like a gas of particles in a box. Particularly observant individuals will note a funny little extrusion at the bottom of the box—ignore it for the moment. When we run the gas, we find that it bounces around in the box for a while, looking convincingly gas-like, and no particles get out through the small hole at the bottom. After running for a minute or so, something very strange starts to happen (Figure 18.9b): the gas seems to be organizing itself into something! A few more seconds, and the transformation is complete (Figure 18.9c). A ball has escaped through the door in the bottom of the box, and is bouncing around outside of the box.

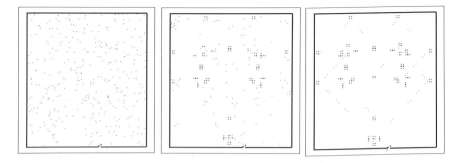

Figure 18.9: Magic-gas experiment: (a) A gas; (b) something happening; and (c) order out of disorder.

It will hardly come as a surprise that this bit of "magic" has been accomplished by running the system backwards. The details, however, may not yet be evident.

The system was actually started in the state pictured in Figure 18.9c, with a 'ball' poised outside of the door, waiting to get into the box. The circuit inside the box is similar to that shown in figure 18.8, except that it has been considerably expanded. This has been done by taking a normal-sized BBM-type circuit, and adding space in a uniform manner between all of the particles. Due to a scale-invariance property of the rule (shared by HPP-GAS and other similar rules) such a transformation results in a new configuration which has an isomorphic evolution: at regular intervals, the new system is an enlarged version of the evolution of the original system. The mirrors of the enlarged system are not unconditionally stable (like those of Figure 18.8). Instead, they are dynamical objects whose integrity can be destroyed by a misguided collision (compare Figures 18.5a and 18.5b). This of course is what we have in mind.

Our missile is poised outside of the doorway to the box. This is a carefully designed doorway which requires exactly the right bounce to get through— only a certain size of ball will make it. Single particles, or even pairs with the wrong spacing, will simply be reflected back the way they came. Our missile will get through, but once it has disrupted things the chances of anything leaking out very soon are rather small. Thus we can let the system run for a while, and wait for the circuit to dissolve into a gas of particles before we stop the simulation. At this point we reverse the direction of motion of all the particles and save the configuration (which is that of Figure 18.9a), ready to impress our friends!

18.3.2   The end of the world

As the sorcerer's apprentice learned, magic can get out of hand. Here we
have an experiment where a miracle causes the end of the world.

```
NEW-EXPERIMENT  N/MOORE  &/HV
                                        0 CONSTANT TIME

                                              : U
                                    CENTER ;
                                              : CW
   &HV TIME XOR {   EAST   SOUTH   NORTH   WEST } ;
                                              : CCW
   &HV TIME XOR {  SOUTH   WEST   EAST   NORTH } ;
                                              : OPP
   &HV TIME XOR { S.EAST S.WEST N.EAST N.WEST } ;
                                              : 2RUL
            CENTER OPP = IF CW ELSE CENTER THEN ;
                                              : BBRUL
     CENTER CW CCW OPP + + + { U OPP 2RUL U U } ;
                                              : EOW
          0 IS TIME BBRUL
          3 IS TIME BBRUL  XOR CENTER' XOR  >PLN0
                                 CENTER  >PLN1 ;
MAKE-TABLE EOW
```

What we have done here is this: we have written the BBM rule as a second-
order reversible rule (see Sections 12.5 and 14.2). This is the complete definition of the experiment—notice that this version of the rule operates on the
N/MOORE neighborhood, and doesn't use an alternating grid at all! How can
this be?

Let us call τ_e the transformation performed on a configuration by the BBM
rule when using the even grid. At an even step, configuration c^t will go into
$c^{t+1} = \tau_e c^t$. Since τ_e coincides with its inverse, we can also write $c^t = \tau_e c^{t+1}$.
Analogous considerations apply to the transformation τ_o performed by the
BBM rule when using the odd grid.

Given three consecutive configurations, c^{t-1}, c^t, c^{t+1}, the following identity holds independently of whether an even or an odd step is performed
first

$$\tau_e c^t + \tau_o c^t = c^{t-1} + c^{t+1}$$

(the sum of two configurations is here taken to be the configuration obtained
by adding corresponding sites, mod 2); in other words, by adding the result
of performing a forward step with that of performing a backward step one
obtains the future plus the past.

We can then define a new transformation $\tau = \tau_{\mathrm{e}} + \tau_{\mathrm{o}}$, so that

$$\tau c^t = c^{t+1} + c^{t-1},$$

or

$$c^{t+1} = \tau c^t - c^{t-1}. \tag{18.2}$$

But this is a second-order reversible rule of the form we have seen in Section 14.2. The alternation of the grid vanishes here, since we have added together an even and an odd step.

If we now run this second-order rule starting from the state of Figure 18.9a (run with ECHO on) we find that the evolution proceeds just as if we were using the BBM rule. We can even reverse the system by interchanging the present and the past data.

Now we will introduce a real miracle. We will change the value of a cell in the present, without making a corresponding change in the past. This is shown in Figures 18.10a and 18.10b. The gas, which looked quite random, was really still quite organized in comparison to how truly random it could get. Most states of this second-order system don't correspond to any state of the BBM gas. When we produced our miracle, a tear appeared in the thin fabric of our BBM simulation, and the world was torn asunder.

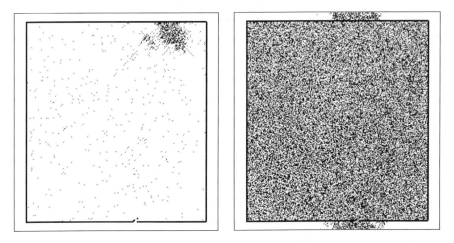

Figure 18.10: End of the world: (a) The fabric begins to unravel; (b) the end.

Conclusions

Cellular automata encourage one in the discipline of making complex objects out of simple materials. In this sense, they are closer in spirit to the mathematical models used in the more abstract branches of theoretical physics than to the more business-minded models used in much of computational physics.

Yet they are much more than useful abstractions. Cellular automata possess two truly fundamental virtues that can lead to eminently practical computer architectures.

Firstly, they are inherently parallel. If we associate one processor with every N cells, we can multiply the size of our simulation indefinitely without increasing the time taken for each complete updating of the space. There is no inevitable overhead associated with splitting the problem up among many processors, or coordinating the activities of many processors. Thus cellular automata models admit massive realizations, limited not by architecture but by economics.

Secondly, cellular automata are inherently local. Due to the speed of light constraint, locality of interconnection of simple processing elements can be translated into speed of operation. In an ordinary computer, the instruction cycle time is limited by the longest signal path, and so fast computers must be small. In cellular automata, the length of signal paths is independent of the size of the computer, and so the machine can be both very big and very fast.

Both of these characteristics, inherent parallelism and locality, stem from the fact that cellular automata are really stylized models of physics, possessing a realistic time and space. As such, they can be mapped more directly onto physical realizations than other architectures. As such, they are also well suited to a variety of physical modeling tasks, as we have discussed in this book.

All of this leads us to believe that cellular automata will be the basis of important parallel architectures. The exact form these architectures will take depends upon a complicated compromise involving such factors as technological dexterity, relative importance of achieving speed versus simulation size, complexity of the operations needed at each site, i/o bandwidth needed for examining and changing variables, and incorporation of non-local (or less local) features for added generality.

It is clear that the invention of useful models that require such machines has been and will continue to be an important stimulus to their evolution. Conversely, the prospect of such dramatic increases in simulation speed and size strongly encourages the further development of models and modeling techniques which exploit the strengths of these machines.

Appendix A

A minimal Forth tutorial

The main purpose of this tutorial is to give you an overall *reading* familiarity with Forth—enough to follow the CAM programming examples given in this book.

Relatively little knowledge of Forth is needed to compose full-fledged CAM experiments: the same few constructs appear over and over with minor variations, while many features of the Forth environment that are prominent in other programming contexts are not required at all.

However, these few constructs must be understood well. In many cases an intuitive presentation will be sufficient, but we shall not hesitate to give the appropriate amount of technical detail in those few cases where this is necessary to insure exact comprehension.

A.1 The command interpreter

You may visualize the Forth *command interpreter* as a competent but not-too-literate technician who sits in the machine room of your computer and has access to all the levers and dials. From the deck, you speak to him through an "intercom"—i.e., your terminal—issuing orders and receiving reports and acknowledgements. For instance, if you say

    BEEP

(type it at the terminal, followed by a carriage return) the terminal will respond with a "beep;" if you say

    0 100 DUMP

the contents of the first 100 memory locations (starting from location 0) will be dumped on the screen. After that, the interpreter will say ok

to tell you it's done and ready for a new command. (From now on, we'll take this carriage-return and ok business for granted.)

The interpreter's "ears" are conditioned to break up the input character stream into *tokens*, using "blank space" (one or more consecutive spaces) as a token separator. The tokens are passed on one by one to the interpreter's "brain" and the spaces are discarded. Thus, the interpreter hears the above command as a sequence of three tokens—0, 100, and DUMP—and would hear the same thing if you typed, say,

        0 100   DUMP

In order to be understood by the interpreter, the two of you must share a *dictionary* of terms and some miscellaneous conventions, which together make up the Forth language. The dictionary's contents reflects the range of things that the interpreter currently knows about. As you take command, you'll find that the Forth interpreter has already gone through "standard training"— and possibly some additional, more specialized training (for example, how to run a CAM machine). This standard training, which is documented in any good Forth manual, is more extensive than that of many common computer languages; in this sense, one speaks of Forth as a programming *environment* rather than just a programming *language*.

A.2   The compiler

The entries that make up the Forth dictionary are called, as you might expect, *words*. To *program* in Forth, you successively add new words to the dictionary—defining each new word in terms of existing ones. In this way you extend the interpreter's knowledge—and at the same time your expressive range—with regard to the set of activities you are interested in. At any stage of this construction you may say something that uses the new words, and check that its actual meaning (i.e., what the *interpreter* does in response to your words) is what *you* had in mind.

For example, to make up a new word for "beep three times" you type

    : 3BEEP   BEEP BEEP BEEP ;

As soon as it sees a colon (':'), the interpreter summons the aid of another technician, called the COLON *compiler*. This technician takes the token that immediately follows, in this case 3BEEP, and starts a new dictionary entry under that name. After that, it expects a phrase describing the action of the new word; this phrase, namely BEEP BEEP BEEP, is not executed at this time, but is compiled in the dictionary as the meaning of 3BEEP. The end of the phrase is marked by a semicolon ('; '), which tells the COLON compiler to return control to the command interpreter.

The language understood by the COLON compiler is slightly different (and somewhat richer) than that understood by the command interpreter; Some things only work with either the compiler or the interpreter, but not with both. Except when noted below, everything we will discuss works well either way.

If you now type

```
3BEEP
```

the interpreter will look up this word in the dictionary, execute it, and respond with the usual ok. If you type, say,

```
4BEEP
```

the interpreter will look it up but won't find it in the dictionary; it will then ask an assistant whether it might possibly be a number (see next section); and finally will print

```
4BEEP ?
```

to tell you it can't make sense of the token 4BEEP .

A.3   The dictionary

If you type FORTH WORDS , you'll get a listing of all the words currently contained in the main section of Forth's dictionary,[1] starting with the ones Forth has learned most recently. Thus, if you had just had the above conversation with the interpreter, the word 3BEEP would be on top of the list. The older word BEEP would appear somewhere down the list.

The following entries

```
BEEP  HERE  +  '  CONSTANT  C@  ;  :  C!  O=
```

taken at random from the dictionary give you an idea of what typical Forth words look like. *Any* token can be entered in the dictionary as a word. In particular, characters that in other languages are used as punctuation marks, such as ': ', can appear as part of a Forth word, or even make up a word all by themselves; the word 'C, ' is very different than the two-word sequence 'C , '.

A word already present in the dictionary may be redefined by you. For instance, if the speaker in your terminal is dead, as a temporary fix you may use a version of BEEP that prints on the screen, on a new line, the message 'Believe it or not, this is a beep!'. This is done by redefining BEEP as follows

---

[1]In addition to this main section, called FORTH , the dictionary may contain some additional specialized sections, as will be explained in a moment.

```
: BEEP CR ." Believe it or not, this is a beep" ;
```

(the construct `." ⟨text⟩"` is an instruction to print ⟨text⟩ on the screen, and can only be used within a COLON definition). If you now define

```
: 4BEEP   BEEP BEEP BEEP BEEP ;
```

this word will be compiled using the *new* version of BEEP , and when executed will print

```
Believe it or not, this is a beep!
Believe it or not, this is a beep!
Believe it or not, this is a beep!
Believe it or not, this is a beep!
```

The old version of BEEP is not deleted from the dictionary, and the previously defined word 3BEEP *will retain its original meaning*—which is tied to the *old* version of BEEP). If you say 3BEEP now, the three beeps will still be routed to the (dead) speaker.

It's all right, and often useful, to redefine a word in terms of its previous namesake. For instance, if you discover that beeps in your terminal have such a long decay time that tree consecutive beeps sound more like a long one, you may redefine BEEP as

```
: BEEP   BEEP 10 TICKS ;
```

(where 10 TICKS means "Wait for ten ticks of internal computer clock"), and a sequence of beeps will now sound "staccato" rather than "legato."

In some English dictionaries, words belonging to certain specialized areas of discourse are listed in separate sections (e.g., geographical names, measurement units, abbreviations). In Forth, these sections are called "vocabularies;" in addition to the main FORTH vocabulary there may be an ASSEMBLER vocabulary containing machine-language op-codes and other assembler-specific terms, an EDITOR vocabulary containing editor-specific terms, etc.

Since word look-up is performed only within the currently "active" vocabularies, the vocabulary structure provides a way to use the same name with different meanings in different contexts, or to make a word unavailable in a certain context. In CAM Forth, certain "neighbor words" (such as S.EAST , &CENTER , etc) are segregated in special vocabularies, in order to make them available only when the corresponding "neighbor wires" are actually connected to the look-up table.

A.4   Numbers

If in an ordinary piece of English text you find a phrase such as 'the motion was passed with 371 votes in favor', you won't look up '371' in the dictionary—and for that matter you wouldn't find it there if you did. The meaning of a number derives from its make-up; this makes it possible for any fool to produce more numbers than any one would want to list, but at the same time makes it unnecessary to list the meaning of individual numbers in a dictionary.

The situation is analogous in Forth: numbers are parsed as they are encountered and their meaning is reconstructed from their make-up by another technician, called NUMBER, summoned by the interpreter as the occasion arises. This "meaning" is nothing but an internal representation in binary form. For instance, if the interpreter sees the token 100 while operating in DECIMAL mode, this token will be recognized as a number and will be internally converted to 0000000001100100 (Forth stores integers in 16-bit cells); however, if you have told the interpreter to operate in HEX mode,[2] the same token will be given the meaning 0000000100000000.

Some numbers that for historical or practical reasons deserve explicit mention, such as 'three', *are* listed (in a spelled-out form) in the English dictionary. In an analogous way, some common numbers such as 0 and 1 have been entered (in this form, i.e., 0 —not ZERO) as *words* in the Forth dictionary.[3] This leads to more efficient execution (their meaning has been established in advance, once and for all, and there is no need to ask for the help of the NUMBER technician) and more compact code.

A.5 The stack

Forth manages to achieve remarkable expressive power and efficiency; yet a Forth *system* (i.e., the language as implemented on a computer) can be amazingly simple and compact. These advantages are bought at the cost of ruthless standardization, in particular in the way nearby words in a phrase communicate to one another the information that binds them together as a syntactical whole.

For the purpose of this communication, all data (characters, Boolean variables, numbers, addresses, etc.) are packaged in a standard-size "carton," called a *cell*, having a capacity of 16 bits, and all data exchanges take place— in a preordained choreography, as we shall see in a moment—through a single clearing-house called the *stack*. This is just a pile of cells that grows or shrinks according to the traffic.

Imagine a stage with this stack in the middle. The Forth interpreter is the ballet conductor; as he reads off the words that make up your phrase, the corresponding actors show up in sequence, do their thing, and disappear. If an actor's part tells him to leave behind certain data for later actors, he'll

---

[2] I.e., base sixteen rather than base ten. In Forth, numbers can be read and printed in any base you choose.

[3] Words of type CONSTANT; cf. Section A.8.

walk to the stack and pile these data, cell by cell, on top of it; if his part expects data from previous actors, he will walk to the stack and pick them up.

Some data that an actor needs may end up, say, buried two cells deep into the stack. The actor won't go fumbling through the stack looking for them (the cartons don't carry a label!); rather, his score will explicitly tell him to lift just the top two cells, grab the cell that is now on top, and put the first two back down.

With this scheme, there is no need for each piece of data to have an *absolute* address—a permanent mailbox with a distinguished name. Instead, all addressing is by position *relative* to the top of the stack. If a new, self-contained piece of choreography is inserted in the old score, at the moment of executing it one will find the stack already built up to a certain height; during execution of this piece one will see the stack grow more, shrink a bit, etc., and by the end of the inserted piece return to its original height. The rest of the score will then resume, finding its own data where they had been left.

A.6   Expressions

The stack discipline is well suited to the communication needs of a hierarchically built program. It allows one to use a particularly simple scoring notation—called *reverse Polish notation*—by which arithmetical and logical expressions of arbitrary depth can be written without making recourse to parentheses or other place markers.

When you type a number to the command interpreter, this number is packaged in one cell and put on top of the stack. The one-character word '.' ("dot") picks up the top cell of the stack and prints its contents *as a number* on the screen. Thus, if you type

    356 .

(where the "dot" is part of what you type) the screen will respond with

    356

(In a more conventional programming language, the equivalent of '356 .' would be something like 'print(356)'.) Note that the stack went up one level with 356, down one level with '.', and is now the same height as before.

The word '+' ("plus") gobbles up the top *two* cells of the stack, adds them together, and places the result—consisting of *one* cell—on top of the stack; thus, it leaves the stack one level lower than it found it. For example, the expression

    2 3 +

will leave the result 5 on the stack (from where you can move it to the screen with '.'). If you want to see how much $1 + 2 + 4$ is, you type

    1 2 + 4 + .

We can picture the evolution of the stack as follows

STACK	INPUT	OUTPUT
. . .	1	
. . . 1	2	
. . . 1 2	+	
. . . 3	4	
. . . 3 4	+	
. . . 7	.	7
. . .		

where each row displays (a) the current state of the stack (with the top element on the right), (b) the text to be interpreted, and (c) what is printed on the screen. The dots on the left indicate the part of the stack that we haven't touched; this indication will be dropped in the following stack examples.

Note that once 3 has been placed on the stack, it does not matter *how* it got there; from a functional viewpoint, the expression 1 2 + is interchangeable with, say, 3, or 1 1 + 1 +, or anything that eventually bows out having left just a 3 on top of whatever else the stack contained before. Note also that the two different expressions

    1 1 + 1 + 1 +   and   1 1 1 1 + + +

produce the same end result even though the second one temporarily builds up the stack to a higher level:

STACK	INPUT	STACK	INPUT
	1		1
1	1	1	1
1 1	+	1 1	1
2	1	1 1 1	1
2 1	+	1 1 1 1	+
3	1	1 1 2	+
3 1	+	1 3	+
4		4	

A.7   Editing and loading

Once you have given a command to the interpreter, you cannot take it back; if something goes wrong, you may not even remember exactly what you said. While immediate interaction with the interpreter is very useful, there are

times where you would like to carefully think out in advance a whole sequence of commands and definitions, review and edit it, and perhaps discuss
it with somebody else before you give it to the interpreter. You want to be
in a position to give *pre-written* orders, and you might have a collection of
different "orders of the day" to be handed to the interpreter according to the
circumstances.

You can do all of this by first writing your text on a disk file, where it can
be inspected and modified by means of the Forth *screen editor*. Then you
can ask the interpreter to use this file (or a portion of it) as the input stream,
instead of what comes from the keyboard; this process is called *loading*. When
you load a file, everything works as if you were typing the file's contents from
the keyboard—except that the interpreter now processes your tokens as they
come, without waiting for a carriage return.[4]

When you compose your text with the editor for subsequent loading, you
may choose to format it in a way that facilitates comprehension, and here
and there add a comment to yourself.

The formatting scheme used in this book is the following

```
                          :  3BEEP
          BEEP BEEP BEEP  ;
                          :  BEEP
                    BEEP
               10 TICKS  ;
                          :  4BEEP
        BEEP BEEP BEEP BEEP  ;
```

where dictionary entries are lined up on the right half of the page and the
"bodies" of the definitions are segregated on the left half.

The Forth word '(' removes from the input stream everything that follows,
up to and including the matching character ')'; thus, you may write a line as
follows

```
    BEEP BEEP ( two beeps ) BEEP BEEP ( two more )
```

and the interpreter will never hear what is "in parentheses."[5]

The word '\' ("backslash") treats as a comment the remainder of the line
on which it appears

---

[4]A typical Forth source file does not contain carriage returns at all; the lines that you see
on the screen when editing are stored one after the other in the file without any intervening
separation marks.

[5]Observe that the following spacing is correct too
```
BEEP BEEP ( two beeps)BEEP BEEP ( two more)
```
even though there is no intervening space between ')' and **BEEP** , since the effect of the word
'(' is precisely to throw away the string 'two beeps)'. On the other hand, the following
spacing
```
BEEP BEEP (two beeps) BEEP BEEP (two more)
```
won't do, since it will make the interpreter think that '(two' is a token to be processed.

```
                  : BEEP  \ New version!
          BEEP            \   plain beep
      10 TICKS ;          \   insert delay
```

A.8   "Constants" and "variables"

In Section A.2 we said that the interpreter "executes" the words you type. Actually, each word in the Forth dictionary carries a notice saying "I am to be executed by technician so-and-so, who knows how to handle me," and the interpreter will just pass the buck to this technician. For words that have been entered in the dictionary by the COLON compiler, the competent technician is the COLON *interpreter*. In general, each type of word has its own compiler and a corresponding interpreter. The buck stops with words that have been compiled by the ASSEMBLER; this technician produces code written directly in machine language (i.e., your microprocessor's native language), and at this point the hardware takes over.

All of this works much more simply than it sounds. Suppose you are writing a telescope-driving program that needs to know your town's latitude, say, 43°. It is good programming practice to give this number a *name*—say, LATITUDE—so that whenever this name appears in your program it will have the same effect as if you had typed '43'. To do this, in Forth you say

```
43 CONSTANT LATITUDE
```

The word LATITUDE will be entered in the dictionary as a constant, and when executed it will place the number 43 on the stack.

What happens is that as soon as it sees the word CONSTANT the command interpreter summons the aid of the CONSTANT compiler, who gobbles up the next token—namely LATITUDE—and starts a new dictionary entry under that name. The entry will consist of two parts: the first (*code field*) contains a notice saying "I am to be executed by the CONSTANT interpreter;" the second (*data cell*) is reserved for the value of the constant. At this point the CONSTANT compiler takes the top cell of the stack—with the 43 you had just put there—and moves it to the data cell in the dictionary. At execution time, the CONSTANT interpreter will look at the data cell and place a copy of it on the stack.

With the above definition of LATITUDE, the command

```
LATITUDE 7 + .
```

will print 50 on the screen.

The term 'CONSTANT' is somewhat of a misnomer (though it is retained for historical reasons), since the contents of the data cell may be altered at will; in the present implementation of Forth, to change the value of LATITUDE to 45° you say

```
45 IS LATITUDE
```

The most relevant aspect of a Forth constant is that it returns the *value* of its data cell, rather than a *pointer* to it (cf. VARIABLE) below).

In CAM, "neighbor words" such as NORTH, SOUTH, etc. act like constants insofar as they return a value; this value will change very many times during the construction of a rule table.[6]

Forth provides another mechanism for accessing a piece of data, namely by its *address*[7] rather than by its *value*. The VARIABLE compiler, used in a construct such as

```
VARIABLE TIME
```

is analogous to the CONSTANT compiler insofar as it constructs a dictionary entry, namely TIME, with a data cell in it. However,

- This data cell is not initialized to a particular value (and therefore the defining word VARIABLE, unlike CONSTANT, does *not* expect a value on the stack).

- When TIME is executed, the VARIABLE interpreter puts on the stack the *address* of the data cell, rather than its contents.

Thus, if we type

```
TIME
```

what will be placed on the stack is not the current value of TIME (which may change several times during execution of the program), but its address (which is always the same).

To get the *value* of TIME you use the word '@' (pronounced "fetch"), as in

```
TIME @  ( data )
```

(i.e., '@' expects an address on the stack, and replaces it with the data at that address), and to set it you use the word '!' ("store"), as in

---

[6]You write a CAM rule in the form of a Forth word (say, LIFE) whose defining phrase will of course use some neighbor words; when MAKE-TABLE generates the look-up table for your rule (cf. Section 4.2) it will execute the word LIFE once for each entry of the look-up table, and the neighbor words will be called into action. These words differ from ordinary constants in that they all share a single data cell. During the construction of the n-th entry of the table the "entry number" n is stored in this cell; when a neighbor word is called, it looks at the entry number and returns the appropriate neighbor value for that entry. If for some perverse reason you decided to tamper with the contents of the "entry number" cell during table construction, the values returned by *all* neighbor words would be affected.

[7]In an ordinary computer, memory locations are sequentially numbered; the address of a piece of data is the number of its location.

```
( data ) TIME !
```

(i.e., '!' expects a piece of data *and* an address, and ships the data to that address). For example, to increment time by one unit you write

```
TIME @ 1 + TIME !
```

Supposing that the TIME data cell is at location 1000 and its initial contents is 5, the evolution of the relevant data is the following

TIME's contents	STACK	INPUT
5		TIME
5	1000	@
5	5	1
5	5 1	+
5	6	TIME
5	6 1000	!
6		

From the viewpoint of CAM's user, Forth VARIABLE's need be used seldom—if ever. In this book, the term 'variable' always has the usual meaning of 'a generic quantity to which we may assign an arbitrary value' rather the the more technical Forth meaning.

A.9 Iteration

Once you've stored a program in the computer's memory, portions of it can be executed over and over, perhaps with some variations.

For instance, you can define

```
: BEEP-STUCK
BEGIN
BEEP
AGAIN ;
```

When this word is called, once the execution reaches AGAIN it jumps back to BEGIN, producing an endless series of beeps. Short of turning off the power, there is no way you can get out of this loop.[8]

The above BEGIN / AGAIN pair delimits a phrase somewhat like a pair of parentheses: the phrase in between gets iterated forever. Note that for readability we vertically aligned the two elements of the pair, flush on the *right* (this is recommended in reverse-Polish-notation style), and indented the phrase inside.

A more flexible pair is DO / LOOP; the word

---

[8]Unless your computer has a working BREAK key—the equivalent of a "panic button."

```
              : 100BEEPS
    100 0 DO
        BEEP
        LOOP ;
```

will beep 100 times.[9] What happens in detail is that DO gobbles up the top two numbers on the stack, 100 (the loop LIMIT) and 0 (the loop INDEX), and saves them for later use. The execution proceeds until LOOP is encountered. At this point, INDEX is incremented by one and compared with LIMIT: if INDEX=LIMIT the loop is terminated; otherwise, execution jumps back to DO.[10]

Pairs of "parentheses" such as BEGIN / AGAIN and DO / LOOP can be nested as ordinary parentheses, and a lot more bells and whistles are available. You can look up the details of these and other flow-control constructs in a Forth manual. Here we shall only mention that flow-control constructs can only appear inside a COLON definition: you cannot say

```
    100 0 DO BEEP LOOP
```

at the command-interpreter level.

A.10   Stack comments

By now, we have encountered many words that expect arguments on the stack or leave results on the stack. Since breaches of stack discipline may send a computation berserk (if you leave an extra item on the stack everyone after you will get his data wrong), it will be convenient to have a notation to remind us of just how many items a word takes from the stack or leaves on it.

The following are examples of *stack comments*:

```
DO        ( n1 n2 -- )
DO        ( limit index --)
BEEP      ( -- )
LATITUDE  ( -- n)
TIME      ( -- addr)
+         ( n1 n2 -- n3)
+         ( m n -- m+n)
2         ( -- n)
2         ( -- 2)
```

---

[9]Of course if you had typed **999BEEPS** you still would have gotten a word that beeps 100 times. A name is a name is a name...

[10]The loop index is a modulo-2^{16} counter. The minimum number of iterations, namely 1, is achieved when the loop is entered with INDEX just one less than *limit*; the maximum, when the loop is entered with INDEX *equal* to LIMIT: 0 0 LOOP will cycle 2^{16} times!

The general convention is as follows. We put in parentheses a "dash" (customarily a double-dash) to indicate the word in question. Before the dash we write a list of what the word *expects* on the stack; after the dash we write a list of what the word *leaves* on it.

What really counts is the *number* of items in each list—which corresponds to the number of cells taken from or given to the stack; but the items themselves may be elaborated upon a little, for extra clarity.

For example, DO takes two items and leaves none. A minimal notation is

```
DO          ( n1 n2 -- )
```

which just tells us that DO expects two items. A better mnemonic is provided by

```
DO          ( limit index --)
```

which reminds us that the first item is used as the *limit* and the second as (the initial value of) the *index* of the loop.

As a final grand example, let us load the following three definitions from a disk file

```
100 CONSTANT HUNDRED  ( -- n)
10000 CONSTANT A-LOT-OF ( -- n)
              : BEEPS    ( n --)
        0 DO
      BEEP LOOP ;
```

and then type the following three commands

```
3 BEEPS
HUNDRED BEEPS
A-LOT-OF BEEPS
```

We have seen above that DO wants two arguments. When we type 3 BEEPS, the first argument is left on the stack by the 3 we typed, while the second is placed on the stack by the 0 appearing within the definition of BEEPS: DO's hunger is satisfied.

Note that if we define words giving a little thought to the "stack interface" (*who* should supply or consume *what* and *when*) and to choosing appropriate names, the flow of a Forth phrase can be given a natural-language flavor that is hard to achieve in other programming languages. Properly trained Forth words can talk to one another under the surface of the phrase, without bothering us with their chatter.

A generally obeyed convention in Forth is to make words "use up" their arguments rather than leave them on the stack. If an object on the stack is needed as an argument by a given word and also by another word that closely follows, a second copy of this object is made—using the word DUP introduced below—before the first copy is used up.

A.11   DUP, DROP, etc.

The Forth word '*' ("times") takes two numbers and returns their product;
to compute the square of 3 you have to type 3 twice: 3 3 *. How about a
word SQR that will take a *single* argument and multiply it by itself?

Forth provides a number of general-purpose words for manipulating the
stack; one of these is DUP (pronounced "dupe"), which looks at the cell on
top of the stack and puts a *duplicate* copy of it on top of it; e.g.,

```
STACK   INPUT
5       DUP
5 5
```

Thus, SQR can be simply

```
      : SQR ( n -- n*n)
DUP * ;
```

since here '*' will see two copies of the argument.

Related to DUP are DROP (which drops the top item from the stack), SWAP
(which swaps the top two items), OVER (which makes a copy of the next-to-
the-top stack item), ROT (which pulls the third item from underneath and
puts in on top of the first two), and a few more. Words of this kind act
somewhat like *pronouns* in English ('this', 'that', 'one another', etc.), in that
they allow one to refer by *position* rather than by *name* to objects introduced
in a different part of the sentence. As an exercise, verify that the function
$y(m,n) = (m+n)(m-n)$ is computed by the following Forth expression

```
( m n )  OVER OVER + ROT ROT - *  ( y )
```

(where the comments tell you what's on the stack before and after).

A.12   Case selection

A flow-control construct that is extensively used in programming CAM is
the *case statement*, which allows one to select for execution one of several
alternative actions. Suppose we have three words called BEEP, HONK, and
WHISTLE; we can then make up a new word, called SOUND, which will take
an integer argument from the stack, with value 0, 1, or 2, and respectively
beep, honk, or whistle:

```
      : SOUND ( n --)
{ BEEP HONK WHISTLE } ;
```

That is, 0 SOUND will execute BEEP, 1 SOUND will execute HONK, and so
on. The selection list may consist of any number n of entries, which are to

be thought of as consecutively numbered from 0 upwards, and is delimited by the two "brace" words, namely '{' and '}'. If you attempt to execute the case statement with an argument that is less than 0 or greater than $n-1$ you get an error message.

Suppose you want to make up a word that returns the number of days in a month. You'd probably try the following

```
            : DAYS ( month -- days)
         1 -
  { 31 28 31 30 31 30
    31 31 30 31 30 31 } ;
```

Assuming that months are numbered 1, 2, ..., 11, 12, you subtract 1 in order to have the numbering 0, 1, ..., 10, 11—better suited to the case statement—and then you look up the number of days. The reasoning is correct, but there is one minor catch: in CAM Forth the case statement only accepts individual dictionary words as items in the selection list; with a few exceptions (mentioned in Section A.4) numbers are *not* in the dictionary. There is an easy fix to this problem: *before* defining **DAYS**, enter the desired numbers in the dictionary as *constants*

```
      28 CONSTANT 28 ( -- 28)
      30 CONSTANT 30 ( -- 30)
      31 CONSTANT 31 ( -- 31)
```

From this moment the token 28 (for one) will be recognized as a *word*—one that leaves a 28 on the stack just as the *number* 28 used to do before. The case statement will now accept it as a list item.

A.13 Conditional statements

The phrase between a **BEGIN** and **AGAIN** pair is iterated forever, that between **DO** and **LOOP** is iterated a number of times as specified by the two arguments that **DO** finds on the stack. A phrase between the words **IF** and **THEN** is executed only if the argument found on the stack by **IF** has the logical value 'true'.[11]

The word

```
=   ( m n -- F|T)
```

compares the two arguments m and n and returns a logical "flag" having the value 'true' if they are equal and 'false' if different. Thus, the following word will beep only when the top two stack items are equal

---

[11]How logical values are encoded in a Forth cell doesn't matter at this point, and is discussed in the next section.

```
                      : BEEP-IF-EQUAL ( m n --)
              = IF
          BEEP THEN ;
```

A richer construct is the IF / ELSE / THEN , used as follows

```
                      : BEEP-OR-WHISTLE ( m n --)
              = IF
          BEEP ELSE
        WHISTLE THEN
      HONK HONK HONK ;
```

This word will beep if *m* and *n* are equal, and whistle if odd; after that, it will honk three times.

There exists also a *conditional-iteration* statement of the form ' BEGIN ... UNTIL ', in which the loop is iterated *until* the value of a logical flag becomes 'true', and one of the form ' BEGIN ... WHILE ... REPEAT ', in which the loop is iterated *as long as* the value of a logical flag remains 'true'.

A.14   Logical expressions

In defining a CAM rule, sometimes it is convenient to treat the contents of a CAM cell as a logical quantity ('on' or 'off', 'true' or 'false') and sometimes as a number (0 or 1—or even 0, 1, 2, or 3 when one is dealing with two bit-planes at once). To understand precisely what is passed on the stack by one word to another in these cases, it is important to be aware of the coding conventions employed in CAM Forth concerning arithmetic and logical expressions.

This lengthy section is meant as a reference for cases where doubts might arise; you may quickly go over it (or skip it altogether) on first reading.

We have seen that the contents of a Forth cell consists of a 16-bit pattern. The same pattern can have different meanings, depending on agreed-upon conventions. For instance, it can be used to encode an integer between 0 and 65,535 ("unsigned number"), an integer between -32,768 and +32768 ("signed number"), one ASCII *character* (using only the lower 8 bits), etc. The cell does not carry a label telling what kind of encoding was used: it is up to the programmer to arrange things so that any "user" of the pattern will know what conventions to use in interpreting it.

For example, suppose that the top cell of the stack contains the pattern 1000000000101010; the three words '.', U. , and EMIT will all print on the terminal the contents of this cell. However, '.' will treat it as a signed number, and print '-32726'; U. will treat it as un unsigned number, and print '32810'; and EMIT will treat it as a character, and print '*' (since the lower eight bits of the pattern, namely 00101010, make up the ASCII code for '*').

In many cases it is convenient to treat the cell pattern just as a collection of separate bits—each one representing an individual binary choice. The words

```
NOT   (   p -- r)
AND   ( p q -- r)
OR    ( p q -- r)
XOR   ( p q -- r)
```

are useful in this context, since they allow one to individually or jointly manipulate these bits. For instance, one can "turn off" the upper eight bits of a pattern by AND'ing it with an appropriate *mask* pattern, namely 0000000011111111, in which the upper eight bits are "off" and the lower eight are "on."

As a reminder, the logical operations NOT, AND, OR, and XOR are defined as follows:

NOT	AND	OR	XOR
$0 \mapsto 1$	$00 \mapsto 0$	$00 \mapsto 0$	$00 \mapsto 0$
$1 \mapsto 0$,	$01 \mapsto 0$,	$01 \mapsto 1$,	$01 \mapsto 1$.
	$10 \mapsto 0$	$10 \mapsto 1$	$10 \mapsto 1$
	$11 \mapsto 1$	$11 \mapsto 1$	$11 \mapsto 0$

In particular, the logical operation NOT complements its one-bit argument, and thus the Forth word NOT complements *each* of the 16 bits of a cell. The other three logical operators act on corresponding bits of two input cells to produce a 16-bit result.

To drive a conditional statement along one or the other of two possible paths (see previous section) all one needs is a binary "flag"—with values 'true' and 'false'.[12] For this purpose, a one-bit token would be sufficient; but Forth cells come in a standard size of 16 bits, and one must have an agreement on which 16-bit pattern(s) should mean 'true' and which 'false'.

The Forth-83 standard stipulates that words that *return* a logical flag (such as '=' and similar "compare" words) should never put on the stack anything but the patterns 1111111111111111 for 'true' or 0000000000000000 for 'false'; for convenience, these patterns have been entered in the dictionary, as CONSTANT words, under the names TRUE and FALSE.[13] On the other hand, words that *expect* a logical flag (such as IF and similar "conditional" words) will treat as 'false' the pattern 0000000000000000 and as 'true' *any other pattern*.

---

[12]When more than two choices present themselves, it is usually more natural to use a case statement (cf. Section A.12) rather than many nested IF statements.

[13]Note that, when printed as signed numbers, TRUE will yield -1 and FALSE will yield 0; as an unsigned number, TRUE will yield 65535 (FFFF in hexadecimal).

As long as one uses only the `TRUE` and `FALSE` patterns for 'true' and 'false', the bitwise logical operations `NOT`, `AND`, etc. can also be used to manipulate such logical flags. However, if one tries to take advantage in an indiscriminate fashion of the wider "catching range" of `IF` [14] some subtle problems may arise. We shall give just one example, as a warning to the reckless programmer.

Consider the word

```
               : BEEP-IF-NOT-EQUAL ( m n --)
     = NOT IF
     BEEP THEN ;
```

(cf. previous section), which beeps only when m and n are *not* equal. This word would work the same if one replaced '`= NOT`' by just '`-`'; In fact, if m and n are equal their difference $m - n$ will be 0, and will be seen as 'false' by `IF`; on the other hand, if they are different $m - n$ will be a pattern containing at least one non-zero bit, and will be seen as 'true' by `IF`.

Well, if '`-`' works "the same" as '`= NOT`', won't '`- NOT`' work the same as '`=`' in `BEEP-IF-EQUAL` of the previous section? If $m = n$, their difference $m - n$ is 0 and its complement as given by `NOT` is the pattern of all 1's (the `TRUE` pattern)—which of course is recognized as 'true' by `IF`, as we intended. If $m \neq n$, the difference pattern *will* contain some 1's but *may* also contain some 0's; thus the complementary pattern returned by `NOT` may contain some 1's—in which case it will again be recognized by `IF` as 'true', which is *not* what we intended.

Since neighbor words such as `CENTER`, `NORTH`, etc. return 1 or 0 as a value, we shall use these values as respectively 'true' and 'false' whenever expedient. Logical operations involving such 1-bit flags work well, except for `NOT` (since it complements all 16 bits). The two word sequence '`1 XOR`' can be used to get the 1-bit complement. Alternatively, comparisons such as '`=`' '`>`' '`<`' and '`<>`' (not equal) can be used to convert 1-bit flags into standard logical flags. [15]

Finally, it will be useful to remember that words such as `>PLNO` and `>AUXO`, which take a stack item and write it as an entry of a CAM lookup table, only use the least significant bit of the item: any garbage that may have accumulated in the remaining bits as a result of arithmetic/logical manipulation tricks will be ignored. ("Joint" versions of these words, such as `>PLNA` and `>AUXA`, use the lowest *two* bits.)

A.15 Further readings

Starting FORTH by Leo Brodie[8] is an excellent practical introduction to

---

[14] As when using arithmetic as a shortcut to logic.

[15] The words '`0=`' '`0>`' etc. also exist as abbreviations for '`0 =`' etc.

Forth, while *Thinking FORTH*, by the same author[9], discusses the methodology that inspires this programming language. *Inside F83*, by C. H. Ting[54] is a thorough description of F83's internal structure.

The periodical *FORTH Dimensions*, published by the Forth Interest Group, P.O. Box 8231, San Jose, CA, is a good source for news, applications, programming techniques, literature listings, and software and hardware developments. The *Journal of Forth Application and Research*, published by the Institute for Applied Forth Research, Inc., is a more academically oriented publication.

Appendix B

Basic CAM architecture

The following considerations apply with some variations both to CAM-6—the machine used for the examples of this book—and to CAM-7, a two-thousand times larger machine which is at an advanced design stage.

While the most natural architecture for a cellular automata machine would be a fully parallel array of simple processors, this approach presents certain technical difficulties—particularly when one contemplates interconnecting enormous numbers of these processors in three dimensions. The CAM architecture maintains the basic conceptual approach of a fully-parallel machine, but with certain variants that lead to a more practical and economical realization and a better utilization of current technological resources. With reference to a fully-parallel approach, this architecture is based on *plane-modules*, an arbitrary number of which can be connected in parallel; each plane-module spans a large number of sites. However, the individual plane-module is a *pipelined* rather than a *parallel* processor.

B.1 The plane-module

For the sake of the present discussion we shall restrict our attention to two-dimensional cellular automata containing one bit of data at each site. More dimensions and larger state-sets are discussed in the following sections.

The whole array is partitioned into rectangular portions of identical size called *sectors*, and a separate hardware plane-module is assigned to each sector. Each plane-module consists of three main sections—*state-variable storage*, *data routing*, and *transition function*.

The storage section contains the state variables of the corresponding sector. In order to perform one updating step on this area, the current values of the state variables are read once, sequentially, and injected into the routing section. The corresponding new values, determined by table look-up, are returned by this section in the same sequential order and written back onto the storage section.

From the above sequential stream of data, the routing section extracts with the appropriate timing the nine values corresponding at each moment to the nine neighbor positions of a site:[1] the site itself, or *Center*; its four nearest neighbors, *North*, *South*, *East*, and *West*; and its four next-nearest neighbors *N.East*, *N.West*, *S.East*, and *S.West*. This section also provides appropriate buffering to make the updating of sites appear *synchronous* even though realized in a sequential manner, and to achieve correct vertical and horizontal wrap-around.

A desired subset of the above nine signals, possibly augmented by signals coming from other plane-modules (cf. Sections B.3, B.4), are submitted in parallel as arguments to the transition-function section, which uses a look-up table to compute the corresponding new value for the center cell. After a brief journey through the routing section, the new value is handed to the storage section, where it replaces the current value of that cell. Note that all ancillary tasks such as argument gathering are performed by the routing section; thus the look-up table, which is the most critical resource in the simulation, is exploited to its full bandwidth. Moreover, since each table is shared by a large number of cells, it becomes practical to employ a large look-up table thus compressing a substantial amount of computation into a single step.

B.2   Larger arrays: edge gluing

An arbitrarily large two-dimensional array can be obtained by *gluing* sectors edge-to-edge, i.e., by exchanging between the pipelines of two adjacent sectors data about those sites that are contained in one plane-module but are neighbors of sites in the other plane-module. The size of a plane-module in CAM-6 is 256×256 sites. In a fully-parallel architecture, this would entail a plane-module with thousands of external terminations; in the pipelined architecture, instead, exchange of information at the edges is serial, and four bidirectional lines, corresponding to the four adjacent sectors, are sufficient.[2]

By gluing sectors in this way, one obtains an arbitrarily large *sheet*; typ-

---

[1]In CAM-7, this part of the function of the routing section will be largely eliminated, since partitioning based on relative offsetting of plane origins (see Section 15.6) will form the basis of neighbor gathering.

[2]This sector-joining technique relies on the fact that the cell memory of the individual plane-modules is logically wrapped around—a cell at the physical edge of the sector sees cells on both that edge and the far edge as neighbors. Since the scanning pattern for cell updates is the same for all plane-modules, all plane-modules have the appropriate edge neighbors available simultaneously to be exchanged. By exchanging pipelines rather than neighbors, we get the same effect with one connection to each immediately adjacent sector *independently* of the size of the neighborhood.

ically, this sheet will be wrapped-around, i.e., the top edge will be joined to the bottom edge and the left to the right; thus, the overall topology of a sheet will be that of a torus. The same gluing technique is used both for array-expansion purposes and for boundary elimination by wraparound.

Observe that the gluing of plane-modules is done once at the routing stage. In this way, both from a logical and a physical viewpoint the transition-function section is *completely decoupled* from a number of implementation details, namely, (a) the fact that a sheet consists of plane-modules glued together, (b) that storage and routing are done on a two-dimensional basis, and independently for each bit plane, and (c) that operations are pipelined.

B.3   More states per cell: sheet ganging

Once sheets of the desired size have been assembled, further hardware configuring of the cellular automata machine is done by selecting suitable signals as arguments to the transition-function. In particular, in order to have a larger state-set for the automaton's cell it is sufficient to *gang* a set of sheets, i.e., connect as inputs to the look-up table of each sheet a selection of neighbor outputs from the other sheets of the group. Such a ganged set will then constitute a *layer* of the cellular automaton, containing a complete cell at each site.

B.4   More dimensions: layer stacking

Finally, layers can be *stacked* on top of one another, by connecting as inputs to the transition function of each layer a selection of neighbor outputs from the layers immediately above and below. This is possible because all plane-modules will be updating corresponding cells at the same time. In this way we can configure CAM-type machines into a three-dimensional cellular automaton. This construction can be further iterated in order to obtain cellular automata in four or more dimensions.

B.5   Display and analysis

Each of the four plane-modules of a CAM-6 machine generates new data at a rate of ≈6 Mbits/sec. If one had to do any substantial reformatting of this information for display purposes, one would need resources of the same order of magnitude as those used for producing it.

In the pipelined architecture, scanning of the array is sequential; with an appropriate choice of scanning parameters this information can be made to appear in the correct framing format for display on a raster-scan device.

In the CAM plane-module, the number of array rows and columns spanned by the plane-module, the scanning sequence, and the timing are such that a tap on the pipeline can directly feed a conventional CRT monitor. Of course, the outputs from a set of ganged plane-modules (cf. Section B.3), which collectively represent the value of a multi-bit state variable, can be combined into an RGB signal and displayed on a single *color* monitor.[3]

The advantages of this set-up are not limited to raw display. On the plane-module, all the neighbor information that is potentially available to the transition function is conveniently accessible, and can be fed to an additional look-up table. In this way, one can compute and send to the display an arbitrary *output* function, instead of just the value of the current center cell. This allows one to do on-the-fly a substantial amount of graphic preprocessing (this approach reminds us of the "staining" techniques used in microscopy for enhancing selected features of the tissue under examination).

Further, the stream of values supplied by such an output function can be sorted into a histogram, accumulated and compared with set threshold values, and in general used for real-time processing and control of the system's dynamics. In particular, one can locate and count occurrences of any specified local pattern.

Finally, since at each updating step all the data on each plane-module are streamed through the pipeline, a single bidirectional tap on this pipeline is sufficient to provide any external device with read and write access to the totality of the data. The collection of these taps, one per plane-module, constitutes an extremely high-speed bus (on CAM-7, which is planned to have 1024 plane-modules of 512×512 sites each, we get an overall word width of 1024 bits and a synchronous word rate of 40 nsec) through which the entire state of the simulated system is continually made accessible to the experimenter while the simulation is in progress—and without slowing it down. This "flywheel bus" is unique to the CAM architecture.

In conclusion, a pipeline fed according to a well-chosen sequencing format and provided with a few well-placed taps constitutes a general-purpose bus on which one can hook up not only the transition function, but also a great variety of display, analysis, and control functions—without any overhead on the simulation process. As in a physical experiment, any portion of the system is potentially accessible to on-line stimulation and measurement.

B.6   Modularity and expandability

Unlike other current schemes for parallel computation, the CAM architecture is truly scale-independent, and a very large cellular automata machine can be

---

[3]When display is not required, CAM's clock could be decoupled from the video rate, to allow—for example—more frequent updating of a smaller array, say at a few thousand frames per second.

built simply by connecting together an appropriate number of plane-modules. The limits are set by economic constraints rather than by electrical problems or issues of logic design. Since there are no "addresses" in a traditional sense, the data space is not limited by the size of an address word. The only timing signal that must be distributed to each block of plane-modules is the clock; and since signals can be reclocked within each block, the system can cope with a timing slack between blocks comparable to the width of the clock pulse.

Bibliography

[1] ALADYEV, Viktor, "Computability in Homogeneous Structures," *Izv. Akad. Nauk. Estonian SSR, Fiz.-Mat.* **21** (1972), 80–83.

[2] AMOROSO, Serafino, and Y. N. PATT, "Decision Procedures for Surjectivity and Injectivity of Parallel Maps for Tessellation Structures," *J. Comp. Syst. Sci.* **10** (1975), 77–82.

[3] BANKS, Edwin, "Information Processing and Transmission in Cellular Automata," *Tech. Rep. MAC TR-81*, MIT Project MAC (1971)

[4] BENNETT, Charles, "Logical Reversibility of Computation," *IBM J. Res. Develop.* 6 (1973), 525–532.

[5] BENNETT, Charles, and Geoff GRINSTEIN, "Role of Irreversibility in Stabilizing Complex and Nonenergodic Behavior in Locally Interacting Discrete Systems," *Phys. Rev. Lett.* **55** (1985), 657–660.

[6] BERLEKAMP, Elwyn, John CONWAY, and Richard GUY, *Winning ways for your mathematical plays*, vol. 2, Academic Press (1982).

[7] BRENDER, Ronald, "A Programming System for the Simulation of Cellular Spaces," *Tech. Rep. 25*, CONCOMP, The Univ. of Michigan (1970).

[8] BRODIE, Leo, *Starting FORTH*, Prentice Hall (1981).

[9] BRODIE, Leo, *Thinking FORTH*, Prentice Hall (1984).

[10] BURKS, Arthur (ed.), *Essays on Cellular Automata*, Univ. Ill. Press (1970).

[11] CODD, E. F., *Cellular Automata*, Academic Press (1968).

[12] COX, J. Theodore, David GRIFFEATH, "Recent results for the stepping stone model," *University of Wisconsin Math Department preprint*.

[13] CREUTZ, Michael, "Deterministic Ising Dynamics," *Annals of Physics* **167** (1986), 62–76.

[14] D'HUMIÈRES, Dominique, Pierre LALLEMAND, and T. SHIMOMURA, "Lattice Gas Cellular Automata, a New Experimental Tool for Hydrodynamics," Preprint LA-UR-85-4051, Los Alamos National Laboratory (1985).

[15] FARMER, Doyne, Tommaso TOFFOLI, and Stephen WOLFRAM (eds.), *Cellular Automata*, North-Holland (1984).

[16] FELLER, William, *An Introduction to Probability Theory and Its Applications*, vol. I, 3rd ed., Wiley (1968).

[17] FREDKIN, Edward, and Tommaso TOFFOLI, "Conservative Logic," *Int. J. Theor. Phys.* **21** (1982), 219–253.

[18] FRISCH, Uriel, Brosl HASSLACHER, and Yves POMEAU, "Lattice-Gas Automata for the Navier-Stokes Equation," *Phys. Rev. Lett.* **56** (1986), 1505–1508.

[19] GACS, Peter, and John REIF, *Proc. 17-th ACM Symp. Theory of Computing* (1985), 388-395.

[20] GARDNER, Martin, "The Fantastic Combinations of John Conway's New Solitaire Game 'Life'," *Sc. Am.* **223**:4 (April 1970), 120–123.

[21] GREENBERG, J., and S. HASTINGS, "Spatial Patterns for Discrete Models of Diffusion in Excitable Media," *SIAM J. Appl. Math.* **34** (1978), 515.

[22] HAYES, Brian, "The cellular automaton offers a model of the world and a world unto itself," *Scientific American* **250**:3 (1984), 12–21.

[23] HARDY, J., O. DE PAZZIS, and Yves POMEAU, "Molecular dynamics of a classical lattice gas: Transport properties and time correlation functions," *Phys. Rev.* **A13** (1976), 1949–1960.

[24] HEDLUND, G. A., K. I. APPEL, and L. R. WELCH, "All Onto Functions of Span Less Than or Equal To Five," Communications Research Division, working paper (July 1963).

[25] HEDLUND, G. A., "Endomorphism and Automorphism of the Shift Dynamical System," *Math. Syst. Theory* **3** (1969), 51–59.

[26] HERRMANN, Hans, "Fast algorithm for the simulation of Ising models," Saclay preprint no. 86-060 (1986).

[27] HOLLAND, John, "Universal Spaces: A Basis for Studies in Adaptation," *Automata Theory*, Academic Press (1966), 218–230.

[28] KADANOFF, Leo, "On two levels," *Physics Today* **39**:9 (September 1986), 7–9.

[29] KIMURA, M., G. WEISS, "The stepping stone model of population structure and the decrease of genetic correlation with distance," *Genetics* **49** (1964), 561–576.

[30] KIRKPATRICK, Scott, C.D. GELATT Jr., M.P. VECCHI, "Optimization by Simulated Annealing," *Science* **220** (1983), 671–680.

[31] KNUTH, Donald, *The Art of Computer Programming*, vol. 2, Seminumerical Algorithms, 2nd ed., Addison-Wesley (1981).

[32] LANDAUER, Rolf, "Irreversibility and heat generation in the computing process," *IBM J. Res. Devel.* **5** (1961), 183–191.

[33] LANDAU, L., E. LIFSHITZ, *Mechanics*, Pergamon Press (1960).

[34] MANDELBROT, Benoit, *The Fractal Geometry of Nature*, W. H. Freeman (1982).

[35] MARGOLUS, Norman "Physics-like models of computation," *Physica* **10D** (1984), 81–95.

[36] MARGOLUS, Norman, Tommaso TOFFOLI, and Gérard VICHNIAC, "Cellular-Automata Supercomputers for Fluid Dynamics Modeling," *Phys. Rev. Lett.* **56** (1986), 1694–1696.

[37] MARGOLUS, Norman, "Quantum Computation," Proceedings of a conference on New Ideas and Techniques in Quantum Measurement Theory (December 1985), to be published in the *Annals of the New York Academy of Sciences* (1986).

[38] MARGOLUS, Norman, "Partitioning Cellular Automata," in preparation.

[39] MARUOKA, Akira, and Masayuki KIMURA, "Conditions for Injectivity of Global Maps for Tessellation Automata," *Info. Control* **32** (1976), 158–162.

[40] MARUOKA, Akira, and Masayuki KIMURA, "Injectivity and Surjectivity of Parallel Maps for Cellular Automata," *J. Comp. Syst. Sci.* **18** (1979), 47–64.

[41] MÉZARD, M., "On the Statistical Physics of Spin Glasses," *Disordered Systems and Biological Organization* (E. BIENENSTOCK et al., ed.), Springer-Verlag (1986), 119–132.

[42] ORSZAG, Steven, and Victor YAKHOT, "Reynolds Numbers Scaling of Cellular-Automaton Hydrodynamics," *Phys. Rev. Lett.* **56** (1986), 1691–1693.

[43] PACKARD, Norman, and Stephen WOLFRAM, "Two-dimensional cellular automata," *J. Stat. Phys.* **38** (1985), 901–946.

[44] PEARSON, Robert, "An Algorithm for Pseudo Random Number Generation Suitable for Large Scale Integration," *J. Computat. Phys.* **3** (1983), 478–489.

[45] POMEAU, Yves, "Invariant in Cellular Automata," *J. Phys.* **A17** (1984), L415–L418.

[46] PRESTON, Kendall, and Michael DUFF, *Modern Cellular Automata, Theory and Applications*, Plenum Press (1984).

[47] REITER, Carla, "Life and death on a computer screen," *Discover* (August 1984), 81–83.

[48] RICHARDSON, D., "Tessellation with Local Transformations," *J. Comp. Syst. Sci.* **6** (1972), 373-388.

[49] ROSENBERG, I., "Spin Glass and Pseudo-Boolean Optimization," *Disordered Systems and Biological Organization* (E. BIENENSTOCK et al., ed.), Springer-Verlag (1986), 327–331.

[50] SALEM, James, and Stephen WOLFRAM, "Thermodynamics and Hydrodynamics of Cellular Automata," *Theory and Applications of Cellular Automata* (Stephen WOLFRAM ed.), World Scientific (1986), 362–366.

[51] SANDER, Leonard, "Fractal growth processes," *Nature* **322** (1986) 789–793.

[52] SMITH, Alvy, "Cellular Automata Theory," *Tech. Rep. 2*, Stanford Electronic Lab., Stanford Univ. (1969).

[53] STANLEY, H. Eugene, and Nicole OSTROWSKY, *On Growth and Form*, Martinus Nijhoff (1986).

[54] TING, C. H., *Inside F83*, Offete Press, 1306 South B. St., San Mateo, CA 94402.

[55] TOFFOLI, Tommaso, "Cellular Automata Mechanics," *Tech. Rep. 208*, Comp. Comm. Sci. Dept., The Univ. of Michigan (1977).

[56] TOFFOLI, Tommaso, "Integration of the Phase-Difference Relations in Asynchronous Sequential Networks," *Automata, Languages, and Programming* (Giorgio AUSIELLO and Corrado BÖHM ed.), Springer-Verlag (1978), 457–463.

[57] TOFFOLI, Tommaso, "Bicontinuous extension of reversible combinatorial functions," *Maths. Syst. Theory* **14** (1981), 13–23.

[58] TOFFOLI, Tommaso, "Reversible Computing," *Automata, Languages and Programming* (DE BAKKER and VAN LEEUWEN eds.), Springer-Verlag (1980), 632–644.

[59] TOFFOLI, Tommaso, "CAM: A high-performance cellular-automaton machine," *Physica* **10D** (1984), 195–204.

[60] TOFFOLI, Tommaso, and Norman MARGOLUS, "The CAM-7 Multiprocessor: A Cellular Automata Machine," *Tech. Memo LCS-TM-289*, MIT Lab. for Comp. Sci. (1985).

[61] TOFFOLI, Tommaso, "Cellular automata as an alternative to (rather than an approximation of) differential equations in modeling physics," *Physica* **10D** (1984), 117–127.

[62] TOFFOLI, Tommaso, and Norman MARGOLUS, *Invertible Cellular Automata*, in preparation.

[63] TUCKER, Jonathan, "Cellular automata machine: the ultimate parallel computer," *High Technology* **4**:6 (1984), 85–87.

[64] ULAM, Stanislaw, "Random Processes and Transformations," *Proc. Int. Congr. Mathem.* (held in 1950) **2** (1952), 264-275.

[65] VAN DYKE, Milton, *An Album of Fluid Motion*, Parabolic Press (1982).

[66] VICHNIAC, Gérard, "Simulating physics with cellular automata," *Physica* **10D** (1984), 96–115.

[67] VICHNIAC, Gérard, "Cellular automata models of disorder and organization," *Disordered Systems and Biological Organization* (BIENENSTOCK et al. eds.), Springer-Verlag (1986), 1–20.

[68] VON NEUMANN, John, *Theory of Self-Reproducing Automata* (edited and completed by Arthur BURKS), Univ. of Illinois Press (1966).

[69] WITTEN, Thomas, and Leonard SANDER, *Phys. Rev. Lett.* **47** (1981), 1400.

[70] WOLFRAM, Stephen, "Statistical mechanics of cellular automata," *Rev. Mod. Phys.* **55** (1983), 601–644.

[71] WOLFRAM, Stephen, "Universality and Complexity in Cellular Automata," *Physica* **10**D (1984), 1–35.

[72] WOLFRAM, Stephen, "Computation Theory of Cellular Automata," *Commun. Math. Phys.* **96** (1984), 15-57.

[73] WOLFRAM, Stephen, "Random-Sequence Generation by Cellular Automata," *Adv. Applied Math.* **7** (1986), 123–169.

[74] WOLFRAM, Stephen (ed.), *Theory and Applications of Cellular Automata*, World Scientific (1986).

[75] ZAIKIN, A., and A. ZHABOTINSKY, *Nature* **225** (1970), 535.

[76] ZUSE, Konrad, *Rechnender Raum*, Vieweg, Braunschweig (1969); translated as "Calculating Space," *Tech. Transl. AZT-70-164-GEMIT*, MIT Project MAC (1970).

Index

The MIT Press, with Peter Denning, general consulting editor, and Brian Randell, European consulting editor, publishes computer science books in the following series:

ACM Doctoral Dissertation Award and Distinguished Dissertation Series

Artificial Intelligence, Patrick Winston and Michael Brady, editors

Charles Babbage Institute Reprint Series for the History of Computing, Martin Campbell-Kelly, editor

Computer Systems, Herb Schwetman, editor

Explorations in Logo, E. Paul Goldenberg, editor

Foundations of Computing, Michael Garey, editor

History of Computing, I. Bernard Cohen and William Aspray, editors

Information Systems, Michael Lesk, editor

Logic Programming, Ehud Shapiro, editor; Fernando Pereira, Koichi Furukawa, and D. H. D. Warren, associate editors

The MIT Electrical Engineering and Computer Science Series

Scientific Computation, Dennis Gannon, editor